FOCUS

Pearson Education Limited
Edinburgh Gate, Harlow
Essex, CM20 2JE, England
and Associated Companies throughout the world

www.english.com/focus

© Pearson Education Limited 2016

The right of Daniel Brayshaw and Bartosz Michałowski to be identified as authors of this work has been asserted by them in accordance with the Copyright, Designs and Patents Act, 1988.

All rights reserved. No part of this publication may be reproduced, stored in a retrieval system, or transmitted in any form or by any means, electronic, mechanical, photocopying, recording or otherwise without the prior written permission of the copyright holders.

First published 2016
ISBN 978-1-4479-9796-2
Sixteenth impression 2023

Set in Avenir
Printed and bound by CPI Group (UK) Ltd, Croydon, CR0 4YY

Acknowledgements

The publisher and authors would like to thank the following people for their feedback and comments during the development of the material:
Humberto Santos Duran, Anna Maria Grochowska, Inga Lande, Magdalena Loska, Rosa Maria Maldonado, Juliana Queiroz Pereira, Tomasz Siuta, Renata Tomaka-Pasternak

Text

We are grateful to the following for permission to reproduce copyright material:
Extract on page 24 adapted from Online passwords: keep it complicated, Guardian (Oliver Burkeman http://www.guardian.co.uk/technology/2012/oct/05/online-security-passwords-tricks-hacking), 5 October 2012, Guardian News and Media Ltd, 2012

In some instances we have been unable to trace the owners of copyright material, and we would appreciate any information that would enable us to do so.

Photo Acknowledgements

The publisher would like to thank the following for their kind permission to reproduce their photographs:
(Key: b-bottom; c-centre; l-left; r-right; t-top)

Alamy Images: Archive Pics 96c, Craig Joiner Photography 47, Beth Dixson 27l, INTERFOTO 96l, Terry Mathews 84 (B), Jenny Matthews 85 (C), Wavebreakmedia Ltd UC2 68 (I); **Daniel Brayshaw:** 51l; **Corbis:** Blend Images / Ariel Skelley 60tr, Juice Images / Ian Lishman 68 (B), moodboard / James Lauritz 60c;
DK Images: Andy Crawford 83, David Henley 6tl, Nigel Hicks 44 (C), 44 (D), Dave King 6br, Mick Loates 22, Ian O'Leary 82, Tony Souter 6cl, Chris Stowers 6tr, 64, James Tye 44 (J), Linda Whitwam 44 (L); **Fotolia.com:** aberson 52, Africa Studio 20tl, AK-DigiArt 68 (F), Anion 23, auremar 63l, BillionPhotos.com 9, corepics 68 (K), determined 32, goodluz 63c, Ralf Gosch 44 (E), gstudio 26r, hjschneider 26l, jiris 125, jojje11 20br, Robert Kneschke 68 (C), 68 (D), Kruwt 6bl, Kurhan 68 (J), mbolina 44 (I), Mechanik 20/3, miklyxa13 20/2, mr.markin 85 (D), Natis 7/6, NEILRAS 126, Sergey Nivens 60br, olly 40, On-Air 98, Gilles Paire 44 (K), pzAxe 44 (A), Andres Rodriguez 68 (A), Gina Sanders 68 (G), senkaya 84 (A), Tomas Sereda 20/4, .shock 72r, waldru 72bc, V. Zhuravlev 20/1; **Getty Images:** English School 96br, Veronica Garbutt 72l, Hulton Archive 48l, Mischa Photo Ltd 28, Nick White 39; **Imagemore Co., Ltd:** 7/3, 7/5, 44 (B); **Mary Evans Picture Library:** The Women's Library@LSE 96tr; **Pearson Education Ltd:** Studio 8 21br, Gareth Boden 59, Cheuk-king Lo 6cr, 7/2, Alice McBroom 44 (F), Jules Selmes 44 (G), 44 (H), 68 (E); **Photolibrary.com:** OJO Images / Chris Ryan 21tl; **Photoshot Holdings Limited:** 27r, UPPA 48br; **Shutterstock.com:** Radu Bercan 51br, BMJ 13, Featureflash 4, Michal Kowalski 63r, Alexey Lysenko 15, Natursports 68 (H), oliveromg 16, William Silver 68 (L), Syda Productions 8, wavebreakmedia 60l, Zerbor 20/5; **Sozaijiten:** 7/1, 7/4; **The Kobal Collection:** 20th Century Fox / Scott Free Productions 37, New Line / MGM / Wingnut Films 33

Illustrations

Illustrated by Sean Sims (c/o New Division Illustration Agency) p. 123, Jacek Krajewski (Studio Gardengraf) p. 8, 12, 34, 45, 46, 62, 75, 87, 93, 99

All other images © Pearson Education

Every effort has been made to trace the copyright holders and we apologise in advance for any unintentional omissions. We would be pleased to insert the appropriate acknowledgement in any subsequent edition of this publication.

CONTENTS

Intro
- **0.1** Family, **0.2** How we met 4
- **0.3** Mr Bean, **0.4** Experiences 5
- **0.5** Adventure, **0.6** Travel 6
- **0.7** Sport, **0.8** Food 7

Unit 1 Personality
- 1.1 Vocabulary 8
- 1.2 Grammar 10
- 1.3 Listening language practice 11
- 1.4 Reading 12
- 1.5 Grammar 14
- 1.6 Speaking language practice 15
- 1.7 Writing 16
- 1.8 Word practice 17
- 1.9 Self-assessment 18
- 1.10 Self-check 19

Unit 2 Invention
- 2.1 Vocabulary 20
- 2.2 Grammar 22
- 2.3 Listening language practice 23
- 2.4 Reading 24
- 2.5 Grammar 26
- 2.6 Speaking language practice 27
- 2.7 Writing 28
- 2.8 Use of English 29
- 2.9 Self-assessment 30
- 2.10 Self-check 31

Unit 3 The arts
- 3.1 Vocabulary 32
- 3.2 Grammar 34
- 3.3 Listening language practice 35
- 3.4 Reading 36
- 3.5 Grammar 38
- 3.6 Speaking language practice 39
- 3.7 Writing 40
- 3.8 Word practice 41
- 3.9 Self-assessment 42
- 3.10 Self-check 43

Unit 4 Living
- 4.1 Vocabulary 44
- 4.2 Grammar 46
- 4.3 Listening language practice 47
- 4.4 Reading 48
- 4.5 Grammar 50
- 4.6 Speaking language practice 51
- 4.7 Writing 52
- 4.8 Use of English 53
- 4.9 Self-assessment 54
- 4.10 Self-check 55

Unit 5 School
- 5.1 Vocabulary 56
- 5.2 Grammar 58
- 5.3 Listening language practice 59
- 5.4 Reading 60
- 5.5 Grammar 62
- 5.6 Speaking language practice 63
- 5.7 Writing 64
- 5.8 Word practice 65
- 5.9 Self-assessment 66
- 5.10 Self-check 67

Unit 6 Working life
- 6.1 Vocabulary 68
- 6.2 Grammar 70
- 6.3 Listening language practice 71
- 6.4 Reading 72
- 6.5 Grammar 74
- 6.6 Speaking language practice 75
- 6.7 Writing 76
- 6.8 Use of English 77
- 6.9 Self-assessment 78
- 6.10 Self-check 79

Unit 7 Shopping
- 7.1 Vocabulary 80
- 7.2 Grammar 82
- 7.3 Listening language practice 83
- 7.4 Reading 84
- 7.5 Grammar 86
- 7.6 Speaking language practice 87
- 7.7 Writing 88
- 7.8 Word practice 89
- 7.9 Self-assessment 90
- 7.10 Self-check 91

Unit 8 Society
- 8.1 Vocabulary 92
- 8.2 Grammar 94
- 8.3 Listening language practice 95
- 8.4 Reading 96
- 8.5 Grammar 98
- 8.6 Speaking language practice 99
- 8.7 Writing 100
- 8.8 Use of English 101
- 8.9 Self-assessment 102
- 8.10 Self-check 103

Exam strategies 104
Function phrase bank, writing 107
Function phrase bank, speaking 109
Vocabulary bank 111
Vocabulary bank – practice exercises 121
Self-checks answer key 128

0.1 Family

Present Simple and Present Continuous • Family

SHOW WHAT YOU KNOW

1 Complete the table. Then complete the sentences.

Male	Female	Together
dad	⁰mum	parents
1 _____	daughter	2 _____
brother	3 _____	–
4 _____	niece	–
grandpa	5 _____	grandparents
6 _____	sister-in-law	–
uncle	7 _____	–

a My brother's wife is my _____ .
b My brother's daughter is my _____ .
c My dad's brother is my _____ .
d My mum and dad are my _____ .
e My grandma and grandpa are my _____ .

2 Choose the correct options.
1 I *don't see / 'm not seeing* my brother every weekend.
2 My dad and my uncle aren't here now; they *play / are playing* tennis.
3 Jo and Ken *don't like / aren't liking* their sister-in-law.
4 Adam *stays / is staying* with his family at the moment.
5 *Do you have / Are you having* a niece?
6 *Does your brother wait / Is your brother waiting* for you now?
7 My grandpa *walks / is walking* 3km every morning.
8 Wow! You look absolutely fantastic! *Do you go / Are you going* to a party?
9 Nina can never sleep late. She *is waking up / wakes up* at 5.15 every morning.

3 Complete the sentences with the Present Simple or Present Continuous form of the verbs in brackets.
0 Harry's dad <u>doesn't work</u> (not work) at the airport. He's a doctor at the hospital.
1 _____ (it/rain) today?
2 Lee and Ann _____ (watch) a film at the moment.
3 It's cold today but my nephew _____ (not wear) a hat.
4 _____ (you/like) tests and exams?
5 Grandma and grandpa _____ (have) four dogs, three cats and a rabbit.
6 My older sister _____ (meet) her boyfriend every Saturday night.
7 Unfortunately, my brother and I _____ (not sit) next to each other on this train.
8 _____ (you/eat) meat or are you a vegetarian?
9 Sorry, he's not here. I think he _____ (repair) the car in the garage. Could you call back in an hour?

0.2 How we met

Past Simple affirmative • Music

SHOW WHAT YOU KNOW

1 Choose the odd one out in each group.
0 folk   jazz   (band)
1 drummer   house   rock
2 punk   hit   pop
3 heavy metal   R & B   record company
4 singer   reggae   hip-hop

2 Complete the sentences with the Past Simple form of the verbs in brackets.
0 Bethany <u>was</u> (be) in a band two years ago.
1 Gary _____ (study) guitar at music school.
2 Will and Wendy _____ (start) watching *The X-Factor* last year.
3 Lucy _____ (receive) a love letter yesterday morning.
4 Hannah and Holly _____ (be) hungry at midnight last night.
5 Uncle Steve _____ (stop) smoking six months ago.
6 When Monica was seven years old, she _____ (want) to be a pilot.
7 I _____ (collect) comics when I was in junior school.

3 Complete the fact file with the Past Simple form of the verbs in the box. There are two extra verbs.

be   become   begin   ~~grow up~~
make   play   wear   win

Katy Perry
A teenage dream come true

Singer Katy Perry ⁰<u>grew up</u> in California. When she was only nine years old, she ¹_____ singing in church. When she was seventeen, she ²_____ her first album and seven years later she finally ³_____ a pop star. In 2008 she ⁴_____ the award for Best New Act at the MTV Europe Music Awards. Her third album, *Teenage Dream* ⁵_____ very popular. More than 5 million people bought it!

0.3 Mr Bean

Past Simple negative and questions • Verbs

SHOW WHAT YOU KNOW

1 Complete the sentences with the Past Simple form of the verbs in the box. There are two extra verbs.

[can   do   have   get   make   play   ~~see~~]

0 I _saw_ the film *Mr Bean on Holiday* at the cinema.
1 Leah _____ read when she was only four years old.
2 My parents _____ married on the beach, in Hawaii.
3 Last weekend Vicky _____ football on Saturday and Sunday.
4 Michelle and Sophie _____ all their homework on the bus to school this morning.

2 Complete the phone conversation with the Past Simple form of the verbs in brackets.

Sunday afternoon:

A: Rachel? Hello, darling. It's Mum. How are you?
B: Hi, Mum. I'm OK, but very tired. How's the holiday?
A: Lovely! Very relaxing. Your dad says hello. ⁰_Did you do_ (you/do) the shopping yesterday morning?
B: Yes.
A: Good. ¹_____ (you/walk) the dog yesterday afternoon?
B: Yes, I did.
A: Oh good. ²_____ (you/visit) your grandma yesterday evening?
B: Yes, Mum, I did!
A: Thank you, darling. Is your brother OK?
B: No, he's lazy! He ³_____ (not cook) on Friday evening.
A: Oh?
B: He ⁴_____ (not clean) his room yesterday morning.
A: Oh dear!
B: And he ⁵_____ (not help) Grandma yesterday evening.
A: Oh dear! Well, darling ... now you know how I feel. You and your brother never help at home.
B: Mum! I promise to help you more in the future. Will you please come home?

3 Find and correct the mistakes in the sentences.

0 Did Mr Bean ~~started~~ as a TV series?   _start_
1 Danielle didn't had a shower this morning.   _____
2 What do you do yesterday?   _____
3 Do Edward and Kate finish their homework last night? _____
4 Paul doesn't play basketball last Friday.   _____
5 Sam didn't ate crisps or chocolate when he was young.   _____
6 Did you really began to play the piano at the age of six? _____

0.4 Experiences

Present Perfect • Leisure activities

SHOW WHAT YOU KNOW

1 Choose the correct options.

1 I can *do / go / play* an instrument, but I can't sing.
2 Sam *does / goes / plays* judo twice a week.
3 Mia and Amy *do / go / play* shopping every Saturday.
4 Can Grandpa *do / go / play* computer games?
5 Nina *does / goes / plays* kite-surfing every summer.
6 Kevin sometimes *does / goes / plays* aerobics with his girlfriend.

2 Complete the sentences with the Present Perfect form of the verbs in brackets. Make positive (✓) or negative (✗) sentences.

0 Max _has won_ (win) a competition. ✓
1 Alex and Nico _____ (act) in a play. ✗
2 Adele _____ (go) to a concert. ✗
3 Mary and Leon _____ (walk) in the mountains. ✓
4 Patricia _____ (read) a book in English. ✗
5 Martin _____ (buy) a new pair of jeans. ✓

3 Complete the sentences with the Present Perfect form of the verbs in brackets.

0 The best party I _have ever been_ (ever/go) to was my best friend's sixteenth birthday.
1 The biggest city my dad _____ (ever/visit) is Tokyo.
2 _____ (Mum/ever/eat) sushi?
3 Grandpa _____ (never/meet) a famous person.
4 Noi comes from Thailand and she _____ (never/see) snow.
5 The most interesting country we _____ (ever/go) to is Iceland.
6 _____ (you/ever/run) 10km?
7 Tim _____ (never/dance) with a girl.
8 _____ (your English teacher/ever/ask) you to do your homework online?
9 We _____ (never/have) a holiday in England.
10 This is the longest book I _____ (ever/read).

5

0.5 Adventure

be going to • Collocations

SHOW WHAT YOU KNOW

1 Read the postcard and choose the correct options.

Hi Mum,
I'm ¹making / doing / having a great time at at the adventure camp. In the morning we ²go / play / do swimming before breakfast. Then we ³go / play / do rock climbing or ⁴go / play / do yoga. Yesterday was great; we ⁵went on / played / made a forest walk. In the evenings we collect firewood and ⁶make / do / have some camp cooking, then we sit by the fire and sing. We organise games every evening and on the last night we are going to ⁷make / do / have a big party.
Can I ⁸go / have / make on holiday to adventure camp every year? ☺
Love from me.

2 Complete the sentences with the positive or negative form of *be going to* and the verbs in brackets.

0 It's warm today. I'm not going to wear (wear) my coat.
1 We _____ (go) sailing. It's cold and we can't swim.
2 Tim _____ (have) a haircut. He wants to look good for the party.
3 Your card _____ (arrive) before Christmas. You posted it too late.
4 Jasmine and Yoko _____ (be) late for school. They missed the bus.
5 You are not concentrating on your homework. You _____ (make) a mistake.

3 Use the prompts to write questions with *be going to*. Then match the questions with the answers.

0 Tom / buy / a new laptop?
   Is Tom going to buy a new laptop? [g]
1 the cake / be / chocolate or fruit?
   _____ [ ]
2 you / forget / my birthday again?
   _____ [ ]
3 what / we / buy / for Dad's birthday?
   _____ [ ]
4 where / they / stay / on their holiday?
   _____ [ ]
5 when / you / clean / your room?
   _____ [ ]
6 Pete / ask / Jill to go to the school dance with him?
   _____ [ ]

a When I've finished my homework.
b Definitely chocolate. It's my favourite!
c Certainly not! When is it again?
d In a hotel by the sea.
e No. He's going with Ellie.
f How about a nice jumper?
g No. He's expecting to get one for Christmas.

0.6 Travel

will for predictions • Travel

SHOW WHAT YOU KNOW

1 Look at the photos and write the means of transport. Some letters are given.

0 b**oa**t
1 s_____p
2 t_____n
3 p_____e
4 c_____r
5 m_____e

2 Put the words in the correct order to complete the predictions.

0 travel / think / we / will / don't
   We don't think we will travel to the moon.
1 I / learn / will / think
   I _____ to drive next year.
2 think / cars / doesn't / fly / will
   Sean _____ in 2050.
3 be / will / there / think
   Sue and Ben _____ high-speed trains in 2050.
4 planes / be / doesn't / will / think
   Lucy _____ transparent.

3 Complete the predictions about schools in 2050 with *will* (✓) or *won't* (✗) and the verbs in the box. There are two extra verbs.

  be   do   have   know   ~~learn~~   pay   use   write

0 Students will learn to speak Chinese. ✓
1 There _____ any paper books. ✗
2 Teachers _____ on whiteboards. ✗
3 All classrooms _____ computers. ✓
4 All parents _____ for their children's education. ✓
5 Students _____ pens and pencils. ✗

0.7 Sport

must, have to and *should* • Sport

SHOW WHAT YOU KNOW

1 Complete the crossword with the correct sports.

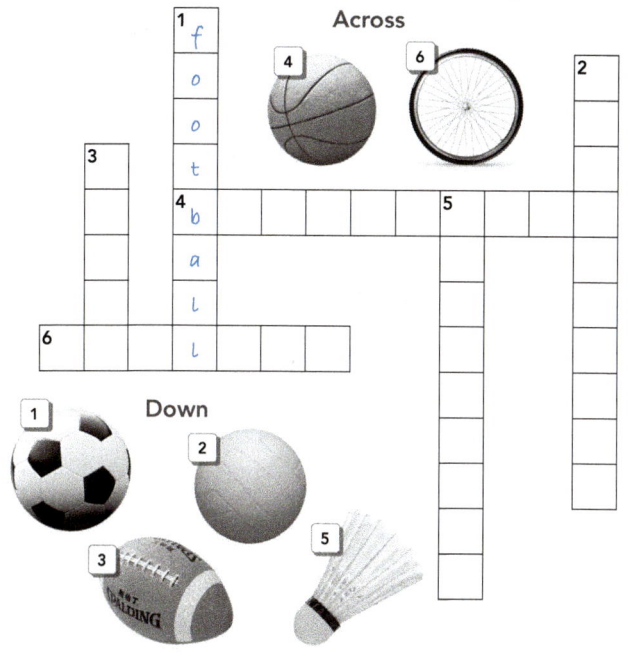

2 Read the comments about sports and choose the correct options.

1 'This is an important game. We *must / mustn't* do our best.'
2 'This is the last kilometre. I *must / mustn't* slow down.'
3 'This is our last chance. We *must / mustn't* score this goal.'
4 'This jump is really big. I *must / mustn't* be careful.'
5 'The marathon is long. I *must / mustn't* run fast at the start.'
6 'The race starts early tomorrow. We *must / mustn't* stay up late tonight.'

3 Read the article and complete the sentences with *should, shouldn't, must, mustn't* or *have to*.

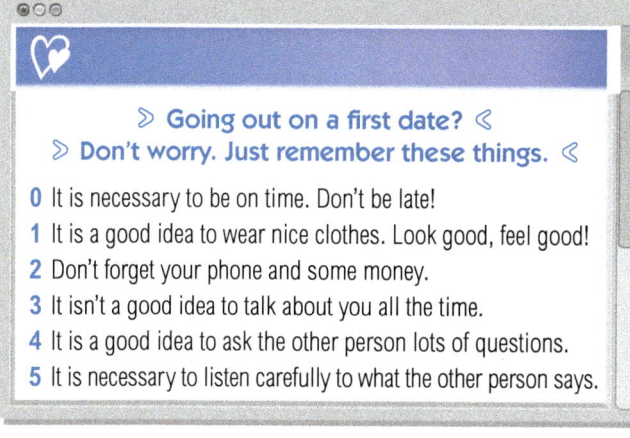

≫ Going out on a first date? ≪
≫ Don't worry. Just remember these things. ≪

0 It is necessary to be on time. Don't be late!
1 It is a good idea to wear nice clothes. Look good, feel good!
2 Don't forget your phone and some money.
3 It isn't a good idea to talk about you all the time.
4 It is a good idea to ask the other person lots of questions.
5 It is necessary to listen carefully to what the other person says.

0 You <u>must/have to</u> be on time.
1 You _____ wear nice clothes.
2 You _____ forget your phone and some money.
3 You _____ talk about you all the time.
4 You _____ ask the other person lots of questions.
5 You _____ listen carefully to what the other person says.

0.8 Food

Countable and uncountable nouns • Articles • Food

SHOW WHAT YOU KNOW

1 Complete the food words in the table. Some letters are given. Then say if they are countable (C) or uncountable (U).

Protein		Carbohydrates	
0 m<u>ea</u>t	u	6 r_____e	
1 y_____t		7 b_____d	
2 e_____g		8 c_____s	

Fruit and vegetables		Other	
3 b_____a		9 c_____e	
4 a_____e		10 w_____r	
5 s_____y		11 j_____e	

2 Read the conversation and choose the correct options.

Dad: Adam, I need to make a shopping list. Can you help, please?
Adam: But Dad, I'm busy!
Dad: Adam, do you want to eat this week?
Adam: OK, OK.
Dad: Look in the fridge, please. ¹*Is / Are* there any milk?
Adam: Yes, there ²*is / are*. We have two bottles of milk, but there ³*isn't / aren't* any juice.
Dad: OK. We need something for breakfast tomorrow. ⁴*Is / Are* there any eggs?
Adam: Yes, there ⁵*is / are*. But there ⁶*isn't / aren't* any onions.
Dad: OK. ⁷*Is / Are* there any pasta?
Adam: Not in the fridge.
Dad: Adam! Please look in the cupboard.

3 Complete the article with *a/an, the,* or Ø (no article).

The Sumo Diet
20,000 calories a day!

⁰Ø Sumo wrestlers need to be big, strong and heavy. To do this, ¹_____ sumo wrestler needs to eat around 20,000 calories each day! In contrast, ²_____ healthy man needs around 3,000 calories each day.

Sumo wrestlers eat ³_____ very large bowl of soup twice a day. ⁴_____ soup is called Chanko-nabe and it's made of chicken, fish, beef and ⁵_____ vegetables. After their meal, sumo wrestlers sleep for three or four hours. ⁶_____ heaviest Sumo wrestler ever was Konishiki Yasokichi – he weighed 287 kg!

1 PERSONALITY

1.1 Vocabulary

Personality adjectives • Adjective + preposition

SHOW WHAT YOU KNOW

1 Choose the correct options.

1 You were *serious / negative / stupid* to walk home on your own late at night. Next time call your parents.
2 Chris is *clever / boring / serious*. He never has anything interesting to say because he spends all his time playing computer games.
3 Megan is so *interesting / clever / unkind*. She's only three and she can already count to fifty.
4 Joe complains about everything. There is always something wrong. He's very *boring / positive / negative*.
5 I think it was very *kind / positive / funny* to help Abi with her homework, Luke. Thank you.

WORD STORE 1A
Adjective antonyms

2 Anna is making a list called *My perfect boyfriend*. Use pairs of opposites from the box to complete her list.

arrogant ~~caring~~ cheerful crazy
hard-working lazy miserable modest
outgoing ~~selfish~~ sensible shy

My perfect boyfriend is ...
~~a movie star, handsome, rich~~

✓ positive	✗ negative
0 caring	not selfish
1 s_____	not _____
2 c_____	not _____
3 o_____	not _____
4 h_____	not _____
5 m_____	not _____

3 A few months after making her list, Anna is having a conversation with her friend Laura. Complete it with the adjectives in the box. There are two extra adjectives.

arrogant caring ~~cheerful~~ hard-working
crazy miserable modest selfish shy

L: So, how are things? Is Simon the perfect boyfriend?
A: Well, nobody's perfect, but you know what? He's really great. First of all, he's really ⁰cheerful , you know, always happy and smiling. And he's very ¹_____ . He wants to be a teacher and he does lots of studying in the evenings.
L: Does he have any time for you then?
A: Oh sure. He's a very ²_____ guy. He calls me every night and asks about my day. And he often buys me flowers.
L: Wow. Lucky you! Dave never asks about my day. He only thinks about himself. He's so ³_____ . Dave thinks he's the best boyfriend in the world. He thinks he's the best at everything. He's really ⁴_____ .
A: Poor you. Simon is exactly the opposite. He's really clever, but he doesn't talk about it. He's very ⁵_____ . I'm really happy, you know.
L: Well, good for you. Unfortunately, I'm not. I'm the opposite. I'm unhappy; really ⁶_____ . I think I need a new boyfriend. I don't know what to do. Does Simon have a twin brother?

WORD STORE 1B
Negative prefixes *un-, in-, ir-, dis-*

4 Add prefixes to make adjectives a–e negative. Then complete sentences 1–4 with the positive or negative form of the adjectives.

a <u>un</u>popular
b ____fair
c ____honest
d ____experienced
e ____responsible

0 Try to be modest. Nobody likes arrogant people. They are nearly always <u>unpopular</u> .
1 Mum trusts my older brother Peter to look after our little sister. He's very _____ ; he never does anything dangerous or silly.
2 Katie never lies. She is a very _____ person.
3 In some jobs men get much more money than women for doing exactly the same work. It's really _____ .
4 Tom passed his driving test eight years ago. He drives to work every day. He is a(n) _____ and safe driver.

8

WORD STORE 1C
Adjective + preposition

5 Complete the advert with the prepositions in the box.

> about (x2)   at   for   in (x2)   on   with

Junior travel writer wanted for *Backpack Magazine*

Are you passionate ⁰*about* travel?
Are you interested ¹_____ cultures?
Are you between 15 and 19 years old?

Yes, yes and yes?

Backpack Magazine is looking for a junior travel writer to join our team during the school summer holidays this year. The successful candidate will be responsible ²_____ writing several magazine articles about what young travellers can do in their country. You will also be involved ³_____ writing articles for our website and smartphone app. You need to be good ⁴_____ written and spoken English and keen ⁵_____ meeting and talking to tourists. At *Backpack Magazine* we are serious ⁶_____ travel, and you won't be disappointed ⁷_____ our offer. Working for us is fun, interesting and well-paid. Write to us and tell us why we should choose you as our junior travel writer.

REMEMBER THIS
You can use **personality adjectives** before a noun, e.g. a **caring** boyfriend, or after the verb *be*, e.g. *My boyfriend is caring*.

6 Read REMEMBER THIS. Put the words in the correct order to form sentences.

0 has / very / parents / Pauline / serious
   Pauline has very serious parents.
1 last / was / hairdresser / inexperienced / Zoe's
   _____
2 two / I / dishonest / had / friends
   _____
3 new / Jamie's / arrogant / girlfriend / extremely / is
   _____

REMEMBER BETTER
To help you remember personality adjectives, try to use them in opposite pairs in sentences about people you know, e.g. *My dad is usually cheerful. He's not a miserable man.*

Choose five pairs of opposite personality adjectives from this lesson and write sentences about people you know. Use the model sentences.

0 *My little sister is shy. She's not a confident girl.*
1 Our History teacher is _____ . He/She's not a(n) _____ person.
2 My best friend is _____ . He/She is not _____ .
3 _____
4 _____
5 _____

SHOW WHAT YOU'VE LEARNT

7 Choose the correct answer, A, B or C, to complete both sentences in each pair.

1 Last night I watched a TV programme ___ robots.
   Are you serious ___ becoming a doctor?
   A on   B about   C with

2 Laura is not very good ___ Maths or Science.
   Jenny likes doing her homework in the coffee shop, but I like doing mine ___ home.
   A for   B in   C at

3 Granddad goes ___ a walk in the afternoon to get some fresh air.
   I'm responsible ___ taking out the rubbish at home.
   A for   B on   C about

4 Many customers were disappointed ___ the new smartphone.
   Ken always eats his chips ___ lots of salt.
   A about   B with   C in

8 Complete the adjectives in the sentences. The first letter of each adjective is given.

1 Why is my brother so l_____ ? He never helps with the housework. He just sleeps on the sofa.
2 Don't be so s_____ . Share the chocolate with your sister!
3 My older sister gets £10 pocket money every week and I only get £5. It's u_____ !
4 Mia is very k_____ on learning English. She learns ten new words every day.
5 Amy is i_____ in three different after-school clubs. She goes to Science club, chess club and Spanish club.
6 Lucy is very p_____ about badminton. She wants to play for the national team.

/10

1.2 Grammar

Present tenses – question forms

SHOW WHAT YOU KNOW

1 Complete the sentences with the correct present form of the verbs in brackets.

1 It's 11 o'clock and the bus hasn't arrived (not arrive) yet. Oh! Wait ... there it is. I can see it now. It _____ (come) round the corner.
2 I _____ (never/try) sushi. I _____ (not like) fish very much.
3 Sorry, Emily _____ (not be) here now. She _____ (run) in the park. Can you call back later?
4 Your dad _____ (already/have) breakfast. He _____ (have) a shower now.
5 Leroy _____ (read) a very good book at the moment. He always _____ (buy) his books online.

2 ★ Complete the questions with the correct form of do, be or have.

0 Why are you always so selfish?
1 _____ Carl ever been involved in a fight?
2 What _____ an appropriate birthday present for my five-year-old nephew?
3 _____ doctors need to be good at Maths?
4 Why _____ Kelly so miserable today?
5 Which sports _____ you keen on?
6 How much _____ they pay for their children's dance lessons?

3 ★★ Read the sentences and complete the questions about the subject and the object.

1 ᵃEmma has eaten ᵇeggs.
 a Who 's eaten eggs ?
 b What _____ ?
2 ᵃLawrence and Lucy are living in ᵇLondon.
 a Who _____ ?
 b Where _____ ?
3 ᵃRay reads about running ᵇmarathons.
 a Who _____ ?
 b What _____ ?
4 ᵃCharles has chosen ᵇchips for lunch.
 a Who _____ ?
 b What _____ ?
5 ᵃHelen is helping ᵇHarry.
 a Who _____ ?
 b Who _____ ?
6 ᵃFreddie feels ᵇfantastic.
 a Who _____ ?
 b How _____ ?
7 ᵃHarriet is on holiday in ᵇHawaii.
 a Who _____ ?
 b Where _____ ?
8 ᵃWilliam works with ᵇWendy.
 a Who _____ ?
 b Who _____ ?

4 ★★ Read the answer and write a question about the underlined part.

0 What are they talking about ?
 They're talking about Emily's birthday party.
1 What _____ ?
 I spend my money on clothes and music.
2 Who _____ ?
 She's waiting for Ken.
3 What _____ ?
 Oscar has read about Istanbul.
4 Which hotel _____ ?
 Liz has heard about the Regent Hotel in London.
5 Which team _____ ?
 We play for the school team.

5 ★★★ Complete the questions in the conversations.

Conversation 1
A: Who ⁰is interested in writing ?
B: My brother is interested in writing.
A: What ¹_____ ?
B: He's writing a short story now.
A: Why ²_____ ?
B: He's writing it because he wants to win a competition at school.
A: Do ³_____ ?
B: Yes, I like writing.
A: Have ⁴_____ ?
B: No, I haven't written a story for the competition.

Conversation 2
A: What ⁵_____ ?
B: I'm baking a cake.
A: Who ⁶_____ ?
B: I'm baking it for my mum.
A: Why ⁷_____ ?
B: It's brown because it's a chocolate cake.
A: Have ⁸_____ ?
B: No, I haven't baked a cake before.

SHOW WHAT YOU'VE LEARNT

6 Read the answer and write a question about the underlined part.

1 _____ ?
 The girls are talking about films.
2 _____ ?
 Dean has spent all his money on that guitar.
3 _____ ?
 Michelle has forgotten to close the door.
4 _____ ?
 Nicola is doing her homework.
5 _____ ?
 Craig believes in ghosts.
6 _____ ?
 People are listening to the band.

/6

1.3 Listening language practice

Prepositions • Suffixes • Negative prefixes

1 Complete Becky's talk with the prepositions in the box. You will need to use some of the prepositions more than once. Then listen and check.

[about   after   for   from   in   on   with]

Students' book recording CD•1.20 MP3•20

Hi, I'm Becky. Your teacher has asked me to talk to you about doing voluntary work in Africa. I worked in South America a few years ago and then in Africa last year for six months. It was amazing! There are lots of jobs ¹_____ volunteers in Africa. I chose to work ²_____ animals and I helped look ³_____ young elephants that had no parents. A lot of people do voluntary work in other countries, but you must think ⁴_____ it carefully. It isn't easy work! You have to work long hours and sometimes things are very different ⁵_____ your own country. For example, the weather is sometimes quite extreme. It can be very hot or very cold. People who volunteer should be fit and healthy, and also interested ⁶_____ different cultures. You learn a lot of new things when you work as a volunteer. Also, you don't work ⁷_____ your own, you work ⁸_____ a team. So, you need to be a good team player and have good communication skills. If you think it's right for you, then I can recommend Volunteer Today, the agency that helped me. They are always looking ⁹_____ responsible young people who want to help others and learn new skills. Go online to Volunteertoday (that's one word) dot com and you can read all ¹⁰_____ their projects. Or you can phone them on 07923341565. I'll give you my number too in case you have any questions. That's 02364 5567213.

2 Complete the sentences with prepositions.

1 I'd like a job where I'm working _____ people, not just on a computer.
2 I'm very interested _____ languages and I can speak three.
3 My brother is looking _____ a summer job. Does your restaurant need any waiters?
4 My mum works from home. She's _____ her own all day and she doesn't like it.
5 I read an article _____ personality yesterday. It was really interesting.
6 Sometimes I look _____ my baby sister in the evenings.

REMEMBER THIS

differ + -ent = different   response + -ible = responsible
health + -y = healthy

3 Read REMEMBER THIS. Complete the sentences. Use suffixes from the box to change the words in brackets into adjectives.

[-ate   -ent   -ive   -y   -ly (x2)]

0 I am <u>passionate</u> (passion) about the environment.
1 I'm more _____ (confidence) than before.
2 There were some very _____ (scare) situations.
3 You get on well with people – you're _____ (cooperation).
4 Were the local people _____ (friend)?
5 I met some _____ (love) people.

REMEMBER BETTER

When you write down new adjectives, notice the suffixes used to make them. Underline them and try to note down a few other adjectives with the same suffix, e.g. help<u>ful</u>, cheer<u>ful</u>; pessim<u>istic</u>, fantastic.

Choose the correct options. Then underline all the suffixes. Use a dictionary if necessary.

Many people find Aung Sang Su Kyi's life and work ¹*inspire / inspiring / inspiration*. Her loyalty to the people of her country is ²*admirable / admiring / admire*.

WORD STORE 1D

Negative prefixes *un-, in-, dis-*

4 Add prefixes to make adjectives a–f negative. Then complete sentences 1–5 with the positive or negative form.

a <u>un</u>fit   d ____sensitive
b ____healthy   e ____cooperative
c ____loyal   f ____successful

0 John stopped going to the gym last year. He is very <u>unfit</u> now because he never does any exercise.
1 When Jenny gets tired, she becomes _____ – she won't do anything you ask her to.
2 It was _____ to ask James about pets. You know his rabbit died last week.
3 Nikki is a very _____ supporter of the basketball team. She goes to watch every game.
4 I know chocolate, cakes and biscuits are _____, but I love them.
5 The climbers tried to reach the top of the mountain, but they were _____. The weather was terrible and they had to return to their camp.

1.4 Reading

Classroom psychology

1 Read the article. Choose from the sentences (A–F) the one which fits each gap (1–5). There is one extra sentence.

A You probably also have a good relationship with your classmates.
B This could be the reason why students who sit here often get lower marks in tests and exams.
C So, if you really want to hear what everyone says in class, choose a different place to sit.
D Research suggests that the chair you choose in the classroom says a lot about you and your personality.
E This means it's a good idea to sit in a different place every day.
F Next time you miss a lesson, borrow notes from someone who sits here.

2 Read the article again. Are the statements true (T) or false (F)?

The article:
1 criticises students at the back of the classroom.
2 suggests that the students on one side usually do well at school.
3 is positive about the students in the middle of the classroom.
4 says that the best students sit at the front.
5 tells readers the best place to sit in the classroom.
6 suggests that intelligent students can sit anywhere and do well at school.

---

teenage-psycho.com – know us, know yourself   HOME | ARTICLES | FORUM | CONTACT

Today's hot article

Where you sit and how you fit

¹___ For more than seventy years, psychologists and teachers have studied the link between the place where students choose to sit in class and what they are like as people and learners. Where do you usually decide to sit? Have you ever really thought about the reasons for your decision?

At the back

People often think that students who sit at the back are lazy. But is this really true? Well, some researchers say it is not. In fact, shy students often choose the back row because it is far away from the teacher and they don't want to answer questions or be involved in discussions. At the back, students probably won't speak much, but in big classrooms, it can be hard to see the board and hear what the teacher is saying. ²___ For students with poor sight or hearing, a seat at the back of the classroom is definitely not a good choice.

On one side

Students who sit on one side of the class are normally interested in lessons, but they like watching and listening rather than joining in. These students are usually also very good at taking notes. ³___ On the sides of the classroom you will generally find modest and thoughtful people. These people usually get good marks at school and are keen on learning.

In the middle

Do you sit in the middle of the classroom? Then the statistics say you probably like your teacher. ⁴___ Caring, outgoing and cheerful people usually sit in the middle. They are normally serious about learning and feel disappointed with low marks in tests and exams.

At the front

Are you passionate about knowledge? Do you like being in control? Are you worried about missing important information in lessons? Yes? Then you probably sit right at the front of the class. Students at the front usually want to discuss things with the teacher and are often very keen on the subject. They want to be in the best place to see and hear everything the teacher does and says. The only problem with sitting at the front is that it can be difficult to see and hear what other students do and say in class. ⁵___

teenage-psycho.com needs YOUR opinion. Tell us what you think of this article. Add your comments below.

3 Complete the table with the underlined nouns and verbs in the article.

Verb	Noun
0 choose	choice
1 know	_____
2 _____	discussion
3 see	_____
4 hear	_____
5 decide	_____

4 Complete the sentences with words from Exercise 3. Change the form of the verbs if necessary.

0 Sorry? What did you say? Could you repeat that, please? My hearing is terrible these days.
1 When Ollie takes Helen out for dinner, she always _____ the most expensive thing on the menu.
2 Stevie Wonder, the famous soul singer, is blind. He lost his _____ when he was a baby.
3 I don't like Peter. He's arrogant. He thinks he _____ everything about everything.
4 Today in class we had an interesting _____ about politics.
5 We can't _____ if we like Kevin's new haircut or not. It is certainly very … different.

REMEMBER BETTER

When you learn a new word, check in a dictionary for other parts of speech from the same word, e.g. a noun or an adjective. The words from the same family will often look similar and so be easy to remember, e.g. *feel – feeling, care – careful*.

A Find the noun forms of the adjectives in a dictionary.

0 popular = popularity
1 fair = _____
2 selfish = _____
3 sensitive = _____
4 honest = _____
5 kind = _____

B Complete the sentences with words from Exercise A. Some letters are given.

0 Everyone likes Mrs Jackson. She's a very **pop**ular teacher.
1 **Fai**_____ is very important in tests and exams.
2 Young children are naturally **sel**_____ . Their parents teach them to share.
3 Be careful what you say to Rachel. She's very **sen**_____ about her appearance.
4 What makes a good friend? Well, **hon**_____ is very important.
5 Thank you very much for all your **kin**_____ . I enjoyed staying with you and your family.

WORD STORE 1E
Word families

5 Complete the sentences with the noun or adjective form of the words in capitals.

1 **GENEROUS**
a We want to thank all our guests for their generosity. We got some wonderful wedding presents.
b Kerry's parents paid for her holiday this year. They have always been very _____ .

2 **LOYAL**
a Real football fans are _____ to their teams when they are doing well and when they are doing badly.
b _____ is very important for young men in the gangs of Los Angeles.

3 **MODEST**
a I really admire Lucy's _____ . She got fantastic exam results, but she didn't tell everyone at school.
b You're too _____ ! Your charity work has helped hundreds of people.

4 **LAZY**
a Most adults think all teenagers are _____ . It's just not true. Most of us work very hard.
b Tim's not really ill – it's _____ . He just doesn't want to do any work.

5 **RESPONSIBLE**
a You are sixteen now and you have to take _____ for your actions.
b My parents are looking for a _____ person to look after our garden.

6 **BRAVE**
a Your little sister was very _____ at the dentist's. She didn't cry or complain.
b Male Emperor Penguins are well known for their _____ . They look after their eggs for months in the long, cold and dark Antarctic winter.

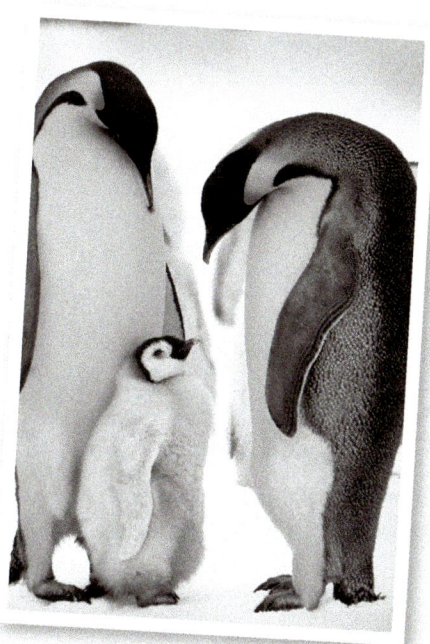

1.5 Grammar

Verb + -ing form or verb + to-infinitive

SHOW WHAT YOU KNOW

1 Choose the correct answer, A, B or C.

1 We ___ town on Saturday afternoons. We hate shopping when it's busy.
   A avoid   B miss   C decide
2 I ___ a burger and a chocolate milkshake, please.
   A like   B 'd like   C love
3 They usually eat in the most expensive restaurants, but we ___ it. We don't have enough money.
   A don't mind   B enjoy   C can't afford
4 My little brother ___ that he's riding a motorbike. He makes motorbike noises and runs around the house.
   A enjoys   B pretends   C spends time
5 Dad still goes running in the winter, but Mum ___ . She won't go because it's too cold.
   A prefers   B refuses   C agrees
6 I don't know how I'll ___ to finish all this homework before school on Monday, but I'll try.
   A hope   B consider   C manage

2 ★ Choose the correct options.

1 Christopher doesn't mind *to pay / paying* for English lessons. He goes on holiday to England every year.
2 Amy avoids *to sunbathe / sunbathing*. She has blonde hair and very white skin.
3 Do you want *to go / going* camping at the weekend?
4 Marco and his mum choose *flying / to fly* when they visit their family in Italy.
5 Carly pretends *to be / being* cheerful when she's away, but I think she really misses home.
6 Do we really need *to take / taking* four big bags with us? We're only going away for three days.

3 ★★ Complete the sentences with the correct form of the verbs in capitals.

1 **SHOP**
   I don't like _shopping_ with my dad. He hates _____ and I refuse _____ with him.
2 **SWIM**
   Lola loves _____ . Yesterday she managed _____ 500 metres. Next weekend she hopes _____ a full kilometre.
3 **BUY**
   Can you afford _____ this expensive coat? You should consider _____ a cheaper one. You need to save money.
4 **MEET**
   Simon enjoys _____ his friends at the skate park. This weekend they've agreed _____ at the skate shop because he wants to buy new wheels for his board.

4 ★★★ Complete the forum post with the correct form of the verbs in the box. There are two extra verbs.

[cook   eat   find   ~~live~~   miss
  see   shop visit write]

LEGALALIENS.COM | FORUM

Are you a foreigner living in Poland?
Tell us what you think about living here and what you miss from home.

ArayaWarsaw writes:

My family comes from Thailand, but we live in Warsaw because my dad works for a Polish electronics company. I like ⁰_living_ in Poland, but I'm not keen on the food. I miss ¹_____ for fresh food in the markets in Bangkok. Luckily, my mum is always busy in the kitchen. She spends a lot of time ²_____ our favourite Thai meals. Unfortunately, she can't always manage ³_____ the right ingredients, and we can't afford
⁴_____ Thailand every time we do our shopping! Anyway, I'm happy to say that there are always chillies in the shops in Poland. My dad won't consider ⁵_____ a meal without chillies!
Are there any other Thai teenagers out there? Would you like ⁶_____ to me and tell me what you miss about Thailand? I promise to reply.

SHOW WHAT YOU'VE LEARNT

5 Complete the sentences with the correct form of the verbs in brackets.

1 I spend a lot of time _____ (talk) on the telephone.
2 Katie loves _____ (walk) in the park in the summer.
3 My mum and dad avoid _____ (discuss) politics.
4 We'd like _____ (meet) you on Sunday afternoon.
5 My little brother misses _____ (play) with my dad when he's away on business.
6 My sister hates _____ (wash) the car when it's cold.

/6

1.6 Speaking language practice

Showing interest

1 Label the expressions *I* for showing interest, *S* for saying you are similar or *D* for saying you are different.

0 Me too. S
1 Is she?
2 Really? I love it.
3 That's cool.
4 Me neither.
5 Wow, that's interesting!
6 Don't you? Oh, I do.
7 Are you? Right …

2 Mark and Diane are at a music festival. They meet in a queue to buy a T-shirt. Complete their conversation with phrases from Exercise 1.

D: Excuse me. Do you know how much the T-shirts cost?
M: Er … no. I mean, yes, I … I think the white ones are £10 and the coloured ones £15. That's what it says on the sign.
D: Oh yes, you're right. I didn't see the sign. Well, I want a blue one.
M: Oh … er … ⁰m<u>e</u> t<u>oo</u>. I don't like white.
D: Ha! ¹M_____ n_____ . I'm Diane, by the way.
M: Er … hi. I'm Mike.
D: What do you think of the festival? I love it. I saw six bands yesterday. My friend is here too. Somewhere!
M: Oh … right … ²I_____ s_____ ?
D: Yeah. She's a DJ. She's playing tonight at 10 o'clock, in tent number 4.
M: Really? ³W_____ , t_____ i_____ !
D: Yeah. She plays techno mostly and a bit of house.
M: Oh right. I see. Well, I … er … don't really like techno.
D: ⁴R_____ ? I l_____ i_____ . I dance to any kind of music, really.
M: ⁵T_____ c_____ . Actually, I don't dance.
D: ⁶D_____ y_____ ? O_____ , I d_____ . I want to be a professional dancer one day. So, what do you do when everyone is dancing then?
M: Well, I stand at the back and listen to the music. I'm quite shy, really, especially with … er … girls.
D: ⁷A_____ y_____ ? R_____ … That's really sweet, Mike. Well, I think I'll … oh, look there's my friend!
M: What about your T-shirt?
D: Er … yes, that's my friend over there. Time to go …
M: Oh, er … OK. Bye then.

3 Put the words in the correct order to form sentences. Then use them to complete the conversations.

A she? / hasn't
that's / really? / cool
Ryan: My sister is having a baby in December.
Emma: ⁰<u>Really? That's cool.</u> My sister hasn't got any children yet.
Ryan: ¹_____ Well, maybe one day. I'm really looking forward to being an uncle.

B interesting / that's / wow
you? / can't
Karen: My parents are keen on music. Dad plays the piano and Mum is a great singer.
Ken: ²_____ I would like to hear them play. Unfortunately, I don't play any instruments and I can't sing.
Karen: ³_____ Well, don't worry, I'm not musical at all. I think my parents are a bit disappointed in me.

C love / really? / it / I
do / right … / you?
Gita: It's getting cold again. This morning there was ice on our car. I hate the winter.
Miko: ⁴_____ Everything looks so beautiful in the winter. I hope it snows soon. I love building snowmen.
Gita: ⁵_____ I prefer to stay inside and watch films.

D too / me
they? / are
Phil: I've finally saved enough money and this weekend I'm buying a new phone.
Paul: ⁶_____ Shall we go to the shops together?
Phil: Sure. How much have you got to spend?
Paul: Er … well, my parents are paying for it.
Phil: ⁷_____ Lucky you.

15

1.7 Writing

A personal email/letter

1 Choose the correct options to complete the tips on writing personal emails/letters.

1. Start the letter/email with a *formal* / *friendly* greeting, e.g. *Dear Mark* or *Hi Ruby*.
2. Use *full forms* / *contractions*, e.g. ~~I am~~ *I'm*.
3. It's a *good* / *bad* idea to ask some questions if you want a reply.
4. Finish the letter/email with a friendly goodbye such as *Yours sincerely* / *Cheers*.

2 Put the words in the correct order to form sentences.

0. Becky / hi   *Hi Becky*
1. writing / I'm / about / to / tell / you / more / bit / a / myself
   _____
2. now / I / going / be / must
   _____
3. hearing / to / forward / from / you / looking
   _____
4. you / your / are / doing / how / and / family?
   _____
5. was / hear / to / good / it / from / you
   _____
6. hello / say / your / family / to
   _____

3 Replace the underlined sentences in the email with more informal alternatives from Exercise 2.

Dear Ms Jones, ᵃ<u>Hi Becky</u>
ᵇ<u>I enjoyed reading your recent email.</u> _____
ᶜ<u>I hope you and your family are very well.</u>
_____ I'm excited about your visit next month, and ᵈ<u>I am writing to give you some information about myself and my life.</u> _____
I'm sixteen and I live with my parents in Madrid. I'm not crazy about living here, but it's OK.
I go to school in the city and I'm involved in lots of after-school activities. I'm not keen on studying, but I'm worried about my exams – I don't want Dad to be disappointed in me, so I work hard. Do you like school?
Sorry it's only a short email, but ᵉ<u>I need to stop writing now.</u>
_____ ᶠ<u>Please give my best wishes to your family.</u> _____
ᵍ<u>I look forward to receiving a reply from you soon.</u>
_____ I will see you next month.
Cheers,
Maria

SHOW WHAT YOU'VE LEARNT

4 You recently received an email from Harry, an English friend. Read part of his email and write your reply.

> My mum and dad tell me that you and your parents are coming to stay with us in the summer. That's great! Write and tell me something about yourself. What do you do in your free time? Who are your favourite bands and actors?

Write your email to Harry in about 100 words.

SHOW THAT YOU'VE CHECKED

In my personal email/letter:

- I have started with a friendly greeting (e.g. *Dear Nick* or *Hi Kate*). ☐
- the first paragraph says why I am writing. ☐
- I have included some information about my likes/dislikes/hobbies, etc. ☐
- I have included some questions to show that I want a reply. ☐
- I have used contractions (e.g. *I'm, aren't, that's*). ☐
- I have finished with a friendly goodbye, e.g. *See you soon/next week/in a few months*. ☐
- I have checked my spelling and punctuation. ☐

1.8 Word practice

Personality

1 Choose the correct answer, A, B or C.

1. Sharon studies every evening until midnight. She's incredibly ___ .
   A caring   B hard-working   C modest
2. Talking to Stephen makes me feel good. He's always ___ , even when he's got problems.
   A crazy   B cheerful   C sociable
3. Robert is too ___ for the job. He's thirty but he's never worked in his life.
   A elderly   B co-operative   C inexperienced
4. Sally is sometimes ___ and her words can hurt you, but she always tells the truth.
   A modest   B dishonest   C insensitive
5. Paul has been a loyal friend ___ our family for a very long time.
   A to   B at   C with
6. Talk to Dylan. He's a ___ person. I'm sure he'll solve your problem.
   A healthy   B sensible   C successful
7. I didn't like your dad's comment. I think it was ___ and rude.
   A unpopular   B unavailable   C unfair
8. We can't blame the government for this tragedy. They aren't ___ the deaths caused by the storms.
   A responsible for   B involved in   C serious about
9. Why are you asking me that question? Are you really ___ my opinion or not?
   A good at   B inspired by   C interested in
10. At home when I'm relaxing I wear an old T-shirt and ___ .
    A a coat   B a suit   C sweatpants
11. I ___ to my sister in the morning. She's always in a bad mood!
    A like speaking   B avoid speaking
    C decide to speak
12. My brother has just moved to Japan but he's not very happy there. He doesn't ___ to new places.
    A adapt easily   B make a good impression
    C have anything in common with
13. When Sarah meets new people, she tries to ___ with her knowledge of Chinese.
    A admire   B inspire   C impress
14. Our charity is looking for a new ___ to answer the phone in our office.
    A role model   B stereotype   C volunteer
15. John has been unemployed for a year so his top ___ now is to find a job.
    A identity   B priority   C opportunity

2 Find nine personality adjectives in the word square.

Q	W	E	R	T	Y	U	S	I	O	P	A
D	S	E	L	F	I	S	H	F	G	C	H
J	K	L	Z	X	O	C	Y	S	V	A	B
N	M	Q	W	E	U	R	T	E	Y	R	U
I	O	P	M	A	T	S	D	N	F	I	G
Z	L	X	O	C	G	V	B	S	M	N	Q
H	A	R	D	W	O	R	K	I	N	G	W
A	Z	P	E	O	I	U	Y	B	T	R	E
S	Y	D	S	F	N	G	H	L	J	K	L
Z	X	C	T	V	G	B	N	E	M	Q	W
E	R	T	Y	U	I	O	P	A	S	D	F
G	H	J	M	I	S	E	R	A	B	L	E

3 Match the adjectives with the prepositions.

0 good — a with
1 passionate   b for
2 disappointed   c in
3 interested   d about
4 keen   e at
5 responsible   f on
6 involved   g about
7 serious   h in

4 Choose three adjective + preposition collocations from Exercise 3 and use them to write true sentences about you.

0 *I'm good at Maths and Geography.*
1 _____
2 _____
3 _____

5 Complete the crossword with negative adjectives.

Across
1 a person who refuses to help

Down
2 a person who eats a lot of fast food and sugar
3 a person who says bad things about their friends when they aren't there
4 a person who doesn't do well in their career
5 a person who doesn't do any exercise or sport
6 a person who doesn't think about the feelings of others

17

1.9 Self-assessment

1 For each learning objective, tick the box that best matches your ability.

☺☺ = I understand and can help a friend.
☺ = I understand and can do it by myself.
☹ = I understand some, but have some questions.
☹☹ = I do not understand.

			☺☺	☺	☹	☹☹	Need help?
1.1	Vocabulary	I can describe people and talk about personal qualities.					Students' Book pages 12–13 Word Store page 3 Workbook pages 8–9
1.2	Grammar	I can ask questions using present tense forms.					Students' Book page 14 Workbook page 10
1.3	Listening	I can identify specific detail in a monologue.					Students' Book page 15 Workbook page 11
1.4	Reading	I can understand the structure of a text.					Students' Book pages 16–17 Workbook pages 12–13
1.5	Grammar	I can use different verb patterns.					Students' Book page 18 Workbook page 14
1.6	Speaking	I can show interest in what somebody is saying and say whether we are similar.					Students' Book page 19 Workbook page 15
1.7	Writing	I can write to someone and tell them about myself.					Students' Book pages 20–21 Workbook page 16

2 What can you remember from this unit?

New words I learned (the words you most want to remember from this unit)	Expressions and phrases I liked (any expressions or phrases you think sound nice, useful or funny)	English I heard or read outside class (e.g. from websites, books, adverts, films, music)

1.10 Self-check

1 Choose the negative adjective in each group.

0	honest	(selfish)	happy	modest
1	caring	cheerful	inexperienced	hard-working
2	unpopular	outgoing	sensible	loyal
3	cooperative	fair	lazy	modest
4	responsible	popular	uncooperative	cheerful
5	brave	generous	dishonest	loyal

/5

2 Choose the correct options.

0 I was very disappointed *at / in /* (with) the phone I bought.
1 Jay is passionate *with / about / on* snowboarding.
2 Carly is very good *at / about / for* cooking.
3 Andrew is responsible *for / on / to* buying the food.
4 Are you serious *on / about / in* becoming a surgeon?
5 We are involved *at / about / in* the school play.

/5

3 Complete the sentences with the words in the box. There are two extra words.

> caring   cheerful   ~~dishonest~~   fair
> healthy   outgoing   sensible   successful

0 Clara lies to her parents. I am not so *dishonest*.
1 Tom never does anything crazy or dangerous. He's a very _____ person.
2 Sarah eats well, exercises and gets plenty of sleep. She's a(n) _____ person and she rarely gets sick.
3 Alfie is _____ . He makes friends easily.
4 Sally is a very _____ person. She likes looking after other people.
5 Jen's dad is a(n) _____ author. His books have sold thousands of copies.

/5

4 Choose the correct answer, A, B or C.

0 ___ you ever tried yoga?
  A Do   (B Have)   C Are
1 Do they ___ their car every weekend?
  A washing   B washes   C wash
2 Which singer ___ a number one hit?
  A have never had   C is never having
  B has never had
3 ___ is he talking to on the phone?
  A Who   B What   C What time
4 ___ do you usually clean your room?
  A Who   B When   C What
5 What TV series ___ at the moment?
  A do you watch   C have you watched
  B are you watching

/5

5 Complete the sentences with the correct form of the verbs in brackets.

0 My sister has decided *to celebrate* (celebrate) her birthday after her exams.
1 Kelly would like _____ (learn) how to play the violin.
2 Sam doesn't enjoy _____ (play) football when it's cold and rainy.
3 Will you manage _____ (carry) the shopping on your own?
4 Have you considered _____ (study) English at university?
5 Jeanette's dad sometimes drives her to school, but really, she prefers _____ (walk).

/5

6 Read the advert and choose the correct answer, A, B or C.

JOIN THE POLICE

Would you like to ⁰___ something to help society and the community you live in?

Have you ever ¹___ about a career in the police?

Police work is challenging – our officers are often in difficult situations and accept ²___ for their actions. Our national police force is serious ³___ reducing crime and we need ⁴___ people to help us do this. Choose ⁵___ for the police and help make your town a safe place to live.

0 (A do)   B doing   C done
1 A think   B thinking   C thought
2 A responsible   B responsibility   C irresponsible
3 A about   B for   C with
4 A uncooperative   B pessimistic   C hard-working
5 A to work   B working   C work

/5

Total /30

2 INVENTION

2.1 Vocabulary

Technology • Compound nouns • Collocations • Phrasal verbs

SHOW WHAT YOU KNOW

1 Look at the photos and write the inventions.

     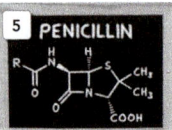

0 refrigerator   1 r_____   2 je_____   3 c_____ s_____   4 n_____ p_____   5 a_____

WORD STORE 2A
Compound nouns – computers

2 Complete the compound nouns in the texts. Some letters are given.

@ **COMPUCLEAN**, we clean all kinds of computers, including ⁰desktop computers and ¹l_____s. Call us now on 073 123 345 456 for more information.

Thank you for joining www.english4U2learn.com, the number one ²w_____e for language learners. We have sent you an email with your ³u_____e and other log-in details. Follow the link in the email and choose a ⁴p_____d of nine characters or more (use numbers and letters).

howitworks.com – internet searches
When you use the touch screen on your phone or the ⁵k_____d on your computer to put a word or phrase into a ⁶s_____h e_____e such as Google, your device connects to an ⁷I_____t s_____r which sends back the information you asked for. If you have ⁸b_____d, this happens very quickly.

our comments on the topic of teenage communication
will328 says:
Emails are only for business people. Most young people use ⁹s_____l n_____g sites like Facebook or we just use our phones to send ¹⁰t_____t m_____s.

WORD STORE 2B
Collocations – computers

3 Complete the instructions with the verbs in the box. There are two extra verbs.

[click   do   download   follow
  ~~go~~   open   speak   visit]

Quick start guide

Touch this icon to connect to the Internet and ⁰go online.

To ¹_____ your favourite websites, touch the website icons, e.g. Twitter.

You can ²_____ music and listen to it with the media player here.

Touch this icon to ³_____ a text document.

To add music from your computer, plug in the USB cable here, ⁴_____ on the phone icon on your laptop or desktop and follow the instructions on the screen.

⁵_____ us on Twitter to get more tips for your new smartphone.

20

WORD STORE 2C
Phrasal verbs – technology

4 Match the verbs with the prepositions to make phrasal verbs about technology.

1 click a up/down
2 switch b on/off
3 scroll c up
4 log d on
5 hang e on/off

REMEMBER THIS
Log on and *log in* both mean 'start using a computer system or website'. Their antonyms are *log off* and *log out*.

REMEMBER BETTER
When you learn phrasal verbs, check their antonyms in a dictionary too. They often include the opposite preposition, e.g. *switch on* ≠ *switch off*.

A Write the opposites. Use a dictionary if necessary.

0 scroll up ≠ scroll down
1 turn up (the volume) ≠ _____
2 turn on ≠ _____
3 log on ≠ _____

B Complete the sentences with phrasal verbs from Exercise A.

0 The information you need is at the bottom of the webpage. You need to scroll down.
1 I can't study with that loud music playing. Will you _____ the volume, please?
2 Use your username and password to _____ to the website.
3 _____ the TV before you go to bed.

SHOW WHAT YOU'VE LEARNT

5 Choose the correct answer, A, B or C.

1 We can't log on to the website. Something is wrong. The message says that there is a problem with our ___.
   A desktop computer B internet server
   C text message
2 I've started using a new ____. I type in what I'm looking for on the Internet and it helps me find the websites.
   A social networking B username
   C search engine
3 Sarah spends a lot of time on ___ sites like Facebook.
   A search engine B social networking
   C Internet server
4 Kevin loves music. He ___ his favourite bands on Twitter.
   A follows B visits C clicks
5 Ben emailed the document to you. Have you got it? OK, please ____ it and scroll down to page 5.
   A log B scroll C open
6 Please don't ____ again. Talk to me!
   A hang up B turn down C switch off
7 To use this service, you need to ____ with your username and password.
   A log off B log on C hang up
8 OK, that is the end of the lesson. Please ____ the system and switch off your computer.
   A switch off B log off C turn off
9 To find the link in this website, you need to ____ down to the bottom of the page.
   A click B scroll C hang
10 You can download photos from your computer if you ____ on the camera icon.
    A scroll B click C switch

/10

2.2 Grammar

Past Continuous and Past Simple

SHOW WHAT YOU KNOW

1 Complete the sentences with the Past Simple form of the verbs in brackets.

1. Graeme <u>went</u> (go) online this morning and _____ (buy) tickets for the concert.
2. Simone and Kay _____ (be) very busy all day yesterday. They _____ (not have) time for a break.
3. _____ (Carly/be) at the Science club last week? _____ (she/give) her presentation?
4. _____ (you/download) those games recently? _____ (they/be) free?

2 ★ Complete the conversation with the Past Continuous form of the verbs in brackets.

At the police station …
A: What ⁰ <u>were you doing</u> (you/do) at six o'clock on 2 May?
B: Erm … I don't remember. I think I was at home. Yes, I ¹_____ (watch) TV.
A: Was anyone at home with you?
B: No, nobody. It was just me. I ²_____ (not work) that day.
A: I see. So nobody saw you at home at 6 p.m. that day?
B: Oh … er … yes, of course. Silly me! My wife was there too. She ³_____ (make) dinner in the kitchen. She ⁴_____ (cook) my favourite pizza.
A: And what about your children?
B: Oh yeah, the kids! They ⁵_____ (do) their homework upstairs in their bedrooms.
A: And your mother-in-law?
B: Oh yes, of course. Er … she ⁶_____ (stand) in the kitchen with my wife. They ⁷_____ (talk).
A: I see. So, can you explain why we have pictures of you waiting in your car outside the bank at 6 p.m.?
B: Er … pictures?

3 ★ Complete the sentences with the Past Continuous form of the verbs in brackets.

0. Alexander Graham Bell <u>was experimenting</u> (experiment) in his laboratory when he made the first successful telephone call.
1. _____ (Archimedes/have) a bath when he shouted 'Eureka!'?
2. Mark Zuckerberg _____ (study) at Harvard University when he created Facebook.
3. _____ (Isaac Newton/sit) under an apple tree when he thought of his theory of gravity?
4. Marie Curie _____ (not live) in Poland when she won her first Nobel prize in 1903.
5. Art Fry created Post-it-notes when he _____ (work) for 3M.
6. George and Diane _____ (visit) a school when terrorists attacked the World Trade Center.

4 ★★ Choose the correct options.

1. Sorry, I *had / was having* a shower when you *called / were calling*.
2. *Did Lola stand / Was Lola standing* outside when it *started / was starting* to rain?
3. When the car *crashed / was crashing* into us, we *waited / were waiting* at the traffic lights.
4. Fortunately, we *didn't ski / weren't skiing* when the bad weather *came / was coming*.

5 ★★★ Complete the story with the Past Simple or Past Continuous form of the verbs in brackets.

What ⁰ <u>were you doing</u> (you/do) the last time you ¹_____ (see) something truly amazing? Well, fisherman and journalist Al McGlashan ²_____ (fish) with friends in his private boat when he ³_____ (find) something very, very strange. At first, the group of fishermen ⁴_____ (not know) what it was, but when they ⁵_____ (look) closely, they saw the body of a giant squid; almost four metres long!

Al took out his video camera and then another amazing thing ⁶_____ (happen). He ⁷_____ (film) the squid when a large blue shark ⁸_____ (arrive) and began eating the dead squid for lunch!

Al ⁹_____ (tell) an Australian newspaper that in all his years of fishing he'd never seen anything like it.

SHOW WHAT YOU'VE LEARNT

6 Find and correct the mistakes in the sentences.

0. He ~~was clicking~~ on an icon and nothing happened.
   <u>clicked</u>
1. Tom was downloading music when his computer was getting the virus. _____
2. Annabelle visited the zoo when she saw an elephant for the first time. _____
3. Grandma, were you watching television when Apollo 11 was landing on the moon? _____
4. They were waiting for the bus when it was starting to snow. _____
5. The girls were playing tennis when Helen was breaking her arm. _____
6. Was the computers working this morning when you arrived? _____

/6

2.3 Listening language practice

Collocations • Word families

1 Read what three speakers said about their jobs and complete gaps a–c with the jobs in the box. There are two extra jobs.

archaeologist   chemist   ecologist
marine biologist   physicist

Extract from Students' Book recording CD•1.36 MP3•36

S1: Everybody's surprised that I'm a scientist – my father's an English teacher and my mother's a translator. But in high school my Chemistry teacher gave me the idea to be a scientist. He gave me books to read ¹*about / with / in* science and I saw that people were ²*making / doing / collecting* new discoveries that were useful to society. When I read that they were ³*protecting / finding / doing* new cures for serious illnesses, I decided I wanted to be a(n) ᵃ_____ .

S3: Science is not just my job. It's the way I see the world. I always want to understand how things work – ⁴*what / which / why* are they like that? How did we get here? ⁵*How / When / Who* old is the universe? You know, the really big questions. I love ⁶*collecting / protecting / doing* experiments, analysing data and finding logical explanations. I don't think I became a(n) ᵇ_____ – I was born that way.

S5: The first time I went scuba diving, I saw a little fish swimming away ⁷*to / into / at* the distance, and ⁸*in / to / at* that moment I thought, 'Oh yes, that's what I want to do – I want to explore oceans, ⁹*collect / protect / make* evidence about global warming and help to ¹⁰*find / protect / make* marine life.' I love my job – I can't understand why everybody isn't a(n) ᶜ_____ .

2 Read the extracts in Exercise 1 again and choose the correct options.

3 Listen and check your answers to Exercises 1 and 2.

4 Cross out the word that cannot be used with the verb.
  1 **make**   research / discoveries / decisions / plans
  2 **find**   cures / answers / decisions / alternatives
  3 **do**   experiments / solutions / research / business
  4 **collect** evidence / signatures / information / science
  5 **protect** marine life / the environment / wildlife / biology

5 Complete the sentences with collocations from Exercise 4.
  0 We have Thursday and Friday off school next week. Shall we make some <u>plans</u>? Let's go to the mountains.
  1 Abi found the _____ to last year's Chemistry exam questions online. It was useful to read them.
  2 Do you want a birthday party or not? Make a _____ so we can make plans and invite all your friends.
  3 My dad is travelling for work again. His company is doing _____ with a Japanese car company.
  4 Emma's got a summer job with a marketing company doing _____ in a shopping centre. She has to stop shoppers and ask them to answer questions.
  5 Our class is collecting _____ for a petition against animal testing. Will you add your name?
  6 The government should not build a new road here. We need to protect _____ and the natural environment.

REMEMBER BETTER

When you learn new nouns (e.g. *cure, research, evidence*), use a dictionary to find verbs that form collocations with them (e.g. *find a cure, do research, collect evidence*). Write sentences using the collocations to help you remember them better.

Write sentences with the noun and verbs below.

text message: ~~write~~/send/get/read
<u>I usually write 20-30 text messages every day.</u>
_____
_____
_____

WORD STORE 2D
Word families

6 Choose the correct options.
  1 When the experiments are finished, we *analyse / analysis* the data and decide what to do.
  2 The *discover / discovery* of penicillin in 1928 changed medicine forever.
  3 Charles Darwin was the first person to explain the *evolved / evolution* of plants and animals.
  4 The US wants to send people to *explore / exploration* Mars by 2030.
  5 *Imagine / Imagination* what technology will be like when you and I are old.
  6 The best way to learn about animal behaviour is to *observe / observation* animals in the wild.
  7 Green groups are working for the *preserve / preservation* of the environment.
  8 Our research tells us that vitamin C gives *protect / protection* against cancer.
  9 There are no simple *solves / solutions* to the problem of global warming.

23

2.4 Reading

All about passwords • Antonyms • Collocations

Glossary

crack (a code or a password) (v) = work out, solve (a code or a password)
fingerprint (n) = a mark made by the pattern of the skin on the end of your fingers
century (n) = 100 years
memorable (adj) = easy to remember

1 Read the article quickly and choose the best title.

1. How to guess someone's password ☐
2. How to create a secure and easy-to-remember password ☐
3. How to remember all your passwords ☐

A

We all know the basic rules for choosing good passwords and keeping them secret. Rule number one: use numbers, symbols and a good mix of letters – upper case (A, B, C) and lower case (a, b, c). Rule number two: use a different password for each of the devices you use or for each website you visit. Rule number three: change your passwords regularly. Rule number four: never write your passwords down. These rules sound easy to follow, right?

B

Well, not really. The rules say that a secure password should look something like this: N0r@5%_fpOe+47d1nk. Do you think you can remember that? Don't forget you should have several different ones, you shouldn't write them down AND you have to change them every few weeks. Does this sound like an impossible task? Well, for most people, it is. So what do most of us do?

C

Recently, researchers had a chance to analyse secret information about passwords. They found that many of us totally ignore the experts' advice and choose simple, easy to remember and extremely insecure passwords. Data shows that one out of every ten people uses *1234* as the pin number for their bank cards and that the passwords *welcome, 123456, ninja* and, of course, *password* are some of the most popular choices.

Even governments choose terrible passwords. It seems hard to believe, but in the 1980s, the American government actually used the 'secret code' 00000000 to unlock its nuclear missiles.

D

So how can we make our passwords secure and memorable? Well, first, the length of your password is important. For a hacker with a computer that can make 1,000 guesses per second, a lower case, five-letter password like *ftmps* takes only around three hours and forty-five minutes to crack. A similar password with twenty letters takes a little longer – around 6.5 thousand trillion centuries!

E

Hackers are very good at guessing when we choose symbols and numbers instead of letters. For example, the password *M@nch3st3r* seems like a good one, but the code is actually very simple – first letter = upper case, @ = a, 3 = E. It is easy for hackers to program their computers to look out for these kinds of codes. Because the length of the password is so important, a group of words written in lower case, e.g. *help cheese monkey swimming* is much more secure than something like *M@nch3st3r*, and probably a bit easier to remember (think of a monkey – it is shouting for help and swimming towards some cheese!).

F

One day, we probably won't have to worry about all this because we won't need passwords. Some laptop computers already have fingerprint readers. Recently, scientists in the US have designed a prototype ring for your finger that sends electricity through your skin to a touch screen to tell computers and phones who you are. For now though, we still need passwords, and if you want one that is secure and memorable, the best advice is to make it loooooong!

24

2 **Match paragraph headings 1–8 with paragraphs A–F of the article. There are two extra headings.**

1. NuM83rs @nd sYmB0ls ☐
2. How to stop hackers ☐
3. No more passwords! ☐
4. Passwords for beginners ☐
5. Bad choices ☐
6. How they do it in the US ☐
7. How good is your memory? ☐
8. Short = bad, long = good ☐

3 **Read the article again and choose the correct answer, A, B, C or D.**

1. Which basic rule for passwords is *not* mentioned?
   A Use a mix of letters, numbers and symbols for passwords.
   B Use different passwords for different websites.
   C Never tell your passwords to another person.
   D Change your passwords often.

2. The article says that most people
   A don't know how to choose a secure password.
   B use the same password for everything.
   C don't follow experts' advice when they choose a password.
   D forget passwords easily.

3. The most popular password is
   A not mentioned.
   B *password*.
   C *1234*.
   D *00000000*.

4. In the 1980s the US government
   A had a secure password for unlocking its nuclear missiles.
   B didn't have a password for unlocking its nuclear missiles.
   C lost the password for unlocking its nuclear missiles.
   D didn't have a secure password for unlocking its nuclear missiles.

5. The article says that hackers
   A choose passwords with symbols and numbers.
   B program their computers to look for symbols and numbers in passwords.
   C choose lower case passwords.
   D program their computers to look for long passwords.

6. According to the article, scientists in the US recently designed
   A fingerprint readers for phones.
   B a prototype keyboard.
   C something people can wear to identify them.
   D a touch screen laptop.

4 **Match the underlined words in the article with their opposites.**

0. fantastic ≠ *terrible*
1. advanced ≠ _____
2. similar ≠ _____
3. forget ≠ _____
4. possible ≠ _____
5. complicated ≠ _____

REMEMBER BETTER

Many words in English have opposites, e.g. *start ≠ finish, easy ≠ difficult, man ≠ woman*. When you learn pairs of opposites, use them both in personal sentences to help you remember them better.

Write personal sentences with the opposites in Exercise 4.

0. *The weather was terrible at the weekend, but we saw a fantastic film on Saturday.*
1. _____
2. _____
3. _____
4. _____
5. _____

WORD STORE 2E
Collocations

5 **Complete the conversation with the phrases in the box. Change the form of the verbs if necessary. There are two extra phrases.**

> find a solution   fix the problem   follow events
> get home   ~~go crazy~~   raise your hand

In the year 2073:

A: Good afternoon. This is Robocorp. How can I help you?
B: Hello? Robocorp? Oh, thank goodness you've answered. Help!
A: What is the problem, madam?
B: My home-help robot has ⁰*gone crazy*! I ¹_____ from work today and all the food from the fridge was all over the kitchen floor and there were broken plates and cups everywhere, and the poor cat was …
A: OK, madam, please try to calm down. I'm sure we can ²_____ to the problem.
B: Calm down? Do you realise I am calling you from the bathroom?
A: The bathroom?
B: Yes! It's the only room with a lock on the door. I'm scared he's going to attack me.
A: Madam, our robots are programmed never to hurt their owners.
B: And are they programmed to go crazy in the kitchen too?
A: Er, no … Stay in the bathroom, madam. I'm sending someone over to ³_____ .
B: Aargh! Quickly! I can hear him … he's coming!

2.5 Grammar

used to

SHOW WHAT YOU KNOW

1. **Tick the sentences that describe routines. Choose the time expressions that show regularity.**
   0. Alastair played computer games <u>every evening</u> before bed. ✓
   1. Karen bought a new laptop last weekend. ☐
   2. Patricia and Matt called each other every Friday night. ☐
   3. Dean always watched football on Saturday afternoons. ☐
   4. Mary dropped her mobile phone down the toilet. ☐

2. ★ **When they went to university, two friends, Carl and Owen, moved into a flat together. Write sentences about them with *used to* or *didn't use to* and the verbs in brackets.**

   When they lived with their parents:
   0. They <u>didn't use to eat</u> (eat) unhealthy food. Now they only eat kebabs and pizzas.
   1. They _____ (do) any cleaning at home. They still don't do much and their flat is a mess.
   2. Their parents _____ (pay) the bills. Now they pay their own bills.
   3. Carl _____ (use) his dad's computer. Now he uses Owen's.
   4. Carl and Owen _____ (argue). Now they argue about the computer.

3. ★★ **Write affirmative sentences, negative sentences and questions about mobile phones in 1983. Use the correct form of *used to* and the prompts.**
   0. mobile phones / have cameras (?)
      <u>Did mobile phones use to have cameras?</u>
   1. mobile phones / cost a lot of money (+)
      _____
   2. most people / own a mobile phone (–)
      _____
   3. people / make fewer phone calls (+)
      _____
   4. mobile phones / be bigger (?)
      _____
   5. mobile phones / have touch screens (–)
      _____
   6. mobile phones / send text messages (?)
      _____

4. ★★★ **Tick the correct sentence in each pair. Sometimes both sentences are correct.**

   When I was in the Science club at school:
   1. a We met every Thursday at 4 p.m. ✓
      b We used to meet every Thursday at 4 p.m. ☐
   2. a We watched videos about great discoveries. ☐
      b We used to watch videos about great discoveries. ☐
   3. a One week, a physicist came to speak to us. ☐
      b One week, a physicist used to come to speak to us. ☐
   4. a Our group went on a trip to the Science Museum in London. ☐
      b Our group used to go on a trip to the Science Museum in London. ☐
   5. a My friend Emma once gave a talk about the sun. ☐
      b My friend Emma once used to give a talk about the sun. ☐

SHOW WHAT YOU'VE LEARNT

5. **Complete the conversation between Jodie and her dad with the correct form of *used to* and the verbs in brackets.**

   J: Dad, ¹_____ (you/use) a laptop when you were my age?
   D: What? No, I didn't. I was your age in 1981. We ²_____ (have) laptops back then.
   J: So, how ³_____ (you/check) your messages?
   D: Jodie! There were no messages or texts, no Facebook or anything. We ⁴_____ (send) letters or faxes.
   J: I see. Wow! Dad, what's a fax?
   D: Er … well, it was a bit like a photocopier. You ⁵_____ (write) your message on a piece of paper, then put it in the fax machine …
   J: And then?
   D: Well, then you ⁶_____ (dial) the number and wait. The machine er … well, it read the piece of paper and sent it to your friend.
   J: What? The piece of paper?
   D: No! Not the same piece of paper, Jodie – just the message.
   J: I see. Wow!

   /6

1983   today

26

2.6 Speaking language practice
Telling a story

1 Put the sentences in the correct order. Which photo are they about?

9/11/01 World Trade Center attacks

26/12/04 South Asian tsunami

a At first I thought it was a movie. ☐
b Let me tell you about the day it happened. 1
c For weeks afterwards everyone in the country was shocked and frightened. ☐
d I was having breakfast with my family. ☐
e The television news was on, but we weren't really watching. ☐
f It was terrible and I hope it will never happen again. ☐
g In the end, both towers fell down and nearly 3,000 people died. ☐
h Suddenly, it happened again; another plane hit the other tower. ☐
i I looked up and saw the pictures of a plane. It had hit one of the two towers. ☐

2 Complete the conversation with the words/phrases in the box. There are two extra words/phrases.

> ~~except for~~   excited   happened   luckily
> next time   nightmare   relieved   shocked
> sounds   suddenly   to start with

A: We had a fantastic time on our summer holiday, ⁰*except for* the day we went to the island.
B: What ¹_____?
A: We were travelling by fast boat to visit a beautiful little island. The captain of the boat was going very fast and the waves were really big. ²_____, the boat hit a giant wave.
B: Oh no!
A: There was a loud bang, the front window broke and lots and lots of water rushed in.
B: Wow! That ³_____ really frightening.
A: Yeah, well, we were ⁴_____ because it happened so quickly and the water hit us really hard. ⁵_____, nobody was seriously hurt.
B: What did you do?
A: Well, in the end we got to the island – wet, but very ⁶_____ to be back on dry land.
B: What a ⁷_____!
A: ⁸_____ we'll take the slow boat.

3 Complete the conversations with one word in each gap.

Conversation 1
A: I once met someone famous.
B: Really? Who?
A: Well, I ⁰*was* sitting in Manchester Airport, waiting for a flight to Berlin. I remember, I was reading *Harry Potter* ¹_____ the time. Suddenly, the lady next to me said, 'Excuse me, ²_____ you enjoying that book?'
B: Who was it?
A: Well, I looked at her and I thought, 'I know you,' and then I realised it was J. K. Rowling.
B: What? The author of the book you ³_____ reading? That's amazing! What did you say?
A: Well, to start ⁴_____, I didn't know what to say, but fortunately, she was really friendly. ⁵_____ the end, we chatted for about ten minutes and I told her how much I love her books.
B: What a great story!
A: I know, and she signed my book too. I'll never forget that day.

Conversation 2
A: I'm afraid ¹_____ horses.
B: What? Why?
A: Well, when I was twelve years old, my neighbour took me riding on her horse.
B: ²_____ happened?
A: It was my first time on a horse. ³_____ first everything was OK. We ⁴_____ going very slowly. My neighbour was holding the horse and I was sitting ⁵_____ its back. I was enjoying the ride, but then, all ⁶_____ a sudden, there was a loud noise and the horse got scared and started running – really fast!
B: That sounds really frightening.
A: It was. Luckily, I didn't fall off. I stay away from horses these days.

27

2.7 Writing

An informal email

1 Where are these linkers used in an email? Mark them as B (beginning), M (middle) or E (end).

- 0 afterwards — M
- 1 eventually ☐
- 2 first ☐
- 3 later ☐
- 4 after that ☐
- 5 finally ☐
- 6 in the end ☐
- 7 then ☐

2 Read the email and choose the correct options.

Subject: Don't go to that club
Attachment: jpeg picture – queuing to the club ☹

Hi Ollie,

Just a quick message to say don't go to that new club. We went there last night and we had a terrible time! ¹*Later / First / After that*, we missed the bus, so we got a very expensive taxi into town. ²*Then / In the end / First*, when we arrived, the queue for the club was really long. We started waiting at 7.30 p.m. and ³*after that / eventually / later* got to the front at 8.30 p.m. – an hour later. ☹ ⁴*Then / Finally / First* we paid £10 each to get in. £10! For under-eighteens night – crazy! ⁵*After that / Eventually / First*, we put our coats in the cloakroom – another £2 each. ⁶*In the end / First / Suddenly*, we didn't have any money for drinks or for a taxi home, so we walked back, thirsty and in the rain! Don't ever try to walk back from town, Ollie. It's a long way!

Next time we'll ask Mum and Dad to go out and we'll have a party at home.

CU Monday,

Pete

3 Write suggestions with imperatives. Use the underlined verbs.

0 We <u>went</u> to the club and it was great.
 Go to the club.
00 We didn't enjoy <u>eating</u> in the restaurant.
 Don't eat in the restaurant.
1 Kelly <u>took</u> the bus and she said it was fine.
 _____
2 Mum <u>visited</u> the museum. She said it was boring.
 _____
3 We <u>ordered</u> the double cheese pizza – delicious!
 _____
4 They enjoyed <u>swimming</u> in the sea.
 _____
5 Fiona's <u>been</u> to Paris four times. She loves it.
 _____
6 I hated <u>sitting</u> at the front. It was too close.
 _____

4 Put the words in the correct order to form sentences.

0 this / email / sorry / is / short / a
 Sorry this is a short email.
1 you / to / hear / great / from _____
2 sure / like / you'll / I'm / it _____
3 a / message / just / quick / say hi / to _____
4 need / help / your / I _____
5 this / useful / is / hope _____

SHOW WHAT YOU'VE LEARNT

5 You recently received an email from your friend Tara. Read part of her email and write your reply.

It's my sister's birthday next week and I want to plan a surprise party for her. I'm looking for ideas! Have you been to any great parties recently? Can you give me any advice?

Write your email in about 100 words.

SHOW THAT YOU'VE CHECKED

In my informal email:

- I have started with a short phrase (e.g. *It's great to hear from you!*). ☐
- I have used imperatives to make suggestions/give advice (e.g. *Make sure you visit the Robot Room!*). ☐
- I have used dashes (–) to add comments or more information (e.g. *We watched another film about black holes – that was scary.*). ☐
- I have used appropriate linkers for the beginning, middle and end. ☐
- I have checked my spelling and punctuation. ☐
- I have written about 100 words. ☐

2.8 Use of English

Four-option multiple choice

1   Read the article below and choose the correct word (A, B, C or D) for each space.

DNA testing

Today police all over the world use DNA tests to ⁰___ crimes. Every person has their own special biological code. This is ¹___ DNA and it can show the police ²___ was in a place and touched different things when a crime happened.

Scientists knew about DNA a long ³___ ago. However, using DNA tests to help the police only began in 1986. Alec Jeffreys was an English scientist and he was ⁴___ with DNA! He ⁵___ a lot of research and discovered a way to show and compare different people's DNA. At that time someone killed two girls in Narborough and the police couldn't find the killer. They knew about Jeffrey's research, so they ⁶___ a big risk: they decided ⁷___ test all the men who lived near the dead girls. It took a lot of time and money, but they didn't ⁸___ up. In the end, they found the man who was responsible ⁹___ the killings.

After this success police in many other countries started to ¹⁰___ people's DNA to find criminals. It is now one of the most important methods they use.

0	A answer	**B solve**	C find	D discover
1	A name	B said	C called	D titled
2	A why	B where	C who	D when
3	A period	B years	C date	D time
4	A enthusiastic	B obsessed	C passionate	D optimistic
5	A did	B made	C experimented	D had
6	A followed	B took	C allowed	D carried
7	A to	B for	C on	D with
8	A stop	B make	C do	D give
9	A of	B at	C for	D on
10	A ask	B analyse	C experiment	D observe

TIPS:

Question 5: Only one of these verbs collocates with *research*.
Question 7: What verb form follows *decide*?
Question 9: What preposition follows the word *responsible*?

Sentence transformations

2   Here are some sentences about Harry and his sister. For each question, complete the second sentence so that it means the same as the first. Use no more than three words.

0   Harry is older than his sister Ruth.
Harry's sister Ruth *is younger than* Harry.

1   Ruth loves playing computer games.
Ruth is mad _____ playing computer games.

2   She doesn't watch so much TV these days.
She _____ watch more TV than she does now.

3   She bought a very expensive new game last weekend.
She spent a lot of _____ a new game last weekend.

4   Now she hasn't got enough money to go to London with her mates.
Now she can't _____ to London with her mates.

5   Harry said he couldn't lend her £100.
Harry refused _____ her £100.

TIPS:

Question 1: You need a preposition here.
Question 2: Which two words can you use to talk about a past habit?
Question 4: What word completes this phrase meaning 'not have enough money to do something'?

2.9 Self-assessment

For each learning objective, tick the box that best matches your ability.

☺☺ = I understand and can help a friend.
☺ = I understand and can do it by myself.
☹ = I understand some, but have some questions.
☹☹ = I do not understand.

			☺☺	☺	☹	☹☹	Need help?
2.1	Vocabulary	I can talk about technology.					Students' Book pages 24–25 Word Store page 5 Workbook pages 20–21
2.2	Grammar	I can use the Past Continuous and the Past Simple to describe past events.					Students' Book page 26 Workbook page 22
2.3	Listening	I can identify specific detail in conversations.					Students' Book page 27 Workbook page 23
2.4	Reading	I can find specific details in a story about space travel.					Students' Book pages 28–29 Workbook pages 24–25
2.5	Grammar	I can talk about past states and repeated actions.					Students' Book page 30 Workbook page 26
2.6	Speaking	I can tell a story and be a good listener.					Students' Book page 31 Workbook page 27
2.7	Writing	I can write to someone and recount a past event.					Students' Book pages 32–33 Workbook page 28

2 What can you remember from this unit?

New words I learned (the words you most want to remember from this unit)	**Expressions and phrases I liked** (any expressions or phrases you think sound nice, useful or funny)	**English I heard or read outside class** (e.g. from websites, books, adverts, films, music)

2.10 Self-check

1 Complete the sentences with the correct form of the words in the box. There are two extra words.

> click   download   follow   open
> raise   ~~scroll down~~   switch   visit

0 For more information, _scroll down_ the page and choose a product from the menu.
1 To open the program, _____ on the icon.
2 Ryan doesn't _____ music. He prefers buying CDs.
3 Jane _____ her favourite musicians on Twitter.
4 When the teacher asks a question, please _____ your hand before you answer.
5 Charge the battery before you _____ on your new phone for the first time.

/5

2 Complete the words in the sentences. Some letters are given.

0 Most of today's **t**ech**nology** did not exist when my parents were young.
1 Send me a **t**_____ **t m**_____**e** when you get off the train.
2 To log on to our website, enter your **u**_____**e** and password.
3 You can use a **s**_____ **e**_____ to look for information online about any topic you want to research.
4 One of the keys on my **k** _____ is missing. I can't type the letter S!
5 **B**_____**d** makes Internet connections much faster than they were in the past.

/5

3 Complete the sentences with the correct form of the verbs in brackets.

0 The _preservation_ (preserve) of the environment is our top priority.
1 The doctor needs to _____ (analyse) Phillip's test results to find out what is wrong with him.
2 The _____ (evolve) of computers means today's models are smaller, faster and more powerful.
3 One student does the experiment and the other _____ (observe) and makes notes.
4 Remember that money will not _____ (solve) all of life's problems.
5 Visiting Mars is the next big challenge in space _____ (explore).

/5

4 Choose the correct options.

0 Peter (didn't go)/ wasn't going to school on Thursday.
1 Adam did / was doing his homework when Simon called / was calling.
2 We slept / were sleeping when the postman rang / was ringing the doorbell.
3 Were they finding / Did they find the pharmacy before it closed / was closing?
4 Chloe and Kyle danced / were dancing together when the music stopped / was stopping.
5 Did Shelly wait / Was Shelly waiting at the station when the train crashed / was crashing?

/5

5 Find and correct the mistakes in the sentences.

0 Did Kay ~~used~~ to cook a big meal on Sundays? _use_
1 Beth used to go to Hong Kong for the first time in 2009. _____
2 Teenagers didn't used to have mobile phones in the 1980s. _____
3 Josh used to play basketball for two years. _____
4 Did use to be milk free at school when you were little? _____
5 When Grandpa was young, films used to were black and white. _____

/5

6 Read the text and choose the correct answer, A, B or C.

> ⁰___ are small, light personal computers for mobile use. They have most of the same components as ¹___ computers, including a screen, speakers and a ²___ to type with. In the 1970s IBM ³___ the first company to make and sell these mobile computers. At first, laptops didn't ⁴___ to have batteries and the screens were black and white and very small. Later, in the 1990s, colour screens ⁵___ more popular. Nowadays, laptops are more popular than any other type of computer.

	A	B	C
0	Desktops	Websites	(Laptops)
1	broadband	desktop	Internet
2	keyboard	search engine	server
3	was	used to be	used to
4	use	used	have
5	were becoming	used to become	became

/5

Total /30

3 THE ARTS

3.1 Vocabulary

Types of books and writers • Films • Music

SHOW WHAT YOU KNOW

1 Put the words in the box under an appropriate heading. There is one extra word.

album   art gallery   best-seller   concert
director   fiction   hit   literature   novel
opera   play   script   stage

Music	Books	Film/theatre
album		

2 Complete the definitions with words from Exercise 1.

0 A(n) <u>opera</u> is a musical play. The 'actors' sing the words.
1 A(n) _____ is a very popular song. Lots of people buy and/or download it.
2 The _____ gives instructions to the actors in a film or play.
3 A(n) _____ is a document with the words of a play or film.
4 A(n) _____ is a long written story, e.g. *Harry Potter* or *Game of Thrones*.
5 You go to a cinema to watch a film. You go to a theatre to watch a(n) _____ .
6 Actors perform on the _____ in a theatre.
7 A(n) _____ is a very popular book. Lots of people buy it.

WORD STORE 3A
Types of writers

3 Read the contents page of a magazine and complete the words. Some letters are given.

Student Arts Magazine — By the students, for the students

In this edition:
Top five teenage books: our own student literary critics write honest book ⁰<u>review</u>s of the latest ¹n_____s for teenagers.
Focus on ... Beethoven: How did the famous composer write ²c_____ l m_____ when he was completely deaf?
Feed your Mind – a selection of poems on the topic of food written by our own Castle College ³p_____s.
'So you want to ... write films or plays' – advice on how to become a ⁴s_____r or ⁵p_____t.
Did you hear that? We print the full lyrics of our ⁶s_____g of the month.
Castle College News – all the latest college news from our own young ⁷j_____s.

WORD STORE 3B
Types of books

4 Complete the table with types of books. Some letters are given.

Fiction	Non-fiction
c<u>lassic</u> novel	aut_____y
c_____ story	t_____ guide
f_____ tale	co_____k
s_____ fiction	e_____a
g_____ story	

5 Complete the sentences with types of books from Exercise 4. Make them plural if necessary.

0 Marie needs a <u>travel guide</u> because she's going to Canada for her holiday and she wants to plan her trip.
1 My dad reads a lot of _____ . He enjoys books from the past that are important in our times.
2 Hannah bought a(n) _____ because she wants to learn how to make Chinese food.
3 Sarah and Vicky enjoy scary stories. They both read _____ .
4 Chloe wants to join the police and be a detective. She loves reading _____ about murders and police investigations.
5 Emily is seven years old. Her mum reads *Pinocchio*, *Snow White* and other _____ to her before she goes to sleep.
6 Jack has always loved _____ . He enjoys reading about aliens, spaceships and the future.
7 I really like _____ . I like reading and learning facts about lots of different subjects.

WORD STORE 3C
'A part of a whole'

6 Complete the phrases with the words in the box.

[act ~~chapter~~ episode scene track verse]

0 a(n) _chapter_ in a book, e.g. a novel
1 a(n) _____ on an album
2 a(n) _____ in a film or play
3 a(n) _____ in a song or poem
4 a(n) _____ in a play
5 a(n) _____ of a sitcom

7 Complete the facts with the words in Exercise 6. Make the words plural if necessary.

0 Shakespeare's *The Comedy of Errors* is a short play, but it still has five _acts_ .
1 There are over 500 _____ of the American cartoon sitcom *The Simpsons*.
2 A rock band called Green Carnation made a one-hour-seven-second song called *Light of Day, Day of Darkness*. This was the only _____ on their album.
3 The book *The Hobbit* by J.R.R. Tolkien has nineteen _____ .
4 The seventeen-minute fight _____ in *The Matrix Reloaded* cost over $40 million to make.
5 *Mahabharata* is a very old and long Indian poem. It has over 100,000 _____ .

REMEMBER THIS

Actors and actresses can **appear/be/play/star** in a film/play/ TV show, and **appear as/be/play** can be used to talk about actors and their characters in a film or play.

Robert Pattinson **stars** in the *Twilight* films. He **plays** a vampire called Edward Cullen.

8 Read REMEMBER THIS. Then read the text and choose the correct options.

I really like director Peter Jackson's *The Hobbit* films. They are fantasy films. Martin Freeman and Ian McKellen star in them. Martin Freeman [1] *appears / plays* as the character Bilbo Baggins and Ian McKellen [2] *appears / plays* Gandalf the wizard. Other famous actors who appear in the films are the Australian actress Cate Blanchett, who [3] *plays / appears* Galadriel the Elf Queen, the American actor Christopher Lee, who [4] *stars / plays* Saruman, and the British actor Benedict Cumberbatch, who [5] *is / appears* the Necromancer.

SHOW WHAT YOU'VE LEARNT

9 Read the conversations and choose the correct options.

Conversation 1
A: Have you read the [1] *book review / literary critic / journalist* of J.K. Rowling's new book?
B: I read [2] *a novel / an article / a poem* about her in the newspaper last week and it said her new book was very good.

Conversation 2
A: My dad listens to a lot of classical music. His favourite [3] *singer / composer / playwright* is Mozart.
B: I don't really listen to classical music, but there's one [4] *poem / track / music* on an album I have that I love. I think it's Beethoven.

Conversation 3
A: I bought two books for Leon for his birthday. One is a [5] *cookbook / ghost story / classic* full of recipes for quick and cheap meals.
B: What's the other one?
A: It's a [6] *travel guide / crime story / fairy tale* about a bank robbery.

Conversation 4
A: Did you watch the final [7] *chapter / episode / act* of *Lost*?
B: I did. The last [8] *track / verse / scene* was so exciting. I will really miss it now that it's finished.

Conversation 5
A: What's you favourite Coldplay [9] *scene / act / track*, Billy?
B: I'm not sure. I really like *Yellow* but I also like *Paradise*. The words in the second [10] *verse / scene / act* are like poetry.

/10

3.2 Grammar

Present Perfect with *just*, *already*, *(not) yet* and Past Simple

SHOW WHAT YOU KNOW

1 Complete the sentences with the Past Simple or Present Perfect form of the verbs in brackets.

0 <u>Did the film win</u> (the film/win) any Oscars at the ceremony last year?
1 _____ (you/ever/read) a play by Shakespeare?
2 Penny _____ (never/borrow) a book from the library.
3 _____ (Peter/write) a novel in 2002?
4 Megan and Sam _____ (not see) the *Twilight* films, but Kim has.

2 ★ Put the words in the correct order to form sentences.

0 already / has / *Star Wars III* / seen / Dylan
<u>Dylan has already seen Star Wars III.</u>
1 *Iron Man III* / has / yet / seen / Katie?
_____
2 *The Hobbit* / already / Carl / seen / has
_____
3 *The Hunger Games* / hasn't / yet / read / Mia
_____
4 listened to / Anna / Lana Del Rey / already / has
_____

3 ★ Look at the pictures and use the prompts to write sentences. Use the Present Perfect and *just*.

0 the play / finish
<u>The play has just finished.</u>

1 the concert / start
_____
_____

2 Dad / fall asleep
_____
_____

3 the actor / forget his lines
_____
_____

4 ★★ Put the words in brackets in the correct place in the sentences, a or b.

0 Has the bus ª <u>just</u> arrived outside the theatre ᵇ_____ ? (just)
1 Elliot hasn't ª_____ listened to all the tracks on the new album ᵇ_____ . (yet)
2 The scary scene has ª_____ finished, so you can open your eyes ᵇ_____ . (already)
3 London's newest art gallery has ª_____ opened ᵇ_____ . (just)
4 Max has ª_____ read seven chapters ᵇ_____ and it's only 10.00 a.m. (already)
5 Have you ª_____ looked at the cookbook I bought you for Christmas ᵇ_____ ? (yet)

5 ★★★ Complete the sentences with the Past Simple or Present Perfect form of the verbs in brackets.

0 Pauline <u>acted</u> (act) in a play last Christmas. She <u>hasn't been</u> (not be) in a film yet.
1 Karen _____ (not see) Madonna in concert. She _____ (not go) to the concert last time Madonna came to Spain.
2 Mike _____ (go) to the Natural History Museum last year. He _____ (not be) to the Modern Art Museum yet.
3 Becky _____ (read) *Game of Thrones*. She _____ (read) it in 2010.
4 _____ (you/speak) to Angela yet today? Believe it or not, she _____ (win) first prize in a radio competition this morning.
5 The builders _____ (start) work in spring. It's November now, and they still _____ (not finish).

SHOW WHAT YOU'VE LEARNT

6 Choose the correct answer, A, B or C.

1 Your mum has ___ fed the dog. Don't give him any more food.
A yet　　　B just　　　C not
2 I ___ writing my poem yet.
A didn't finish　　B have finished　　C haven't finished
3 Alice has ___ been to Paris five times. Her aunt and uncle live there.
A already　　B just　　C yet
4 ___ to the bookshop on Saturday?
A Have you been　B Did you go　C Were you
5 Have you finished reading that book about the history of Facebook ___ ?
A yet　　　B just　　　C next
6 Ken and Michelle ___ to the opera last weekend.
A haven't been　B have been　C didn't go

/6

3.3 Listening language practice

Art and music

1 Complete the extract from an interview with the correct form of *be, do* or *have*. Then listen and check.

Extract from Students' Book recording CD•2.4 MP3•48

A: It's 2.30 on Saturday afternoon and you're listening to the Culture Programme. In this part of the programme, we invite a guest to talk about their 'Artist of the Week'. This week we have Katy West in the studio. Katy is the editor of *Photo Monthly Magazine*. Welcome to the Culture Programme.

B: Thank you.

A: Katy, tell us about your 'Artist of the Week'.

B: My 'Artist of the Week' is a French photographer. He takes photographs and makes them enormous. Then he pastes them in public places.

A: ¹_____ he have a name?

B: Ah, well, he's called JR. […]

A: So what kind of photographs ²_____ he take, and where can we see them?

B: He takes black and white portraits of people and pastes them on buildings, walls and bridges. He ³_____ had exhibitions in museums such as the Pompidou Centre in Paris, but his favourite art gallery is in the street. He wants people who ⁴_____ usually go to museums to see his work. […] He ⁵_____ worked in many different places of the world. In Africa he did a project called *Women are heroes*. […]

2 Complete questions 1–5 with the correct present form of *be, do* or *have*. Then match the questions with answers a–e.

1 What *is* this street artist called? e
2 _____ JR take photographs of famous people?
3 What _____ he do with the photographs?
4 What _____ he done recently?
5 _____ he worked in Africa?

a He pastes them in public places.
b This year he's done projects in Paris, Hong Kong and the US.
c No, he usually takes photographs of ordinary people with difficult lives.
d Yes, he has.
e His name is JR.

REMEMBER BETTER

Use diagrams like word webs to record groups of connected words. This can help you to remember them better.

A Complete the word web with the underlined words in Exercise 1 and the words in the box. There are two extra words.

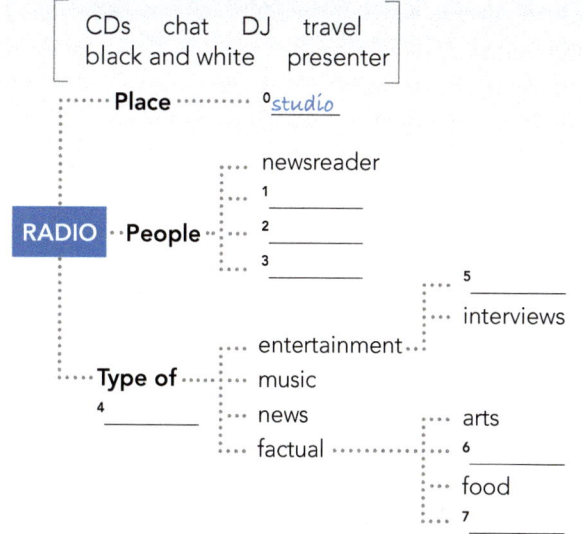

CDs   chat   DJ   travel
black and white   presenter

B Draw your own word web for the topic of books. Use words and phrases from this unit and add any others you know.

WORD STORE 3D
Art and music

3 Choose the correct options.

1 Good *painters / photographers / sculptors* need a wide selection of colours and brushes.
2 This *painting / sculpture / photograph* is made of stone.
3 I like looking at pictures of people. Let's go to the *portrait / landscape / sculpture* section of the gallery.
4 There are four people in our *singer / band / composer*.
5 The first films had no sound and were *black and white / colour*.
6 I can't stop singing that Beatles *song / opera / symphony* that my dad always plays.
7 I love the picture that hangs in my parents' living room. It's an eighteenth-century *photo / painting / landscape* of a group of children sitting in front of their house.
8 One of the most difficult things about being a *composer / songwriter / playwright* is making the characters and the dialogues seem real.
9 Andy has always wanted to be a *singer / composer / songwriter* but unfortunately he has a terrible voice.
10 *A symphony / An opera* has singers and a story.

35

3.4 Reading

Readers, books, films and reviews

1 Read book reviews A–F. Are the books fiction (*F*) or non-fiction (*N*)?

A ☐   D ☐
B ☐   E ☐
C ☐   F ☐

2 Read the reviews again and the descriptions below. Decide which book (A–F) would be most suitable for each person (1–5). There is one extra review.

1 Gareth ☐   4 Sean ☐
2 Karen ☐   5 Jemma ☐
3 Nathan ☐

1 Gareth, 16

I'm training to be a professional chef, so I'm very busy. When I find time to read, I like books that help me forget about my work and studies. I love reading about the real lives of successful, famous people. I'm not really into romantic stories.

2 Karen, 18

I'm a student and I don't have much time to read for pleasure. I enjoy practical books. One of my favourites is *101 Things Every Student Needs to Know*. I hate books about monsters and space.

3 Nathan, 16

I love getting lost in great stories. I enjoy reading stories about the lives, love and relationships of people from the past. I like a book to make me laugh, cry and to show me what life was like in other countries, at other times.

4 Sean, 15

I like books where the heroes are teenagers like me. I prefer stories that don't follow the rules of the real world. My favourite books have incredible people, strange aliens and amazing events. I don't like stories with romance in them.

5 Jemma, 18

I'm studying Science, but I prefer fictional books that make me forget about the real world. When I was a little girl, I used to imagine I had magic powers. I killed monsters and fought dragons – things like that. Now I'm older, I like stories that mix romance with fantasy.

A

The Great Gatsby, by F. Scott Fitzgerald

The Great Gatsby is the story of rich, successful Jay Gatsby and his beautiful friend Daisy Buchanan. They live in a magical world of love, jazz and champagne in 1920s New York. There is romance and happiness, but like in many classic novels, there is also sadness and heartbreak.

B

Real Food, Real Fast, by Sam Stern

Teenage chef Sam Stern introduces delicious healthy recipes which you can have on your plate in just a few minutes. This useful book is great for amateur chefs and busy students. Sam's recipes are cheap, fast and delicious.

C

Ritz Paris: Haute Cuisine

Do you want to learn to cook like a professional chef? Are you interested in the history of great French food? This is not a cookbook for the average home cook. The recipes are long and challenging, the ingredients are unusual and expensive and the food … is absolutely delicious!

D

Twilight, by Stephenie Meyer

This is a fantastic story about a young student called Bella. She falls in love with Edward and then finds out he's a vampire. Vampires are usually found in stories of the past, but Stephenie Meyer's book brings them to modern America. This book will make you laugh, cry and dream of romance with vampires! We think it is a future classic.

E

Night of the Purple Moon, by Scott Cramer

Scientists say a comet from deep space is passing Earth and it will make the moon purple. Teenager Abby Leigh is looking forward to watching this happen. But the comet carries a terrible secret – an alien virus that kills all the world's adults. Abby is suddenly responsible for her brother and young sister's survival in this world without adults.

F

Steve Jobs: The Exclusive Biography, by Walter Isaacson

This is the life story of Apple's former boss, Steve Jobs. Walter Isaacson tells us about the professional and personal life of one of modern America's most successful businessmen. We learn about Jobs' family, his loves and the ideas he had for the future of Apple before his sad death in 2011.

3 Book E is a science fiction book. Underline five more words or phrases in the review connected to this type of book. *Comet* is underlined as an example.

4 Books B and C are cookbooks. Find words in the reviews that match these definitions.

0	an adjective; delicious	tasty
1	an adjective; good for you	_____
2	a noun; instructions for how to make food	_____
3	a noun; you eat your dinner off a …	_____
4	a noun; this person's job is to cook food	_____
5	a noun; the different foods you put together to make a meal	_____

REMEMBER BETTER

Go to an English language website such as amazon.co.uk and find the section on books. Look at the different types of books in the best-sellers menu. Read some of the reviews and make a note of useful vocabulary. Check any words you don't understand in a dictionary.

Match the words in the box with the books below. Use a dictionary if necessary.

| ~~attractions~~ | beach | clue | flavour | food | hotel |
| investigate | killer | map | meal | murder | recipes |

Cookbook	Crime story	Travel guide
Jamie's 15 Minute Meals, by Jamie Oliver	*The Girl with the Dragon Tattoo*, by Stieg Larsson	*The Rough Guide to Thailand*, by Paul Gray and Lucy Ridout
		attractions

WORD STORE 3E
Adjectives with positive or negative meanings

5 Put the words in the box under an appropriate heading.

~~amusing~~	boring	emotional	entertaining
funny	inspiring	moving	predictable
relaxing	unoriginal	unrealistic	

Positive	Negative
amusing	

6 Read the comments and choose the correct options.

***Prometheus*, by Ridley Scott**

Your comments:

comedyfan246 says:
I enjoyed *Prometheus*, but I think every film should have funny moments and there was nothing to laugh at in this one. So, not an ¹*unrealistic / amusing / moving* film, but enjoyable.

LaraNYC says:
I loved it! I felt scared, excited, happy and sad; a very ²*predictable / relaxing / emotional* film. I didn't expect to feel all those different things.

jellybean_21 says:
Some science fiction is very ³*entertaining / unrealistic / funny* but I thought *Prometheus* seemed very real – very human. Often, with this kind of film, you know what is going to happen next, but *Prometheus* was not ⁴*predictable / moving / relaxing*. I didn't know how it was going to finish until the last five minutes.

debsterHK says:
Prometheus is the same as all the other sci-fi films I've seen – I thought it was very predictable; very ⁵*unrealistic / inspiring / unoriginal* – in other words, nothing new.

ianbSMC says:
Normally, I enjoy chilling out when I watch a film, so I prefer ⁶*entertaining / relaxing / amusing* films and I often fall asleep before the end! *Prometheus* was not this kind of film. BUT it was great. It took me to another world for two hours. Not a chilled out film, but a very good one.

3.5 Grammar

Comparative and superlative adjectives • *too* and *enough*

SHOW WHAT YOU KNOW

1 Match each of the adjectives 1–4 with two of its opposites in the box.

> busy   clever   confident   exciting   far   ~~noisy~~
> intelligent   interesting   outgoing   popular

1. quiet ≠ *noisy* / _____
2. stupid ≠ _____ / _____
3. boring ≠ _____ / _____
4. shy ≠ _____ / _____

2 ★ Read the information about two museums in London and complete the sentences. Write *S* for The Science Museum and *N* for The Natural History Museum.

	The Natural History Museum	The Science Museum
Number of visitors per year	5 million	3 million
Started in	1881	1857
Distance from Victoria Station	2.2 miles	2.0 miles
Distance from Buckingham Palace	1.7 miles	1.8 miles
Opening hours	10.00 a.m. – 5.50 p.m.	10.00 a.m. – 6.00 p.m.

1. The *S* Museum is not as popular as the ___ Museum.
2. The ___ Museum is not as old as the ___ Museum.
3. The ___ Museum is not as far from Victoria Station as the ___ Museum.
4. The ___ Museum is not as far from Buckingham Palace as the ___ Museum.
5. The ___ Museum is not open as long as the ___ Museum.

3 ★ Complete the sentences with the superlative form of the adjectives in brackets.

0. Bob Marley is probably the *greatest* (great) reggae artist of all time.
1. I think the violin makes the _____ (beautiful) sound of all instruments.
2. The guitar is one of the _____ (easy) instruments to learn.
3. *Thriller* by Michael Jackson is the _____ (popular) album ever written.
4. The Pacific Ocean is the _____ (big) ocean on our planet.

4 ★★ Complete the sentences with *too* or *not enough* and the adjectives in brackets.

0. The book is *too long* (long). I don't have much time for reading.
1. Ken's MP3 player is _____ (loud). He can't hear his music on the bus.
2. I'm _____ (young) to remember the 1980s. I was born in 1997.
3. Your dog is _____ (clever) to learn that trick. It's cute, but very stupid.
4. My trousers are _____ (small). I need to buy a new pair.

5 ★★ Complete the conversation with the comparative or superlative form of the adjectives in brackets.

In the Modern Art Museum:

A: What do you think of the exhibition, James?
B: Yeah, great, actually. It's ⁰*better* (good) than I expected.
A: Yeah, I think it's ¹_____ (funny) than last year. Actually, it's the ²_____ (good) exhibition I've ever been to. I really liked the photos of the dogs in the water.
B: Personally, I thought the giant baby sculptures were the ³_____ (interesting) thing in the exhibition.
A: I didn't see those. Where are they?
B: They're down this corridor, on the left. They're ⁴_____ (big) than you, so you can't miss them!

SHOW WHAT YOU'VE LEARNT

6 Complete the second sentence so that it has a similar meaning to the first using the word in capitals.

0. Of course, for younger listeners, rap is more popular than opera. **AS**
   Of course, for younger listeners, opera is *not as popular as* rap.
1. The tree in this painting is not tall enough. It doesn't look real. **SHORT**
   The tree in this painting is _____ . It doesn't look real.
2. Henry's poem is longer than Bethany's. **LONG**
   Bethany's poem _____ Henry's.
3. I don't know anyone more intelligent than Laura. **THE**
   Laura is _____ girl I know.
4. The screens in Central Cinema aren't as big as the screens in Empire Cinema. **THAN**
   The screens in Central Cinema _____ the screens in Empire Cinema.
5. There isn't a photograph more beautiful than the one of the snowy mountains. **MOST**
   The photograph of the snowy mountains _____ .
6. It's too noisy to study in the library at lunch time. **QUIET**
   It's _____ to study in the library at lunch time.

/6

3.6 Speaking language practice

Describing a photo

1 Choose the correct options.
1. They're probably watching something scary on TV because the boy on the left looks *frightened / miserable / proud*.
2. There are hundreds of people cheering and dancing, so I think they're at a concert. It's only a small place and it looks very *empty / crowded / excited*.
3. She looks familiar. I've seen her face on TV and in magazines. I don't know her name, but I think she's *quiet / shy / famous*.
4. There is a girl sitting in a dentist's chair. She's biting her nails and she looks worried. I imagine she feels *tired / bored / nervous*.
5. The man in the foreground is not happy. He's shouting and pointing. He looks very *irritated / proud / shy*.
6. They are standing next to the aeroplane. They are wearing those things to cover their ears, so it's probably very *noisy / quiet / empty* there.

2 Complete the descriptions with the adjectives in the box. There are two extra adjectives.

[empty   famous   miserable   noisy
  ~~proud~~   quiet   shy   tired]

0. I think the man in the foreground has won first prize. He has a medal and he looks very <u>proud</u>.
1. They are standing in a forest and there is nobody else there. It's a very _____ place. I imagine there is only the sound of the wind in the trees.
2. There is nobody in the restaurant – not one customer. It's completely _____ . The waiter has nothing to do and he looks bored.
3. She's sitting next to this handsome guy, but she looks very uncomfortable and her face is red. Perhaps she's _____ and she doesn't know what to say.
4. They have just finished running a race, I think, so they probably feel very _____ .
5. It looks cold and wet. I don't think the family sitting on the beach are enjoying their day out. They all look really _____ .

3 Put the words in brackets in the correct order to complete the descriptions.

0. (shows / a / this / classroom / photo)
   <u>This photo shows a classroom</u> . The children are young and it looks noisy.
1. (of / photo, / can / I / this / in / see / lots / photographers)
   _____ .
   They are all trying to take a picture of this lady.
2. (in / I / so / think / he's)
   There are books everywhere, _____ a library, or maybe a bookshop.
3. (nurse / middle / the / in / the)
   _____ looks very friendly.
4. (so / looks / he / perhaps / smart / very)
   _____ it is a job interview.
5. (my / in / opinion)
   _____ , shopping is a boring way to spend your time.

REMEMBER THIS
I think he's in a bookshop. (+)
I don't think he's in a library. (–)
~~I think he isn't in a library.~~

4 Read REMEMBER THIS. Then find and correct the mistakes in the sentences.
0. I think he isn't at home.
   <u>I don't think he's at home.</u>
1. I think the women aren't happy.
   _____
2. I think those bags aren't his.
   _____
3. I think it isn't winter.
   _____

5 Complete the description with the words/phrases in the box. There are two extra words/phrases.

[happy   I imagine   in the middle
  looks   next to   on the left   personally
  so I think   they are   ~~this photo shows~~]

⁰<u>This photo shows</u> people watching a film at the cinema. There are children in the audience, ¹_____ it's a family film. In the foreground there is a family. ²_____ there is a man holding a drink. He's probably the dad. ³_____ is a little boy. He ⁴_____ about six or seven years old. His mum is sitting ⁵_____ him. They all look really ⁶_____ . They are laughing, so ⁷_____ they're watching a comedy.

39

3.7 Writing

An informal letter/email

1 Complete the phrases in the email. The first letter of each word is given.

Dear Sarah,

⁰**H**ow are **t**hings **w**ith you? ¹**T**_____ very much **f**_____ the photos. I've put some of them in frames and they look great in the living room.

²I **m**_____ **t**_____ you **a**_____ London. Dave and I went to see his uncle last weekend and we had a fantastic time. We went on the London Eye – the views were amazing. His uncle also took us for sushi – delicious!

³It's a **s**_____ you lost your phone. Have you got all your friends' numbers again yet? I sent an email with mine.

We're having a birthday party for Alex next month. He's going to be eighteen. ⁴**W**_____ you **l**_____ to **c**_____? It's on the twenty-first. ⁵I **m**_____ be **g**_____ now.

⁶**H**_____ to **s**_____ you soon.

Love,

Polly x

---

2 Match sentences 1–6 in the email with functions a–f.

a starting an email — *How are things with you?*
b expressing sympathy _____
c inviting somebody _____
d giving recent news _____
e closing an email _____ / _____
f thanking somebody _____

3 Put the words in the correct order to form sentences. Then match them with functions a–f in Exercise 2.

0 well / I / you / are / hope [a]
  I hope you are well.

1 make / hope / can / you / I / it ☐
  _____

2 seeing / forward / you … / look / to / I ☐
  _____

3 from … / just / back / come / I've ☐
  _____

4 that's / for / now / all ☐
  _____

5 was / it / kind / you / me … / to / of / very / send ☐
  _____

6 hear / that … / to / I'm / sorry ☐
  _____

SHOW WHAT YOU'VE LEARNT

4 You recently received a letter from Carla, a girl you met at a summer camp in France. Read part of her letter and write your reply.

> I'm attaching some great photos I took in France – some of them are really funny! Which one do you like best? Sadly, Dave and I have broken up – after eighteen months together! Let me know your news.

Write your letter in about 100 words.

SHOW THAT YOU'VE CHECKED

In my informal email/letter:

- I have started with a friendly greeting, (e.g. *Dear Richard* or *Hi Jean*). ☐
- addressed all the points in the question (e.g. written my news, made a suggestion, answered a question, replied to an invitation). ☐
- I have used contractions (e.g. *I'm, aren't, that's*). ☐
- I have finished with a friendly goodbye, (e.g. *Look forward to seeing you next week, Hope to see you soon*). ☐
- I have checked my spelling and punctuation. ☐
- I have written about 100 words. ☐

3.8 Word practice

The arts

1 Choose the correct answer, A, B or C.

1. My grandad doesn't like jazz but he's fond of ___ .
   A script   B song   C classical music
2. I've found a new job. I'm going to write ___ for the local newspaper.
   A novels   B reviews   C chapters
3. Is this film based ___ a true story?
   A at   B in   C on
4. What kinds of musical ___ can you play?
   A bands   B scripts   C instruments
5. Do you think Damien Rose will ___ a good performance as King Arthur in the film?
   A do   B have   C give
6. It's a great ___ book for young readers about dragons and magic.
   A crime   B fantasy   C science fiction
7. Jessica is a talented ___ and she often writes for British theatres.
   A critic   B novelist   C playwright
8. You can learn how to make lots of Spanish dishes form this ___ .
   A cookbook   B short story   C encyclopedia
9. Ann is a ___ . She has written the music and words for many different singers.
   A singer   B composer   C songwriter
10. There are twelve ___ on this CD but only three are good.
    A verses   B ranges   C tracks
11. Jason is very funny. He should become a ___ .
    A presenter   B comedian   C journalist
12. The documentary on London crime was good but it showed too much ___ .
    A suspense   B violence   C tension
13. It's an ___ story because women didn't go to university in the fifteenth century!
    A unrealistic   B entertaining   C emotional
14. If a film is moving, it makes you feel ___ .
    A you want to travel
    B like trying something new
    C strong emotions
15. Michael Bourne is interested in real people and events. He specialises in ___ films.
    A factual   B relaxing   C enjoyable

2 How much do you remember about the arts? Do the quiz to find out.

QUIZ

1. What does a literary critic write?
2. What is the name for a person who writes plays for the theatre?
3. What is the word for the sections in a book?
4. What is a track in the world of music?
5. What is the difference between a composer and a songwriter?
6. What is the word for the parts of a play?
7. What is the name for a person who writes newspaper articles?
8. What is a verse in poetry?

3 Read the titles. What type of book do you think each one is?

0. *Plant of the Star Lords* — science fiction
1. *Exploring South America on foot* — _____
2. *A Taste of Italy* — _____
3. *Inspector Morgan – The Davenport Diamond Mystery* — _____
4. *The White Lady* — _____
5. *My Life* — _____

4 Complete the word web with words about the arts. Write as many words as you can.

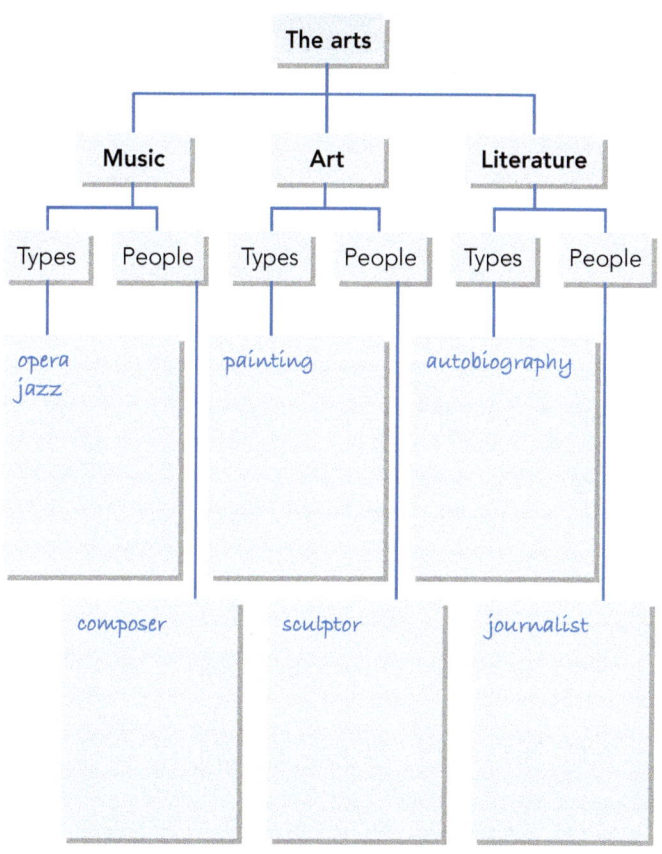

3.9 Self-assessment

1 For each learning objective, tick the box that best matches your ability.

☺☺ = I understand and can help a friend.
☺ = I understand and can do it by myself.
☹ = I understand some, but have some questions.
☹☹ = I do not understand.

			☺☺	☺	☹	☹☹	Need help?
3.1	Vocabulary	I can talk about books, films and music.					Students' Book pages 36–37 Word Store page 7 Workbook pages 32–33
3.2	Grammar	I can use the Present Perfect and the Past Simple to talk about past actions.					Students' Book page 38 Workbook page 34
3.3	Listening	I can identify specific detail in a radio programme about a street artist.					Students' Book page 39 Workbook page 35
3.4	Reading	I can identify specific detail in film descriptions and reviews.					Students' Book pages 40–41 Workbook pages 36–37
3.5	Grammar	I can make comparisons.					Students' Book page 42 Workbook page 38
3.6	Speaking	I can describe a situation in a photo and speculate about what is happening.					Students' Book page 43 Workbook page 39
3.7	Writing	I can write to someone and thank them, give news, express sympathy or invite them somewhere.					Students' Book pages 44–45 Workbook page 40

2 What can you remember from this unit?

New words I learned (the words you most want to remember from this unit)	Expressions and phrases I liked (any expressions or phrases you think sound nice, useful or funny)	English I heard or read outside class (e.g. from websites, books, adverts, films, music)

3.10 Self-check

1 Complete the words in the sentences. Some letters are given.

0 Paul loves writing stories. I think he should become a n<u>ovelis</u>t.
1 Dad says c_____l music is serious and important and people will still listen to it many years from now. He doesn't like pop music.
2 Donna's reading an exciting c_____e story at the moment. It's about a police detective working in Vienna.
3 The new play at the city theatre is an a_____n of a famous book by a Russian author.
4 At the art gallery, Ben liked the landscape paintings best, but I liked the p_____s. I love paintings of real people.
5 What a terrible comedy! It wasn't f_____y at all. We didn't laugh once.

/5

2 Choose the correct options.

0 In my opinion, the last (track) / play / film on the album is the best.
1 Many literature / literary / review critics say that Harry Potter is one of the best series ever written for children and teenagers.
2 This collection of children's fairy tales / tracks / guides is a magical book for young readers.
3 Tonight is the final chapter / act / episode of my favourite TV show. I really want to know how it will end.
4 Gavin thought the verse / scene / tale with the vampires was the scariest part of the film.
5 This is a very boring / unrealistic / emotional film. You will laugh, cry, feel scared and feel happy – all in 104 minutes!

/5

3 Complete the sentences with the words in the box. There are two extra words.

autobiography   band   moving   playwright
<s>photo</s>   photographer   symphony   unrealistic

0 Please delete that <u>photo</u> from Facebook. I look terrible!
1 Fiona's uncle was a(n) _____ and an actor. He wrote and acted in plays about the war in Vietnam.
2 My grandpa has had a very interesting life. I think he should write it all down in a(n) _____.
3 Peter plays the drums in a rock _____.
4 You take some brilliant pictures. Have you ever thought about becoming a professional _____?
5 The special effects in those old Japanese monster movies were amazing fifty years ago, but now they look very _____.

/5

4 Complete the sentences with the Present Perfect form of the verbs in brackets. Choose one of the time expressions in italics and put it in the correct place in the sentence.

0 <u>I've already found</u> (find) a suitable birthday present for Emily _____. (already/yet)
1 I _____ (finish) a new poem _____. Would you like to be the first person to hear it? (just/yet)
2 Eileen _____ (see) the new James Bond film _____. (already/yet)
3 _____ (Rosa/look) at a travel guide for Spain _____? (already/yet)
4 Mum _____ (pay) for the theatre tickets _____. I gave her the money back last week. (already/just)
5 We _____ (not meet) any of the other guests _____. We only arrived at the party two minutes ago. (just/yet)

/5

5 Choose the correct options.

0 Tomorrow will be as cold than / (as) / with today.
1 The cake I made was too / than / as dry. Even the dog didn't want to eat it!
2 Ola is not fit / fitter / fittest enough to run a marathon.
3 The far / further / furthest Leo has ever swum is 3km.
4 I think a hot bath is most / more / as relaxing than watching TV.
5 That was as / the / than most entertaining film I've seen in ages.

/5

6 Choose the correct answer, A, B or C, to complete both sentences in each pair.

0 Do they always ___ football on Thursday evening?
   We saw a new ___ at the theatre yesterday.
   (A play)   B watch   C film
1 The first ___ of the play is fifty minutes long.
   She looks very sad in the last ___ of the comedy.
   A scene   B act   C write
2 Tony loves science ___ films.
   Fantasy novels are in the ___ section of the bookshop.
   A classic   B stories   C fiction
3 We ___ just come back from a very loud concert and I still can't hear very well.
   Do you ___ any books about the history of football?
   A had   B have   C haven't
4 Is there ___ bread left to make some sandwiches?
   Excuse me, waiter, this pasta is not hot ___.
   A enough   B any   C too
5 Chris is the same age ___ me.
   History is not as difficult ___ Maths.
   A than   B like   C as

/5

Total   /30

4 LIVING

4.1 Vocabulary

Houses and homes • Phrases with *make* and *do*

SHOW WHAT YOU KNOW

1 Choose the odd one out in each group.

0	fridge	oven	dishwasher	(desk)
1	shower	coffee table	armchair	sofa
2	wardrobe	bedside table	microwave	bed
3	bath	dining table	washbasin	toilet
4	kitchen	living room	plant	bedroom
5	lamp	bathroom	study	hall

WORD STORE 4A
Describing houses

2 Label the photos with the words in the box.

> bungalow ~~concrete~~ cottage
> the countryside housing estate mud
> semi-detached house stone suburbs
> terraced house wood village

Material	Houses	Location
 concrete	E	I
B		
C		K 
	 	L 

3 Complete the words in the texts. Some letters are given.

This week's Hot Homes
See our list of the top five houses/flats for sale.

22 Greenways Road – This is a lovely ⁰s<u>emi</u>-d<u>etache</u>d house, with neighbours on the south side only. Greenways Road is in the quiet ¹s_____s of the city, and good transport links get you to the city centre in only fifteen minutes.

78 Darrington Avenue – This small ²t_____d house (quiet neighbours on both sides) is made of red ³b_____k and has a private garden at the back and a real fire in the living room – very ⁴c_____y on cold winter nights!

8 Denholme Street – With solar panels, wood-burners and water from a spring, this ⁵e_____e is ideal if you care about the environment. It's very near the ⁶s_____a with wonderful views across the water. There are big windows at the back, so there's a lot of natural ⁷l_____t inside.

Oak House, Long Lane – A large and very ⁸s_____s home (eight big rooms!) in a small, friendly ⁹v_____e only thirty miles from London. This ¹⁰d_____d house has large gardens all round. Built in the 1800s, this is a very ¹¹t_____l English home.

128/14 Ivy Close – These new ¹²f_____s (seven in each building) are very ¹³m_____n and have hi-tech kitchens and bathrooms. Kitchen, living room and dining room are ¹⁴o_____n plan, so there's one very big living space. Ivy Close is right in the city ¹⁵c_____e, close to shops and offices, so it's perfect for young professionals.

44

WORD STORE 4B
Things inside and outside a house

4 Match the items in the picture with the words in the box. There are three extra words. In which room do the three extra items go?

- ☐ bookcase
- ☐ carpet
- ☐ cupboard
- ☐ cooker
- ☐ kitchen sink
- ☐ floorboards
- ☐ path
- ☐ pond
- ☐ porch
- ☐ shelves
- ☐ stairs
- ☐ worktop

WORD STORE 4C
Phrases with *make* and *do*

5 Choose the correct options.
1 Gordon's food is delicious, but he always *does* / *makes* a mess in the kitchen when he *does* / *makes* the cooking.
2 When Mum and Dad *do* / *make* the housework, they *do* / *make* lots of noise and I can't concentrate on my homework.
3 Helen never *does* / *makes* the shopping on Saturdays. She prefers to *do* / *make* the gardening if the weather is nice.
4 I would like to *do* / *make* a complaint about this meal. My burger is cold and my cola is warm.

6 Complete the diagrams with words that collocate with *make* or *do*.

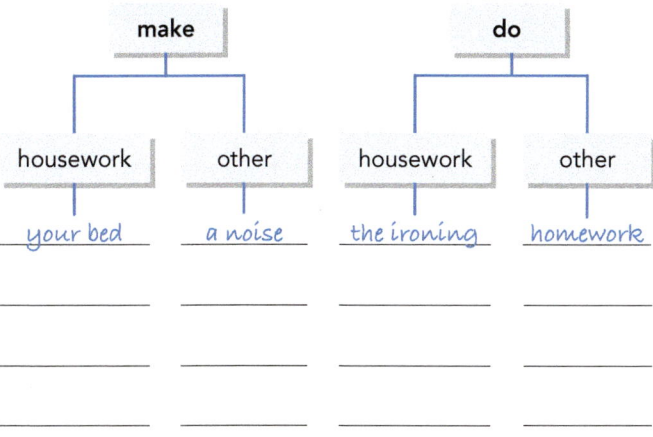

REMEMBER THIS
stay at home = not leave your house/flat
leave home = leave your house/flat
go home = go back to your house/flat
get home = arrive at your house/flat

7 Read REMEMBER THIS. Complete the sentences with the verbs in bold.
0 Tomorrow I need to <u>leave</u> home at 6.00 a.m. My flight is at 8.15 a.m. and it takes about half an hour to get to the airport.
1 Kim doesn't feel like going out, so we're going to _____ at home and watch a film.
2 It's 11.00 p.m. I think you should _____ home and get some sleep.
3 I'm hungry, Alex. When we _____ home, I'll start cooking dinner straight away, OK?

REMEMBER BETTER
To remember the collocations with *home*, write sentences about a typical day or weekend in your life and the things you do inside or outside your home.

Complete the sentences to make them true about you.
0 On school days I leave home at <u>7.30</u> a.m. (time).
1 After school I usually go home by _____ (means of transport).
2 On weekdays I usually get home at _____ (time).
3 Sometimes I go out at the weekend, but sometimes I like to stay at home and _____ (activity).

SHOW WHAT YOU'VE LEARNT

8 Choose the correct options.
1 My grandma chose *an eco-house* / *a bungalow* / *a detached house* because this type of house is on the ground floor and doesn't have stairs.
2 Jo's flat is *in a village* / *in the country* / *in the city centre*. It's only one minute from the central station.
3 Granddad built his own shed out of *wood* / *concrete* / *stone* from trees from the local forest.
4 In their back garden, Ellie and Scott have a *patio* / *pond* / *shed* full of expensive Japanese fish.
5 Sue decided to change the old gas fire for a *bookcase* / *windowsill* / *wood-burner*.
6 The *porch* / *path* / *door* on the front of our house is made of glass. It's a great place for growing tomatoes.
7 Kevin, the washing is dry and it's your turn to *do the shopping* / *do the cooking* / *do the ironing*. Dad needs a shirt and a pair of trousers for work tomorrow.
8 Please ask your dad to put the car in the *cupboard* / *garage* / *house*. It is going to be very cold tonight.

/8

4.2 Grammar

Present Perfect with *for* and *since*

SHOW WHAT YOU KNOW

1 Decide if the underlined part of each sentence describes *a point in time* or *a period of time*.

0 I was born in <u>1997</u>. **(point)** / period
00 The film was <u>two hours</u> long. point / **(period)**
1 I like living in the city, so <u>a week</u> in the country is long enough. point / period
2 Sasha moved into her flat in <u>2012</u>. point / period
3 It took us <u>three days</u> to paint the walls in my bedroom. point / period
4 Zara finished her homework at <u>6.00 p.m.</u> point / period
5 The village is <u>375 years</u> old. point / period
6 My parents bought the house <u>when they got married</u>. point / period

2 ★ Choose the correct options.

1 Luke has lived in this cottage *for* / *since* he was three years old.
2 I haven't done the washing *for* / *since* two weeks. I have no clean clothes.
3 We have wanted to live in a village near the sea *for* / *since* so many years!
4 Annie has been in bed *for* / *since* yesterday morning. She's really sick.
5 People have built houses out of mud *for* / *since* thousands of years.
6 My brother hasn't had a bath *for* / *since* at least six months. He prefers the shower.
7 They've had a wood-burner *for* / *since* three years and they've already saved a lot of money on heating.
8 That pasta has been in the cupboard *for* / *since* we moved into this flat four years ago.
9 Dad hasn't cut the grass *for* / *since* he lost the key to the shed.

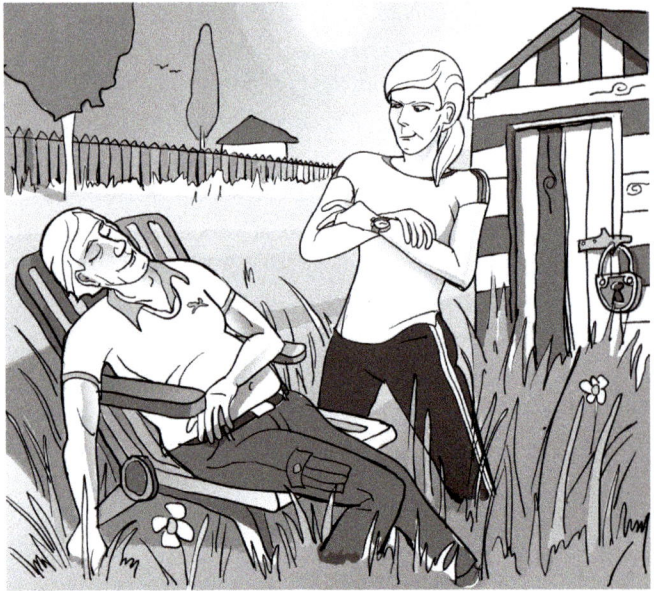

3 ★★ Complete the sentences with the Present Perfect form of the verbs in brackets and *for* or *since*.

0 Kevin's in his room, but he <u>hasn't made</u> (not make) a noise <u>since</u> one o'clock. Do you think he's OK?
1 We _____ (have) frogs in our pond _____ two weeks.
2 Harry _____ (write) lots of miserable poems _____ he stopped seeing Ellen.
3 Chloe _____ (not make) her bed _____ three days.
4 Lewis and Oliver _____ (play) for the school football team _____ two years.
5 _____ last month, there _____ (be) a market in the city centre.

4 ★★★ Complete the conversations with the Present Perfect form of the verbs in brackets. Add *for* or *since* where necessary.

0 A: How long <u>have you lived</u> (you/live) in London?
   B: We<u>'ve lived in London for</u> five years.
1 A: How long _____ (Olivia/want) to be an architect?
   B: Oh, Olivia _____ she visited Barcelona.
2 A: How long _____ (your parents/be) married?
   B: I don't really know, but they _____ a long time.
3 A: How long _____ (Alice/know) Samuel?
   B: She _____ they started school.
4 A: How long _____ (your sister/have) long hair?
   B: She _____ at least six months.

SHOW WHAT YOU'VE LEARNT

5 Complete the sentences using the information in brackets. Use the Present Perfect and *for* or *since* where necessary.

0 <u>I've been passionate about poetry for</u> (be/passionate about poetry) three years.
1 I _____ (not be/to school) two weeks.
2 Molly _____ (not read/a good book) last year.
3 How long _____ (Polly/be/busy) in the kitchen?
4 The World Wide Web _____ (exist) 1989.
5 Lauren _____ (not see/Oliver) four days.
6 How long _____ (your grandparents/live) in a bungalow?

/6

46

4.3 Listening language practice

Verb-noun collocations

1 Read the extract and choose the correct options. Then listen and check.

Extract from Students' Book recording CD•2.18 MP3•62

1
I ¹*have / am / do* a big family – there are seven of us in this house, and we're all very noisy people. It's OK when you're feeling sociable, but sometimes I want to ²*have / be / spend* on my own and have some quiet time. So I ³*shut / open / enter* <u>my bedroom door</u>, ⁴*do / listen / put* <u>my headphones on</u> and listen to music or ⁵*chat / see / spend* <u>with my friends</u>. I have a sign on the door that says 'Keep out' and it's not just for my parents. My brothers and sisters ⁶*do / are / have* not welcome either. My room is a place for me to get away from other people.

2 Read the extract and complete it with the verbs in the box. There are two extra verbs. Then listen and check.

[~~decorate~~   have   make   painted
  played   showed   write]

Extract from Students' Book recording CD•2.18 MP3•62

3
I think my room reflects my personality. My parents let me ⁰<u>decorate</u> it in my favourite colour, so I ¹_____ the walls black and put different coloured lights everywhere. I love making things – I use my room as a kind of studio. I paint, ²_____ music lyrics. On my computer, I ³_____ music mixes and create light shows to go with them. It's awesome! When my friends ⁴_____ a party, they always ask me to do the music.

3 Complete gaps 1–4 in the word webs with the verbs in the box. There are two extra verbs. Then complete gaps a–d with the underlined words in the extracts in Exercises 1 and 2.

[chat   listen   ~~paint~~   play   put   shut   write]

0 *paint* ······· the walls
              a picture
              your fingernails

1 _____ ······· a _____
              a blog
              a 'to do' list

2 _____ ······· b _____
              the window

3 _____ ······· c _____
              posters on the walls
              a sign on your door

4 _____ ······· d _____
              with my parents
              about school

REMEMBER BETTER

Use word webs to record verb-noun collocations. Thanks to the visual presentation, you will remember them better.

Add three more items to each word web.

1 play ······· together
           computer games
           music
           a _____
           b _____
           c _____

2 listen to ······· my MP3 player
              my parents
              music
              d _____
              e _____
              f _____

WORD STORE 4D
Adjective order

4 Put the adjectives in the box under an appropriate heading.

[~~automatic~~   big   blue   cotton   horrible
  lovely   old   plastic   red   Samsung]

Opinion	Size/Age	Colour	Material	Make/type
				automatic

5 Put the adjectives in the correct order to complete the sentences.

0 (leather / fantastic / biker's / black)
   Roxy's got a <u>fantastic black leather biker's</u> jacket.
1 (stone / small / beautiful / grey)
   Kathy and Paul live in a _____ cottage.
2 (awful / pink and white / designer)
   Kate bought a(n) _____ shirt.
3 (little / silver / cool / Sony)
   Julia's got a _____ laptop.
4 (party / red / elegant / silk)
   Lucy bought a(n) _____ dress.
5 (modern / nice / orange and yellow)
   Paul's got a(n) _____ bedroom.

47

4.4 Reading

W.J.C. Scott-Bentinck • The city and the country

Glossary

duke (n) = a very important English aristocrat
wig (n) = false hair worn on the head
servant (n) = in the past people paid servants to cook, clean, etc. for them

underground (adj, adv) = below the ground, e.g. you can leave your car in the underground car park; rabbits live underground

1 Read the text quickly and choose the best title.

1 England's shyest man ☐   2 England's most unusual duke ☐   3 England's strangest house ☐

A **W.J.C. Scott-Bentinck**, the fifth Duke of Portland, was a very <u>wealthy</u> and very <u>odd</u> Englishman. He was born in 1800 and lived to be nearly eighty years old. The Duke was a successful businessman with lots of money and an amazing home, but he was not an average aristocrat.

B The first unusual thing about him was his choice of clothes. He often wore two or more coats at the same time and a very strange hat – it was <u>nearly</u> a metre tall. He also liked wearing wigs and pieces of material tied around his ankles (nobody knows why!).

C Another unusual thing about him was his incredible shyness. He lived in a <u>huge</u> house called Welbeck Abbey, but spent most of his time in just one or two of the rooms. He had many servants, but he was too shy to talk to them. Instead, he communicated with them by ringing a bell and leaving note in special boxes. If servants did meet him anywhere in the house or garden, they had to stand completely still, say nothing and look down at the ground until he was gone. Inside Welbeck Abbey there was a mini-railway and, to avoid any face to face contact, the servants from the kitchen used to send meals to his room on the mini-train.

D As well as this unusual form of transport, there were many other amazing things in the Duke's house. For instance, he built an underground ballroom with space for 2,000 guests, but he never used it because he was too shy to invite anyone. Also underground, he built many tunnels and used them to move around his giant house and garden without seeing anyone. One of the tunnels went all the way from Welbeck Abbey to the nearby town of Worksop, almost 3km away! Wellbeck Abbey wasn't the Duke's only home. He had another beautiful house in London and sometimes he stayed there. He didn't build this one though; the Duke's grandfather won it in a game of cards! In total, nearly 1,500 people worked for W.J.C Scott-Bentinck. Sometimes he was a moody and unusual boss, but at other times he was very kind. For example, he gave each servant an umbrella and bought horses for them to ride through the gardens and in tunnels under his house. He also built a boating lake, an area for ice-skating and a horse-riding school for his servants to use. The horse-riding school had a glass roof over 100m long!

E When the Duke died in 1879, his <u>relatives</u> found that most of the rooms in his house had no furniture and the walls were all pink. In one room there was only a toilet – nothing else at all! in another room there were hundreds of green boxes and in each one there was a dark brown wig. Nobody knows how many of them he actually wore.

2 Read the text again. For questions 1–4, choose from the paragraphs (A–E).

Which section mentions that:
1. the Duke had developed an unusual form of communication?
2. he had strange taste in decorating?
3. his personality stopped him from using one of his underground developments?
4. his fashion sense was different from other people at the time?

3 Read the text again. Find and underline the answers to the questions.

1. What was unusual about the Duke's hat?
2. Why did he write notes to his servants?
3. How did his servants deliver his food?
4. Why was the underground ballroom never used?
5. How did the Duke's grandfather get the house in London?
6. How long was the roof of the riding school?
7. What was in the room with the toilet?

4 Match the underlined words in the text with their synonyms.

0. strange = odd
1. very big = _____
2. family members = _____
3. almost = _____
4. rich = _____

5 Complete the conversation with the answers to Exercise 4.

Phil: What do you think about the Duke of Portland?
Gary: Well, I think he was very ⁰odd with his unusual clothes and his underground tunnels! Why did he live in just one or two rooms when he had a ¹_____ house like Welbeck Abbey?
Phil: I don't know. I guess he wasn't lonely though, with ²_____ 1,500 people working for him.
Gary: Well, no, but he was shy, so he didn't want to see anyone else – not even his ³_____ . I read that his sister lived very near, but he hardly ever saw her.
Phil: Really strange. I wonder why he spent so much money on a ballroom and never used it.
Gary: I suppose he was so rich that he didn't care. Maybe he liked dancing on his own!
Phil: Perhaps. I'd love to be ⁴_____ like that. I wouldn't spend my money on a ballroom though.
Gary: No? I thought you liked dancing.
Phil: Yeah, breakdancing, not ballroom dancing!

WORD STORE 4E
Places in the city and in the country

REMEMBER BETTER
When you record new vocabulary, categorise words under headings to help you remember them and their meanings.

Label the words as M for manmade or N for natural.

architecture M   back streets ☐   beach ☐   rock ☐
bridge ☐   canyon ☐   rainforest ☐   harbour ☐
island ☐   monument ☐   mountain ☐   river ☐
neighbourhood ☐   slum ☐   statue ☐   square ☐
coast ☐   reef ☐   ruins ☐   temple ☐   valley ☐

6 Cross out one incorrect option in each sentence.

1. Mum, can we take a boat along the *river / coast / mountain*? It would be so much fun!
2. There are some interesting *rainforests / statues / monuments* in the centre of London.
3. The girls are meeting *in the square / by the bridge / on the reef*. Then they are going shopping.
4. It is a difficult walk through the *canyon / valley / temple*, so you'll need strong walking boots.
5. Be careful in *this neighbourhood / these back streets / this rock*. It can be dangerous at night.
6. Most tourists come here to see the beautiful, modern *slum / architecture / harbour*.

7 Choose the correct options.

1. Without electricity or clean water, life in the *slum / architecture / river* is very difficult.
2. Environmental groups are trying to protect the trees that grow in the world's *rocks / beaches / rainforests*.
3. Snowboarding and skiing on the local *ruins / reefs / mountains* is a very popular activity in winter.
4. Divers can explore the amazing *reef / temple / canyon* and the beautiful fish that live there.
5. We are now walking through the *rocks / valley / ruins* of a 600-year-old Inca city.
6. There aren't any real beaches here, but you can swim from the *rocks / mountain / architecture*.
7. The *bridge / island / harbour* doesn't have an airport, so the only way to get there is by boat.
8. We spent most of our holiday reading and sunbathing on the *canyon / slum / beach*.

49

4.5 Grammar

Present Continuous, *be going* to and *will*

SHOW WHAT YOU KNOW

1 Complete the sentences with the Present Continuous form of the verbs in brackets.

0 Charles! Your fish and chips <u>are getting</u> (get) cold now. Hurry up!
1 I _____ (not lie) now. Really! I promise it's true.
2 Hello? _____ (you/come)? I'm waiting here but I can't see you.
3 Lisa can't come to the phone now. She _____ (run) in the park.
4 Ian and Emma _____ (not talk) at the moment. They disagree about the bathroom.
5 _____ (Mum and Dad/sleep)? I want to practise playing my drums.

2 ★ Read the conversations and choose the correct options.

Conversation 1
A: I hear your parents have just bought a new house. When ¹*are you moving / will you move* in?
B: Oh, we ²*won't move / aren't moving* in until next month. On the twenty-eighth, I think.

Conversation 2
A: Are you coming to class? It's almost 9 o'clock.
B: Yes. ³*I'm seeing / I'll see* you later, Caroline, OK?
C: OK, bye.

Conversation 3
A: Oh no! That man has just stolen my bag!
B: ⁴*I'm calling / I'll call* the police.

Conversation 4
A: What ⁵*will we have / are we having* for dinner today?
B: Oh, I don't know. ⁶*We'll see / We're seeing* what's in the freezer.

3 ★★ Complete the pairs of sentences with the correct form of the verbs in brackets. Use *be going to* or the Present Continuous.

1 a We<u>'re going to eat</u> (eat) in a restaurant, but we haven't decided which one.
  b We _____ (eat) in a restaurant tonight. The table is booked for 7.00.
2 a Nathan _____ (visit) his friend in the UK next week. He reserved a seat yesterday.
  b Nathan _____ (visit) his friend in the UK if he can find a cheap flight.
3 a Penny and Jill _____ (play) tennis if it stops raining.
  b Penny and Jill _____ (play) tennis at 4.30 at the sports centre.

4 ★★★ Complete the messages with the most appropriate future forms of the verbs in brackets.

Hi, Lily. Got any plans for today?

Hi, Alex. I ⁰<u>'m meeting</u> (meet) Fran at 4 p.m. We ¹_____ (see) the new James Bond film if there are any seats left. Wanna come?

Love to. :) Do you need a lift to town? I ²_____ (pick) you up if you want.

Cool. Katie's here now – we ³_____ (do) some homework after lunch (at least that's the plan!). I think we ⁴_____ (be) free by 3 p.m. though.

OK. By the way, Pete ⁵_____ (have) a party tonight. His parents are away. We can all go after the film.

Fantastic! Fran loves parties. And she likes Pete. ;)

SHOW WHAT YOU'VE LEARNT

5 Choose the correct answer, A, B or C.

1 There's someone at the front door. ____ it?
  A Are you going to get   B Will you get
  C Are you getting
2 Jasmine and William ____ house tomorrow.
  A are going to move   B will move
  C are moving
3 I think I ____ a ham and mushroom pizza. No, actually, salami and pepper.
  A 'm going to have   B 'll have
  C 'm having
4 Becky ____ a bookcase when she has time.
  A 's going to buy   B 'll buy
  C 's buying
5 We ____ on Saturday night anymore. The airline moved the flight to Sunday morning.
  A aren't going to fly   B won't fly
  C aren't flying
6 I'm afraid your sister ____ . She called to say she's sick.
  A isn't going to come   B won't come
  C isn't coming

/6

4.6 Speaking language practice

Making suggestions

1 Choose the correct options.

1. **A:** I think we should stop for a break. We've already walked for hours.
   B: *I'd rather keep going. / That sounds good.* My feet hurt and I'm thirsty.
2. **A:** Let's go ice skating. I haven't done it for years.
   B: *Why not! / I'm sorry, I'm not keen on ice skating.* Can we get the bus there?
3. **A:** What about visiting Grandma this weekend?
   B: *I'm not sure about that. / Good idea!* I've got lots of homework to do and I'm going to a party.
4. **A:** Do you fancy having a BBQ on the patio?
   B: *Let's get a takeaway instead. / Sounds great.* Have we got any sausages?
5. **A:** Why don't we invite Naomi to the party?
   B: *I don't really like Naomi. / That's a great idea.* She's so arrogant.
6. **A:** How about going to the school disco with me?
   B: *Great idea! / I'd rather go on my own.* Sorry.

2 Put the sentences in the conversation in the correct order.

Kyle: That's a great idea! Where do you want to go? [2]
Kyle: Three hours? Wow! I'm not sure about that. Perhaps I'll ask Dad if I can borrow his car. We could drive there quicker ourselves.
Marcin: What are you doing on Saturday, Kyle? Kuba and I are thinking of going snowboarding for the day. Do you fancy coming with us?
Kyle: Why not! I'll ask Mum to make us some sandwiches.
Marcin: Well, I think we should go to Harrachov, in the Czech Republic. There's a bus. It takes about three hours.
Marcin: Good idea. Don't forget to tell her that Kuba is vegetarian.
Marcin: Sounds good. Why don't we take some food from home? It's expensive to eat on the mountain.

3 Complete suggestions 1–6 with the correct form of the verbs in brackets. Then match the suggestions with responses a–g.

0. Why don't we *go* (go) out for dinner tonight? [g]
1. Let's _____ (fly) to Spain and have a few days in the sun. There are cheap flights at the moment.
2. How about _____ (sit) down for ten minutes? I need a rest.
3. We could _____ (do) our homework together. You could help me.
4. I think we should _____ (camp). It's cheaper than staying in a hotel.
5. Do you fancy _____ (cook) fish tonight? We should have something healthy.
6. What about _____ (buy) Dan a book for his birthday?

a. To be honest, I'd rather have steak.
b. That's a good idea. I am better at Maths than you.
c. Why not! Has he read the new J.K. Rowling novel?
d. That sounds great. There are some seats over there. Do you want a coffee?
e. I'm sorry, I'm not keen on sleeping outside. We could look for a cheap hostel.
f. We went there last year. Let's go to Croatia instead.
g. I'm not sure about that. We've already eaten out twice this week.

4 Complete the phrases in the conversation. The first letter of each word is given.

Lydia: I can't believe I didn't win the race. All that training and I was only fifth!
Sophie: Don't worry, Lydia. There'll be other races. ⁰**W**hy **d**on't we do something fun to cheer you up? ¹W_____ a_____ going for ice cream?
Lydia: I don't ²r_____ l_____ ice cream. ³I_____ r_____ go shopping.
Sophie: ⁴T_____ a good i_____ . I need something new to wear to the party on Saturday.
Lydia: ⁵D_____ you f_____ going to the new shopping centre? There are sales at the moment, I think.
Sophie: ⁶W_____ n_____ ! And then ⁷w_____ c_____ go for a pizza or something.
Lydia: ⁸T_____ s_____ great. Thanks, Sophie.
Sophie: My pleasure. Really! Let's get going then.

4.7 Writing

A story

1 Complete the story with the words in the box.

> and extremely immediately one
> suddenly then when ~~year~~

A BIT OF A SHOCK

Last ⁰ _year_ I was staying with my English friend in her lovely old house in the country. My room was on the second floor. It was very quiet up there. ¹_____ I was in bed, I could only hear the night birds outside.

²_____ night, I was just going to sleep when ³_____, I heard a noise in my room. Someone was walking across the floorboards. I was so scared that I couldn't move. ⁴_____ something soft touched my hair. I screamed and sat up.

My friend ⁵_____ rushed into my room ⁶_____ switched on the light. She laughed! Her cat, Rosie, was sitting on the end of my bed, looking very surprised. I felt ⁷_____ silly!

2 Find these things in the story.
1. an adverb that means 'very'
   _____
2. a short sentence
   _____
3. an example of the past continuous
   _____
4. an adjective that means 'frightened'
   _____
5. a word which tells us what happened next
   _____
6. an adverb that means 'very quickly'
   _____
7. a verb that means 'came quickly'
   _____

3 Choose the correct options.
1. *While / After* I was looking for my friend, I saw her bag on the floor.
2. I knocked at the door. *When / Then* I looked in the window.
3. *Although / While* it was noisy outside, I slept deeply.
4. In the *finally / end*, I realised he wasn't coming.
5. I went into the garden *because / and* I wanted to see the flowers.
6. I had a shower. *When / After that* I went downstairs for breakfast.

SHOW WHAT YOU'VE LEARNT

4 Your teacher has asked you to write a story. Your story must begin with this sentence.

> I was doing my homework in the garden when something fell on the grass beside me.

Write your story in about 100 words.

SHOW THAT YOU'VE CHECKED

In my story:
- I have used an interesting title. ☐
- I have used different tenses. ☐
- I have used some short dramatic sentences. ☐
- I have used linking words to connect sentences. ☐
- I have used a range of adjectives. ☐
- I have used some adverbs to add interest. ☐
- I have used paragraphs. ☐
- I have written about 100 words. ☐
- I have checked my spelling and punctuation. ☐
- I have checked that my handwriting is clear enough for someone else to read. ☐

4.8 Use of English

Four-option multiple choice

1 Read the text below and choose the correct word (A, B, C or D) for each space.

Houses of the future?

Our cities and towns are ⁰___ more and more crowded. There isn't enough space to build more ¹___ for people. However, some people are using their ²___ to design very unusual houses in big cities. They are creating ³___ places to live under the ground!

A recent newspaper ⁴___ described a house in central London with just a small entrance from the street. Stairs go down to a lounge, kitchen and bathroom. Then more stairs go down to bedrooms and play rooms! ⁵___ a wonderful idea! Unfortunately, the ⁶___ don't think so. They have ⁷___ lots of complaints about it. When builders work on houses like this, it ⁸___ a very long time. It's also very noisy!

So when designers come ⁹___ with clever new ideas like this, they need to be ¹⁰___ to other people's feelings. Would you like to live in a place like this? Post a comment to let us know.

0	A going	B being	**C getting**	D developing
1	A suburbs	B accommodation	C slums	D architecture
2	A ideas	B opportunities	C learning	D imaginations
3	A shallow	B spacious	C successful	D sociable
4	A article	B programme	C episode	D action
5	A How	B What	C Why	D Which
6	A critics	B population	C journalists	D neighbours
7	A made	B taken	C done	D put
8	A is	B gets	C takes	D uses
9	A on	B in	C at	D up
10	A sensible	B loyal	C honest	D sensitive

TIPS:

Question 1: You need the word which means 'somewhere for people to stay'.
Question 4: What do you read in newspapers?
Question 9: Which preposition completes this phrasal verb meaning 'think of'?

Sentence transformations

2 Here are some sentences about moving house. For each question, complete the second sentence so that it means the same as the first. Use no more than three words.

0 We live on the edge of a big town.
   We live in _the suburbs_ of a big town.
1 We moved to this house ten years ago.
   We _____ in this house for ten years.
2 Now my parents have decided to buy a house five kilometres away.
   Now my parents are _____ buy a house five kilometres away.
3 They say that this house is too small for our family.
   They say that this house isn't _____ for our family.
4 I think it's great to live near the town.
   I enjoy _____ near the town.
5 Here I can travel to school by bus.
   Here I can use the public _____ to get to school.

TIPS:

Question 1: You need to use the Present Perfect here.
Question 2: What verb form do you use to talk about future plans and intentions?
Question 4: What verb form follows *enjoy*?

4.9 Self-assessment

1 For each learning objective, tick (✓) the box that best matches your ability.

☺☺ = I understand and can help a friend.   ☹ = I understand some, but have some questions.
☺ = I understand and can do it by myself.   ☹☹ = I do not understand.

			☺☺	☺	☹	☹☹	Need help?
4.1	Vocabulary	I can describe houses and use phrases with *make* and *do*.					Students' Book pages 48–49 Word Store page 9 Workbook pages 44–45
4.2	Grammar	I can talk about actions that started in the past and continue until now.					Students' Book page 50 Workbook page 46
4.3	Listening	I can identify specific detail in short monologues.					Students' Book page 51 Workbook page 47
4.4	Reading	I can find specific detail in an article.					Students' Book pages 52–53 Workbook pages 48–49
4.5	Grammar	I can talk about future arrangements, intentions and spontaneous decisions.					Students' Book page 54 Workbook page 50
4.6	Speaking	I can make and respond to suggestions.					Students' Book page 55 Workbook page 51
4.7	Writing	I can write a short story.					Students' Book pages 56–57 Workbook page 52

2 What can you remember from this unit?

New words I learned (the words you most want to remember from this unit)	Expressions and phrases I liked (any expressions or phrases you think sound nice, useful or funny)	English I heard or read outside class (e.g. from websites, books, adverts, films, music)

4.10 Self-check

1 Choose the correct options.

0 We live in a flat, so we don't have a garden, but we like to put plants in pots on the cupboards /(windowsills)/ floorboards.
1 Poor Susan burned her hand on the carpet / cupboard / cooker yesterday evening.
2 The patio / porch / pond is full of plants, so we can't see the fish in the water!
3 Mum always does the cooking and after dinner Dad and I do the mess / washing-up / kitchen sink.
4 Our village / stone wall / eco-house has solar panels, a wood burner and a compost toilet.
5 Anastasia loves reading. The shelves / bookcase / worktop in her bedroom is full.

/5

2 Complete the words in the sentences. Some letters are given.

0 **S**e**mi-d**etache**d** houses are often quieter because there are no neighbours on one side.
1 The fishing boats leave the **h_____r** in the middle of the night.
2 Do you want to visit them or not? Please make a **d_____n** so we can plan our weekend.
3 Jasmine doesn't mind doing the washing but she hates doing the **i_____g** afterwards.
4 Please take off your shoes and leave them out here on the **p_____h**.
5 Now I live with my family in the **s_____s**, but when I'm older, I want to live in the city centre.

/5

3 Complete the sentences with the words in the box. There are two extra words.

> bridge   cosy   countryside   island
> mud   patio   river   single

0 Ben and Theo often go fishing in the river in the forest on Sundays.
1 We skied all morning, then stopped for lunch in a warm and _____ little restaurant at the top of the mountain.
2 This morning the _____ was closed because of the wind. Dad had to drive an extra 30km to take me to school.
3 The air in the _____ is much cleaner than in the city.
4 In many parts of the world people make their houses out of _____ .
5 When she was a little girl, my grandma shared a _____ bed with two of her sisters.

/5

4 Use the prompts to write sentences in the Present Perfect. Add for or since.

0 Rick / work / as a builder / 2010
   Rick has worked as a builder since 2010.
1 the statue of the King / be / in the square / 1754
   _____
2 their pond / not have / fish in it / two years
   _____
3 the cat / sit / on the windowsill / this morning
   _____
4 Nina / live / in a flat / ten years
   _____
5 I / not feel / well / last weekend
   _____

/5

5 Choose the correct answer, A, B or C.

0 What shall we have for dinner? Perhaps I ___ pizza. Does that sound OK?
   A 'm making   B 'm going to make   C('ll make)
1 Hannah and I ___ to a concert on Friday night. Hannah's uncle has bought us tickets.
   A 're going   B 're going to go   C 'll go
2 Oliver has a plan for next weekend. He ___ to the campsite on the coast.
   A 's cycling   B 's going to cycle   C 'll cycle
3 You look terrible. I think I ___ the doctor.
   A 'm calling   B 'm going to call   C 'll call
4 Ryan ___ football tomorrow because he's broken his leg.
   A isn't playing   B isn't going to play   C won't play
5 We ___ to visit Auntie Joan on Thursday.
   A 're planning   B 're going to plan   C 'll plan

/5

6 Read the text and choose the correct answer, A, B or C.

> We ⁰___ in this old ¹___ on the ninth floor of a block in the city centre since I was born, but tonight is our very last night here. Tomorrow morning at 8 a.m. we ²___ to a new house in a small ³___ , twenty-five miles from the city. I'm looking forward to living there, but I'll miss this old place. I ⁴___ to the same school for the last five years and I'm worried because I ⁵___ at a new school next Monday.

0 A live   B lived   C(have lived)
1 A cottage   B flat   C bungalow
2 A 're moving   B 're going to move C 'll move
3 A village   B suburbs   C island
4 A go   B went   C 've gone
5 A 'm starting   B 'm going to start C 'll start

/5

Total /30

5 SCHOOL

5.1 Vocabulary

Education • Phrasal verbs • Phrases with *get*

SHOW WHAT YOU KNOW

1 Match the headings in the box with the word groups. There are two extra headings.

> ~~Architecture~~   Business   Design and Technology
> Engineering   English   Law   Medicine   Writing
> Physical Education (PE)   Reading   Science

0 Architecture : buildings, design, drawing
1 _____ : illness, doctor, hospital
2 _____ : roads, bridges, machines
3 _____ : athlete, fitness, sport
4 _____ : books, magazines, websites
5 _____ : electronics, graphics, product design
6 _____ : crime, judge, court
7 _____ : pronunciation, phrasal verbs, intonation
8 _____ : pen, keyboard, typing

2 Complete the school subjects in the sentences. The first letter of each word is given.

0 Katy's not good with numbers, so she hates **M**aths.
1 I think we can learn a lot when we study the past. That's why I decided to take **H**_____ .
2 Our **A**_____ teacher says we are both very good at painting and drawing.
3 You really think that Paris is in Japan? Don't you study **G**_____ at school?
4 Which **S**_____ exam have you got tomorrow? Some students have Chemistry and others have Physics.

WORD STORE 5A
Phrasal verbs

3 Choose the correct options.

1 If you get too cold during the exam, *get into* / *put on* your jumper.
2 Mia is my classmate and my friend. I *get on* / *carry on* very well with her.
3 This Saturday afternoon I'm *meeting up* / *getting up* with friends to study Maths.
4 It is very difficult to *get into* / *get on with* the best universities. You need really good exam results.
5 I want to *carry on* / *get up* studying English after my exams. I want to get to a really high level.
6 *Take off* / *Meet up* your sunglasses in the classroom.
7 I'm so happy that it's the weekend. I don't have to *take off* / *get up* early tomorrow.

WORD STORE 5B
Education

4 Choose the correct options.

1 My best friend and I are *classmates* / *classrooms* / *classes*. We are in the same class at school.
2 At our school uniforms are *demanding* / *compulsory* / *secondary*. We have to wear them.
3 Today the teacher gave us a list of ten new words to *study* / *revise* / *learn* by heart for a test next lesson.
4 Phil's timetable is very *demanding* / *compulsory* / *secondary*. He is always busy at school and often tired.
5 Ruby doesn't have enough time for Art this year, so she has decided to *revise* / *drop* / *pass* it.
6 Jacob wasn't in the Maths lesson again today. He often *passes* / *drops* / *skips* lessons. I don't think he'll pass the exam.
7 My cousin *does* / *learns* / *passes* a course in photography in the evenings at the local college.

5 Complete the word web with the words in the box. Then complete the text with the correct form of verbs from the word web.

> an exam   a lesson   a subject

drop ···· 1 _____
do ····
revise for ····
take/do ···· 2 _____
pass ····
fail ····
skip ···· 3 _____

---

teen talk [ask]

Welcome to Teentalk, online advice for teenagers. You can ask us anything you like!

My older sister isn't doing well at school this year. She often gets into trouble because she ⁰ skips lessons and goes to meet her boyfriend at the shopping centre. She never does any homework and she doesn't ¹_____ for any of her tests or exams. Most students ²_____ eight subjects in their final year, but my sister wants to ³_____ Science because it's too difficult and she doesn't think she will ⁴_____ the exam. She's going to ⁵_____ her final exams at the end of this year and Mum thinks she'll ⁶_____ all of them. It's difficult for a younger sister to give advice to an older sister. How can I help her?

56

WORD STORE 5C
Phrases with *get*

6 Complete the text with the phrases in the box. Change the form of *get* if necessary. There are two extra phrases.

> get better   get home   get late   get tired
> ~~get to the station~~   get to work
> not get a text message   not get to school

MyEnglishLab

English homework:

Write 150 words about somebody very similar or very different to you.

I am sixteen and my brother Charles is twenty-five. He is much older than me, but people say we have a lot in common. I'm not sure about that, but on a normal day, our lives are quite similar. We get up at seven, have breakfast together and then walk for the train. We ⁰*get to the station* at eight and catch the same train into town. Charles ¹_____ at half past eight, but I meet my friends, so I ²_____ so early. When school finishes, my brother and I usually meet at the school gate and travel home together. This means that we normally ³_____ at the same time. We have dinner, I do my homework and then we often watch TV together. When it ⁴_____ , at around 11 o'clock, he usually ⁵_____ , so he goes to bed. I usually stay up a bit later. Perhaps our days are so similar because he is a teacher at my school!

ALWAYS LEARNING   PEARSON

7 Complete the diagram with examples for each category.

```
                    get
      ┌──────────────┼──────────────┐
get + adjective/   get + noun    get (to) + noun
past participle
   get ready      get a text message   get to work
   _____        _____      _____
   _____        _____      _____
   _____        _____      _____
```

REMEMBER THIS
wake up = stop sleeping
get up = get out of bed
stand up = stop sitting and be on your feet

8 Read REMEMBER THIS. Complete the sentences with the phrasal verbs in bold.
1 Our school is quite formal. We have to _____ when the teacher comes into the classroom.
2 On Sundays I don't rush to _____ . I like lying in bed and reading.
2 I really need an alarm clock if I have to _____ early.

SHOW WHAT YOU'VE LEARNT

9 Complete the second sentence so that it has a similar meaning to the first, using the word in capitals. Do not change the word in capitals.

0 Lucy and I are in the same class at school. **CLASSMATES**
  Lucy and I *are classmates* .

1 John will send me a text message when he's ready to leave. **GET**
  I'll _____ from John when he's ready to leave.

2 Simon's parents can't continue paying for private lessons. **CARRY**
  Simon's parents _____ paying for private lessons.

3 Please remove your headphones when I'm talking to you. **TAKE**
  Please _____ your headphones when I'm talking to you.

4 Why is it so difficult to get out of bed on Monday? **UP**
  Why is it so hard to _____ on Monday?

5 Please arrive at school by 9 a.m. on exam day. **TO**
  Please _____ school by 9 a.m. on exam day.

6 How can I improve my English? **GET**
  How can I _____ at English?

7 It's not easy to pass the driving test first time. **FAIL**
  It's _____ the driving test first time.

8 You must revise if you want to do well in the test. **MARKS**
  You must revise if you want to _____ in the test.

9 Last time I missed the train. This time I'm going to arrive at the station early. **GET**
  Last time I missed the train. This time I'm going to _____ early.

10 I think we should arrive at about 10 o'clock. **GET**
   I think we should _____ at about 10 o'clock.

/10

5.2 Grammar

First Conditional

SHOW WHAT YOU KNOW

1 **Change the underlined verbs to make negative sentences. Use short forms.**

0 They're classmates. They are in the same class.
They aren't classmates, but they meet after school.

1 My sister gets up early on Mondays. She has to get the bus to school.
My sister _____ early on Mondays.

2 We'll live together next year. We are going to university in the same town.
We _____ live together next year. We are going to university in different towns.

3 She's a good student. She likes studying.
She _____ a good student. She hates studying.

2 ★ **Put the words in the correct order to complete the First Conditional sentences.**

0 you / pass / you'll / study / hard, / your / final
If you study hard, you'll pass your final exams.

1 write / forget / number / if / my / he / it / doesn't
He'll _____
_____ down.

2 hurry up / she'll / her / miss / doesn't / Samantha
If _____
_____ train.

3 how / you / he'll / sure / understand / him / tell / if / you
I'm _____
_____ feel.

4 listen / don't / know / you / carefully, / what / to / you / you / won't
If _____
_____ do.

5 with / dance / ask / you / you / won't / don't / if
Anita _____
_____ her.

6 go / he / will / feels / if / tomorrow / back / school / to
Sam _____
_____ better.

3 ★★ **Complete the First Conditional sentences with the correct form of the verbs in brackets.**

0 If Stacey gets (get) good grades this year, she 'll get (get) into university next year.

1 What _____ (Charlotte/do) if she _____ (fail) her exams?

2 We _____ (get) into trouble if we _____ (skip) another lesson.

3 If Julia and Toby _____ (not have) extra lessons at a private academy, they _____ (not pass) their exams.

4 If you _____ (not look) at the timetable, you _____ (not know) what classes you have.

4 ★★★ **Complete the forum posts with the correct form of the verbs in the box. There are two extra verbs.**

be   learn   not enjoy   not get   not pass
pay   pass   stop   take   ~~want~~

ASK ANYTHING

jayne17 asks …
What will I have to do if I ⁰ want to learn to drive? I'm seventeen years old. Can anyone help?

MOST HELPFUL ANSWERS

Hi, Jayne. Before you learn to drive, you'll need to choose a driving instructor. It's important to choose carefully because if you ¹ _____ on with your instructor, you ² _____ the lessons. My instructor was great and I really enjoyed learning to drive. Good luck! ☺

You will probably feel nervous the first time you drive, but if your instructor ³ _____ you to a quiet place to practise, it ⁴ _____ much less stressful.

My brother is learning to drive and he's worried about the theory test (the one you do on a computer). I think that he ⁵ _____ the test without any problems if he ⁶ _____ the rules of the road.

jayne17 asks …
Thanks for the advice. One more question. If I ⁷ _____ the test, will I have to pay again?

SHOW WHAT YOU'VE LEARNT

5 **Match intentions 1–6 with conditions a–f. Then write First Conditional sentences.**

0 visit Brazil — g
1 see kangaroos and koalas
2 drive to school every day
3 study at a private academy
4 get a tattoo
5 make sandwiches every morning
6 want to learn to snowboard

a need to have strong legs
b pass the driving test
c have to pay tuition fees
d not have to eat in the school canteen
e do a gap year in Australia
f have it forever
g learn some basic Portuguese

0 If Mark visits Brazil, he 'll learn some basic Portuguese.
1 She _____ if she _____ .
2 I _____ if I _____ .
3 If Sarah and Ken _____ , they _____ .
4 If Katie _____ , she _____ .
5 If you _____ , you _____ .
6 If your friend _____ , he _____ .

/6

5.3 Listening language practice

Expressions with prepositions • Synonyms • Phrases with *get*

1 Read the conversation and choose the correct options. Then listen and check.

Extract from Students' Book recording CD•2.36 MP3•80

A: Hi, Tom. Are you coming out ¹*with / by / for* us tonight?
B: Oh no, I can't. I'm revising ²*to / about / for* exams. I need to learn fifty French verbs ³*on / by / with* heart tonight.
A: But the exams don't <u>start</u> until next month.
B: I know, but I get really nervous ⁴*on / about / for* exams. If I don't <u>revise</u> every night, I'll get stressed.
A: I don't know why you're so worried. You always get good marks in class.
B: I know, but that's different. In exams, I panic. And I really want to get good grades for my A-levels. I want to get ⁵*into / with / in* a good university.
A: Listen, you need to relax. If you continue like this, you'll get <u>ill</u>.
B: Well, what can I do?
A: OK, first, you need to make a revision timetable. If you make a timetable, you'll see that you have <u>plenty of</u> time to do everything.
B: Um, yeah, that's quite a good idea.
A: And I think you spend too much time alone – sometimes it's good to study ⁶*about / by / with* other people.
B: Is it? I'm not so sure. They might know more than I do!
A: You're so <u>negative</u>.
B: Well, it's OK for you, you don't get nervous.
A: Of course I get nervous. But I try to be <u>positive</u>. For example, before an exam, I imagine myself ⁷*to / in / on* the exam – I know all the answers and I pass the exam ⁸*on / by / with* the best marks.
B: Hm. It's true, I'm not very confident. […]

2 Complete the sentences with prepositions.
1 I am getting nervous <u>about</u> tomorrow. Jake asked me to study _____ him. He's so handsome. I don't think I'll learn anything!
2 Vince stayed up too late and then he actually fell asleep _____ the English exam.
3 Our exams don't start until May, so we've still got three months to revise _____ them. I'm going to study hard because I want to pass _____ the best marks and get _____ university to study Medicine.
4 I have to learn fifteen words _____ heart for a test tomorrow. I'll come out _____ you another time.

3 Match the underlined words in the conversation in Exercise 1 with their definitions.
0 sick = <u>ill</u>
1 more than enough = _____
2 optimistic = _____
3 study for exams = _____
4 begin = _____
5 pessimistic = _____

> **REMEMBER BETTER**
>
> Synonyms are different words with the same or very similar meanings. When you learn a new word, it's a good idea to check its synonym(s) in a dictionary. Knowledge of synonyms will help you understand more when you read and listen to more difficult texts.
>
> **Replace the underlined words in the sentences with synonyms. The first letter of each word is given.**
>
> 0 Today Naomi and Leon had their final exams, so tonight they are going to go out and <u>enjoy themselves</u>. (h<u>ave</u> a g<u>ood</u> t<u>ime</u>)
> 1 The teacher said we should try to <u>relax</u> the night before the exam. (t_____ it e_____)
> 2 I don't like studying with other people. I work best <u>alone</u>. (o_____ m_____ o_____)

WORD STORE 5D
More phrases with *get*

4 Complete the conversations with the phrases in the box. Change the form of *get* if necessary.

> get a lot out of   get a tattoo   get ill
> get into trouble   get plenty of sleep   ~~get rid of~~

0 A: Did you <u>get rid of</u> those horrible old slippers?
    B: Yes, I got a new pair for my birthday. Not the most exciting present, but useful.
1 A: Were you sick after the school field trip?
    B: Yes, I was cold and wet all day. I think that was when I _____ . I still feel pretty bad.
2 A: Are you going to bed early tonight?
    B: No, I _____ last night. Tonight I'm going to stay up and revise.
3 A: How is your nephew doing at school?
    B: Not very well. He often _____ with his teachers. They say he talks too much during lessons.
4 A: Are you still going to the after-school chess club?
    B: Yes. I really _____ it. I meet new people, learn more about chess and, believe it or not, I even met a nice girl there.
5 A: Are you busy tomorrow evening?
    B: Well, yes, I am, and I'm very excited about it. I _____ on my back. I have an appointment at Ink Forever at 8 p.m. Will you come with me?

5.4 Reading

Studying in the UK • Verbs with prepositions • Word families

Glossary
work placement (n) = when students work for a short time as part of their studies
footwear (n) = a formal word for shoes and boots
field trip (n) = when students go somewhere (e.g. a museum or historic site) to learn about a particular subject

1 Read the article quickly and decide why it was written.
1 to explain how to get a job you love ☐
2 to give advice on where to study the subject you love ☐
3 to present the benefits of studying a subject you love ☐

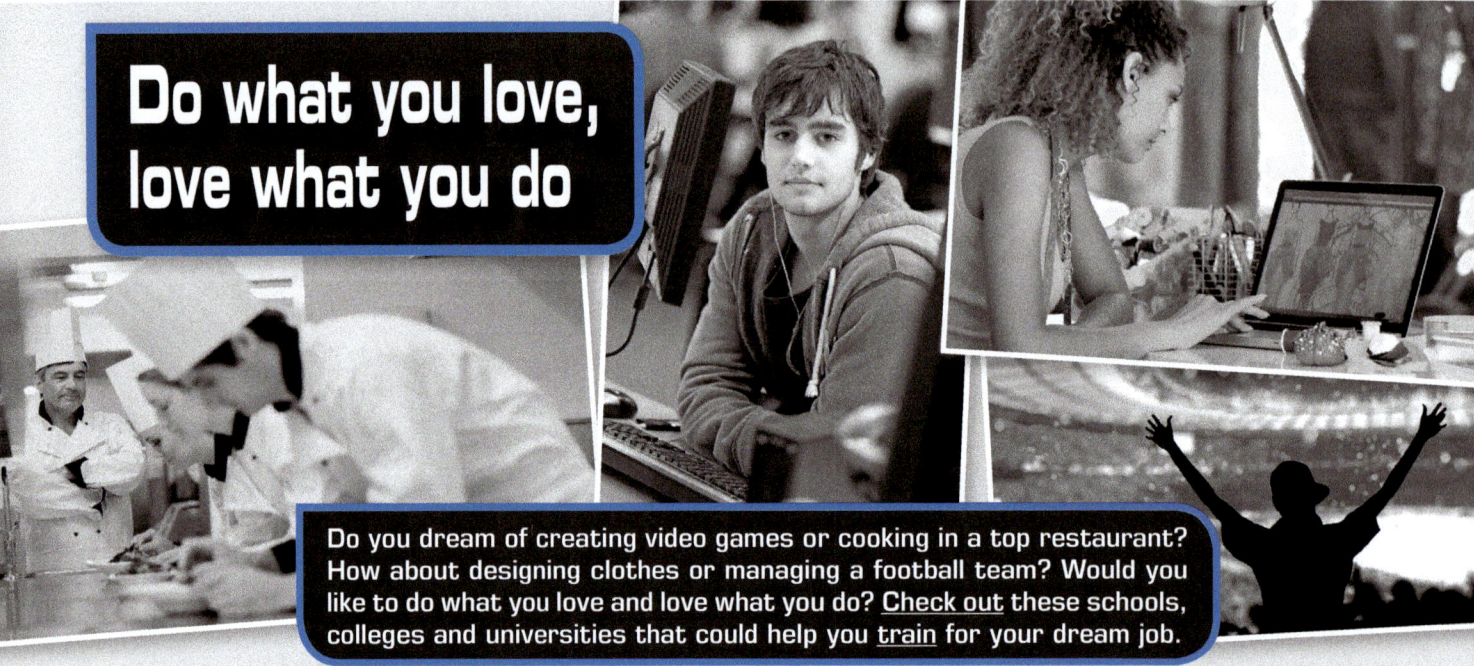

Do what you love, love what you do

Do you dream of creating video games or cooking in a top restaurant? How about designing clothes or managing a football team? Would you like to do what you love and love what you do? <u>Check out</u> these schools, colleges and universities that could help you <u>train</u> for your dream job.

A So you love ... video games?

A new course at the University of Derby in the UK could be <u>ideal</u> for you if you dream of a job in the video game industry. The School of Computing and Mathematics offers a degree in Computer Games Modelling and Animation. Students on the course develop their artistic skills and learn how to create game characters and digital worlds using the university's powerful computers and software. Lecturers on the course have years of industry experience and the company that created Lara Croft from the famous *Tomb Raider* games helped to design the course. Students can choose to take their third year as a work placement year and get some experience of what it's really like to work in the video games industry. If you want to apply for a place on the course, you will need a good grade in A-level Art and Design, and, of course, you will need to love computers and video games!

B So you love ... cooking?

If you are happier in the kitchen than in front of a computer screen, you might be interested in a course organised by the London School of Hospitality and Tourism. Many students on the Culinary Arts and Professional Cookery course go on to work in top restaurants after they <u>graduate</u>. The school has its own award-winning training restaurant called Pillars. Pillars is a real working restaurant, so you'll experience what it's like to work in the restaurant industry and customers will come and pay to eat your homework! On the course, you'll study French and Italian cooking and if you decide on this course, you'll need to buy chef's whites, the traditional all-white uniform of professional chefs.

C So you love ... clothes?

The UK's capital city is the place to study if you want to be the next Armani or Versace. London College of Fashion offers a wide range of degree courses for the fashion industry. If you love shoes then you could try the degree in Footwear Design and Development. <u>Perhaps</u> you are more interested in designing clothing for sports – check out the course in Fashion Sportswear. There are design courses for menswear, womenswear and even for underwear! The course is popular with international students, so it's not unusual to hear lots of foreign languages at the college. Every year the college organises fashion shows and some of the biggest clothing companies and buyers with years of experience are there to look at students' designs.

D So you love ... football?

Do you love football? Do you dream of managing Manchester United or Real Madrid? Southampton Solent University could help to make your dreams come true. Football is part of the history of Southampton and if you get a place to do the Football Studies degree, you'll go on field trips to the most <u>well-known</u> stadiums and football clubs in the region. Famous managers and players from the world of football regularly give guest lectures at the university. Students have the opportunity to hear about their years of experience in the football industry. Many students find jobs with big international football clubs such as Chelsea FC or FC Spartak Moscow after they finish the course. For this reason, graduates who speak another language have a real advantage in the world of modern football.

2 Read the article again and match statements 1–6 with courses A–D.
1 Large companies will be interested to see your work on this course. ☐
2 A company helped to develop this course. ☐
3 You'll go on field trips on this course. ☐
4 You'll have to buy special clothes for this course. ☐
5 You'll probably meet someone famous on this course. ☐
6 A year of work experience is an option on this course. ☐

3 Read the text again. Are the statements true (T) or false (F)?
1 A lecturer from the University of Derby created the famous game character Lara Croft. ☐
2 Students need their own computer for the course Computer Games Modelling and Animation. ☐
3 Pillars training restaurant is open to the public. ☐
4 Foreign languages are part of the Culinary Arts and Professional Cookery course. ☐
5 You have to be good at sports if you want to study Fashion Sportswear. ☐
6 Graduates from the degree Football Studies at Southampton Solent University will benefit from knowing a foreign language. ☐

4 Replace the crossed out words in the sentences with the underlined words in the article.
1 I think Australia is the ~~perfect~~ *ideal* place for a gap year. There is so much to see and do there.
1 If you want to ~~learn the skills you need~~ _____ to be an actor, you'll have to go to drama school.
2 ~~Maybe~~ _____ it's not a good idea to go out tonight. I have a Maths test tomorrow and I need to revise.
3 You should ~~look at~~ _____ the school's new website. There are some funny pictures of all the teachers.
4 The French Alps are ~~famous~~ _____ for some of the best skiing and snowboarding in Europe.
5 I'm not planning to do a gap year. I want to ~~complete my studies~~ _____ first and then go travelling.

5 Match the sentence halves. Look at the words in italics to help you.
0 Check out these schools, colleges and universities that could help you *train* [f]
1 A new course at the University of Derby in the UK could be ideal for you if you *dream* ☐
2 If you want to *apply* ☐
3 If you *decide* ☐
4 Buyers with years of experience are there to *look* ☐
5 Students have the opportunity to *hear* ☐
a *for* a place on the course, you will need a good grade in A-level Art and Design.
b *on* this course, you'll need to buy chef's whites.
c *about* their years of experience in the football industry.
d *of* a job in the video game industry.
e *at* students' designs.
f *for* your dream job.

REMEMBER THIS
After some verbs, we put a preposition before the object. Try to learn these verbs and prepositions together.
verb + **preposition** + object
I want to *apply* **for** a place on the course.

6 Read REMEMBER THIS and complete the sentences with prepositions. Use a dictionary if necessary.
0 Greg Mortenson didn't succeed *in* his plan to reach the summit of K2.
1 After he got lost, he stayed ___ the tiny village of Korphe.
2 He thought ___ how he could help the villagers who looked after him.
3 His programme Pennies for Pakistan helped to pay ___ a new school for girls in the village.

WORD STORE 5E
Word families

7 Choose the correct options.
1 I stayed up all night revising. I was so *exhaustion / exhausted / exhaust* that I fell asleep in the exam.
2 Nick, please *explain / explains / explanation* why you missed the last lesson. I hope you have a good excuse!
3 I can't stay in the mountains for long. The *isolate / isolated / isolation* is driving me crazy.
4 We will *provision / provide / provided* accommodation for all the guests at our wedding.

8 Complete the sentences with the correct form of the words in capitals.
1 COLLECT
a My brother loves superheroes. He has a giant *collection* of comic books.
b My rich uncle _____ sports cars.

2 DECIDE
a Last summer I _____ to get a tattoo of a flower on my shoulder.
b Choosing the right course can be a difficult _____ .

3 DONATE
a I think millionaire Susan Richie should _____ some of her money to charity instead of spending it all on clothes and holidays.
b If you enjoyed tonight's free concert, please make a small _____ to help poor families in the area.

4 EDUCATE
a Our organisation helps to _____ young people about the dangers of drugs.
b We think the government should spend less money on soldiers and guns, and more money on _____ .

5.5 Grammar
Relative clauses

SHOW WHAT YOU KNOW

1 Match the words in the box with their definitions.

a bungalow ☐   a classmate ☐   a cooker ☐
a critic ☐   a pond ☐   the coast [1]

1. a place where the sea meets the land
2. a machine that you use to heat food
3. a person who is in your class at school
4. a house which has only one floor
5. a place in a garden where fish and frogs live
6. a person that writes book or film reviews

2 ★ Choose the correct options.

1. Mr Jones is the teacher *which / who* broke his leg on the field trip. He still can't walk properly.
2. Rose's Place is the café *that / where* I worked during the summer holidays. I saved a lot of money.
3. Look! That's the guy *that / which* cheated in the exam. He still got bad marks though.
4. Here's the textbook *where / that* you left at my house. Now you can do your homework.
5. Do you remember the number of the room *which / where* the exam is today? I'm so stressed I can't remember anything.
6. This is the computer *which / where* always goes wrong. Someone should fix it.

3 ★★ Complete the advert with *which/that, who/that* or *where*.

- Do you own a dog ⁰*which/that* you can't control?
- Do you have a postman ¹_____ worries every time he has to visit your house?
- Does your dog take you for a walk?

If the answer is **yes**, then maybe we can help.

Good Dog Academy is a school ²_____ helps to train difficult dogs. We work with dog owners ³_____ have big problems with their pets. Come and visit the Good Dog Academy, a place ⁴_____ difficult dogs can become perfect pets in only two weeks!

Phone **0801 333 333** for details.

4 ★★ Use the prompts to write sentences with relative clauses.

0. Sydney / the city / my father was born
   Sydney is the city where my father was born.
1. football / a sport / is cheap and fun
   _____
2. a pupil / a child / goes to primary school
   _____
3. a tattoo / a picture under your skin / never disappears
   _____
4. Mrs Kemp / the teacher / always gives us lots of homework
   _____
5. Oxford / the city / has the oldest university in the UK
   _____
6. the Japanese / the people / invented sushi
   _____
7. an architect / a person / designs buildings
   _____
8. an ice rink / a surface / you can ice skate
   _____

5 ★★★ Cross out the relative pronoun where it is not necessary.

0. This is a photo of the girl ~~that~~ I met last weekend at Sasha's party.
1. If Mum can't pick me up from school, I get the bus which stops outside our house.
2. I've written down the phone number of the private tutor that my cousin recommended.
3. This is the hospital where I was born. It's much bigger now than in the past.
4. Can you buy some apples, some cheese and the eggs that say 'organic' on the box?
5. This is the puppy which I chose. Isn't he cute?

SHOW WHAT YOU'VE LEARNT

6 Complete the sentences with relative pronouns.

1. This is the bag _____ I bought on Saturday.
2. Where is the student _____ lost the MP3 player?
3. Take me to the place _____ we ate lunch last week.
4. Can I see the new phone _____ you bought?
5. This is the teacher _____ taught us last week.
6. That is the classroom _____ I have my English lessons.

/6

5.6 Speaking language practice

Giving an opinion • Agreeing and disagreeing

1 Label the phrases *A* for agreeing, *DP* for disagreeing politely or *D* for disagreeing.

0 That's a good point. — A
1 I see what you mean, but …
2 I totally disagree.
3 Oh come on! That's nonsense.
4 I'm not so sure.
5 That's true, but …
6 I couldn't agree more.

2 Complete the phrases for expressing opinions, agreeing and disagreeing in the conversation. The first letter of each word is given.

A: ⁰I̲f̲ y̲ou̲ a̲sk̲ m̲e̲, I t̲hink̲ learning a language on your own, without a teacher, is really difficult.

B: Really? ¹I t_____ d_____. ²I_____ m_____ o_____, it's a good way to learn because you can choose what and when you study. If you have a busy day, you don't have to do a lesson, but if you have some free time, for example at the weekend, you can study then.

A: ³T_____ t_____, b_____ what if you need to ask a question? ⁴P_____, I t_____ that learning with a teacher is better. You can ask questions and the teacher can explain things and correct your mistakes. ⁵I t_____ private lessons are best. You get lots of attention from the teacher if you are the only student.

B: Well, ⁶I s_____ w_____ y_____ m_____, b_____ I get stressed if it's just me and the teacher. I'd prefer to learn in a group. In a group you can stay quiet. You don't have to speak if you don't want to.

A: ⁷O_____ c_____ o_____! T_____ n_____. If you don't practise speaking in lessons, you will never pass your speaking exam.

B: Hmm, you sound like our teacher.

3 Put the words in the correct order to make phrases. Then use them to complete the conversations. There is one extra phrase for each conversation.

Conversation 1
I / believe / really
that's / come / oh / on! / nonsense
agree / more / couldn't / I

A: Students worry too much about fashion and not enough about studying. ¹_____ that wearing a uniform to school would help to improve exam results.

B: ²_____. It is possible to be fashionable and hard-working, you know.

Conversation 2
I / you / if / me, / ask / think
point / a / that's / good
so / not / I'm / sure

A: ³_____ doing a gap year is a great idea. Young people get a lot out of travel.

B: ⁴_____. Isn't it better to get your qualifications first and then travel?

Conversation 3
couldn't / more / agree / I
doesn't / think / she
true, / but / that's

A: Well, I spoke to my sister and ⁵_____ single-sex schools are a good idea at all. She thinks girls and boys should learn to live, study and work together from a young age.

B: ⁶_____ exam results are often better at single-sex schools. What is more important?

Conversation 4
think / personally, / I
totally / I / disagree
agree / I / more / couldn't

A: ⁷_____ doing sport at school is as important as learning to read and write.

B: ⁸_____. If kids are going to do well at school, they need to be fit and healthy.

5.7 Writing

An email/letter of enquiry

1 Put the words in the correct order to form useful phrases for an email of enquiry.

0   Sir / Dear / Madam, / or
    Dear Sir or Madam,

1   enquire / to / I / writing / am / about …
    _____

2   in … / interested / am / particularly / I
    _____

3   would / I / grateful / if … / be
    _____

4   look / to / you / forward / I / hearing / from
    _____

5   faithfully / yours
    _____

2 Complete the indirect questions.

0   Do I need to bring a laptop?
    Could you tell me if *I need to bring a laptop* ?

1   How many hours of English will we study each day?
    I would like to know _____ .

2   Is there a TV in the room?
    Could you tell me if _____ ?

3   How much does an average meal cost in the canteen?
    I would also like to know _____ .

4   Will someone pick me up from the airport?
    Could you also tell me if _____ ?

5   Do I need to buy insurance?
    Finally, I would like to ask _____ .

3 Use the phrases in Exercise 1 and indirect questions to improve the underlined parts of the email.

⁰Hello there,

I am a nineteen-year old Italian student, and ¹I want to know about your Surf and Study course in the south of England this summer. ²I want to do an international English exam, and if I can get better at surfing at the same time, I'll be very happy. I have tried windsurfing before, but never surfing.

I would like to know how many hours of English we will study each day. ³Will I be able to do the exam at the end of the course? I would also like to know if I need to bring my own surfboard. ⁴Finally, is the sea warm in the summer?

⁵Please write back and answer my questions.

⁶Yours sincerely,

Carla Ambrosi

0   *Dear Sir or Madam,*
1   _____
2   _____
3   Could you tell me _____
4   Finally, I would like _____
5   _____
6   _____

SHOW WHAT YOU'VE LEARNT

4 You recently received an email from your Australian friend Brett. Read part of his email and the advert below and write an email to the Australian Centre.

I know you want to come here to study English, so I'm sending you an advert I saw last week. Why don't you write to them and ask about their courses – you know, how long they are and what they cost. It's probably a good idea to ask about their social programme too! That's really important! I hope this helps.

Write your email in about 100 words.

The Australian Centre

Study English in incredible Sydney. Experience one of the world's great cities and improve your English at the same time.

We offer experienced teachers, city-centre accommodation and a lively social programme. For information about courses, fees and availability, write to: David Cochran at davidc@tacs.edu.

SHOW THAT YOU'VE CHECKED

In my email of enquiry:

- the beginning matches the end (*Dear Mr Smith* → *Yours sincerely*; *Dear Sir or Madam* → *Yours faithfully*). ☐
- the first paragraph gives information about me and why I am writing. ☐
- the second paragraph asks politely for the information I need. ☐
- the third paragraph says what I would like the reader to do. ☐
- I have asked indirect (not direct) questions. ☐
- I have not used contractions (e.g. *I'm, aren't, that's*) or abbreviations (e.g. *info, cu, v. good*). ☐
- I have checked my spelling and punctuation. ☐
- I have written about 100 words. ☐

5.8 Word practice

Education • Phrases with get • Word families

1 Choose the correct answer, A, B or C.

1 Joe's hoping to __ Oxford University next term.
   A get on with   B carry on   C get into
2 When we go to Amsterdam, we can __ with my friend Peter. I haven't seen him for years!
   A match   B meet up   C get on
3 Bad news. I've __ my French exam again.
   A taken   B failed   C passed
4 Is Maths a(n) __ subject to get onto a course in Medicine at university?
   A extra   B compulsory   C demanding
5 Martin doesn't like getting up in the morning. He often __ his first lesson at college.
   A drops   B scrapes   C skips
6 My school __ is terrible this year! I've got Maths at half past eight four days a week!
   A uniform   B revision   C timetable
7 How do you __ to school every day, Lisa?
   A take   B get   C do
8 I think we should go home soon. It's getting __ .
   A ill   B late   C tired
9 I'm sorry, I don't understand. Can you __ it again in a different way?
   A tell   B provide   C explain
10 I didn't like the film. It was a complete __ of time.
   A waste   B spend   C exhaustion
11 Let's not discuss this now. It's not __ to the topic.
   A remote   B relevant   C refer
12 I want you all to learn it by __ this poem.
   A eye   B reading   C heart
13 Students need __ to enter the science laboratories in my school.
   A beanbags   B bicycles   C swipe cards
14 Boys of this age like competing __ other children.
   A for   B to   C against
15 The weather was very bad, so we couldn't __ the top of the mountain.
   A reach   B arrive   C isolate

2 Find eight phrases with get in the word path.

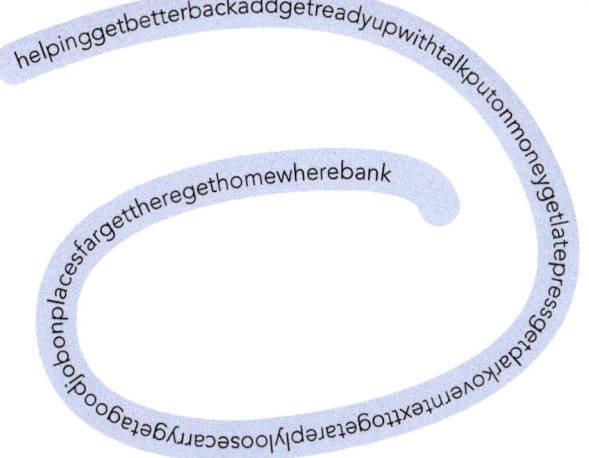

3 Complete the crossword with words about education.

Across
1 busy, intense and tiring
2 another student in your class
3 stop doing a subject

Down
1 study (a course)
4 necessary, not optional
5 miss a lesson
6 be successful in an exam
7 prepare for an exam

4 Complete the second column of the table.

Verb	Noun	Example
collect	collection	
decide		
donate		
educate		
exhaust		
explain		
isolate		
provide		

5 Complete the sentences with the nouns from the table in Exercise 4. Then write the sentences in the table, to help you remember the meanings.

1 The patient with the Ebola virus is still in _____ in hospital.
2 Can you give me a(n) _____ for your bad behaviour?
3 Would you like to make a(n) _____ of £5 to our charity?
4 The most important thing in the fight against poverty is free _____ for all children.
5 My aunt has got a(n) _____ of ceramic teapots from all over the world.
6 The cyclist was taken to hospital after the race because he was suffering from _____ .
7 The government is responsible for the _____ of health care.
8 Will you marry me? I need to know your _____ by tomorrow.

5.9 Self-assessment

1. For each learning objective, tick the box that best matches your ability.

   ☺☺ = I understand and can help a friend.
   ☺ = I understand and can do it by myself.
   ☹ = I understand some, but have some questions.
   ☹☹ = I do not understand.

			☺☺	☺	☹	☹☹	Need help?
5.1	Vocabulary	I can talk about schools in different countries.					Students' Book pages 60–61 Word Store page 11 Workbook pages 56–57
5.2	Grammar	I can use the First Conditional to talk about the possible results of an action.					Students' Book page 62 Workbook page 58
5.3	Listening	I can identify specific detail in a conversation.					Students' Book page 63 Workbook page 59
5.4	Reading	I can find specific details in an article.					Students' Book pages 64–65 Workbook pages 60–61
5.5	Grammar	I can use relative clauses to give more information.					Students' Book page 66 Workbook page 62
5.6	Speaking	I can give opinions and agree or disagree with others' opinions.					Students' Book page 67 Workbook page 63
5.7	Writing	I can write a polite email/letter asking for information.					Students' Book pages 68–69 Workbook page 64

2. What can you remember from this unit?

New words I learned (the words you most want to remember from this unit)	Expressions and phrases I liked (any expressions or phrases you think sound nice, useful or funny)	English I heard or read outside class (e.g. from websites, books, adverts, films, music)

5.10 Self-check

1 Complete the sentences with the words in the box. There are two extra words.

> ~~cold~~   home   late   nervous
> reply   rid   station   tired

0 Sam! Come and eat your dinner now before it gets _cold_.
1 Will you get _____ of those old shoes? They smell terrible!
2 I need to get _____ early on Friday. Kelly is coming over and my room is a real mess.
3 Anthony always gets _____ when the teacher asks him a question in class.
4 I emailed the driving school about lessons, but I haven't got a _____ yet.
5 What time does your train get to the _____ ? I'll come and meet you if you want.

/5

2 Complete the second sentence so that it has a similar meaning to the first using the word in capitals. Do not change the word in capitals.

0 Did Jack buy you a present on Valentine's Day? **GET**
  Did _you get a present_ from Jack on Valentine's day?
1 Please remove your shoes. **TAKE**
  Please _____ your shoes.
2 My piano teacher and I are good friends. **GET**
  I _____ my piano teacher.
3 Work hard and you'll pass your exams. **FAIL**
  Work hard and you _____ your exams.
4 Max can't continue being late for lessons. **CARRY**
  Max can't _____ being late for lessons.
5 Jamie always sees his girlfriend on Saturdays. **WITH**
  Jamie always _____ his girlfriend on Saturdays.

/5

3 Complete the words in the sentences. The first letter of each word is given.

0 Our government believes that free e_ducation_ for all children from six to sixteen years old is essential.
1 At my school Physical Education isn't c_____ , so some of the students don't get any exercise.
2 I can't d_____ which language to study: French or Spanish?
3 When I work, I like to be alone somewhere quiet. The i_____ helps me to concentrate.
4 Can anyone e_____ how this machine works?
5 Don't give up until you have t_____ all the possibilities!

/5

4 Complete the conversation with the correct form of the verbs in brackets.

A: You look unhappy, Ellie. What's the matter?
B: Well, I'm starting university next year and I have some difficult choices to make. The first decision is where to study. If I ⁰_go_ (go) to university in my hometown, I'll stay with Mum and Dad, but if I study in London, I ¹_____ (rent) a flat with my friend Lena. I ²_____ (save) more money if I live at home with my parents, but Lena says we'll have more fun if we ³_____ (get) a flat together in London.
A: So you have to decide what's more important for you.
B: Well, another problem is, Lena is a good friend, but she's not a very good student and she ⁴_____ (not pass) her exams if she doesn't revise a lot. If she ⁵_____ (fail) her exams, she won't go to university at all and then I'll be on my own in London.
A: Hmm ... Do you really want to go to university and live with someone who is not a good student? Think about it carefully.

/5

5 Find and correct the mistakes in the sentences

0 This is the park ~~that~~ I usually walk the dog. _where_
1 I love Indian food who isn't too spicy. _____
2 This is the language academy that my cousin studied Japanese. _____
3 That's the girl which won the race. _____
4 Is this the university where has the best medical courses? _____
5 I'd like a teacher what doesn't give us too much homework. _____

/5

6 Read the text and choose the correct answer, A, B or C.

> Anna goes to ballet school in Moscow. She has to work hard because the timetable is very ⁰___ . Every morning she ¹___ at 5.30 and travels across the city to the place ²___ the school is. At school, she ³___ normal subjects for five hours every day and then ballet for another four hours. If she ⁴___ the exams at the end of the year, she'll stay in Moscow for another year. She wants to be a professional ballerina, but her parents say that a good ⁵___ is important too.

0 A compulsory   (B demanding)   C decision
1 A gets better   B gets late   C gets up
2 A where   B when   C who
3 A educates   B drops   C does
4 A 'll pass   B passes   C 's passing
5 A decision   B explanation   C education

/5

Total /30

67

6 WORKING LIFE

6.1 Vocabulary

work + prepositions • Job conditions • *job* versus *work*

SHOW WHAT YOU KNOW

1 Complete the jobs. Some letters are given.

 A h<u>airdress</u>er
 B f_____er
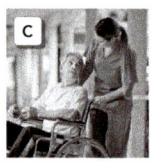 C n_____e a_____nt
 D s_____p

 E b_____er
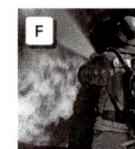 F f_____-_____er
 G o_____w_____r
 H j_____st

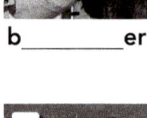 I t_____r
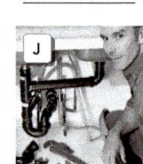 J p_____er
 K w_____er
 L t_____r g_____e

WORD STORE 6A
What do you do?

2 Complete the sentences with *in*, *at* or *for*. Sometimes more than one answer is possible.

0 Annabel works <u>for</u> her aunt.
1 Shaun works _____ a shoe shop.
2 Colin works _____ a chemical company.
3 Megan works _____ marketing.
4 Neil works _____ NASA.
5 Peter works _____ a petrol station.

3 Read the business cards and complete the sentences.

0 Amber <u>is a computer programmer</u> (job).
1 She works _____ (company name).
2 She works _____ company (type of company).
3 George _____ (job).
4 He works _____ (company name).
5 He works _____ (area of business).

WORD STORE 6B
Collocations – terms and conditions

4 Read the text and choose the correct options.

www.jobsa2z.com

Planning your future? Going for your first job? Changing jobs? We tell you the truth about jobs: the pluses and minuses from A–Z!

You searched for three jobs. Here are the best results:

Tour guide:

Pluses: Many tour guides ¹*get / are / do* self-employed so they can ²*be / take / work* flexible hours and it's easy to ³*take / do / work* days off.

Minuses: Most tour guides ⁴*get / are / earn* badly-paid. Because they ⁵*earn / do / take* low wages, many tour guides ⁶*do / earn / get* overtime or have a second job. Tour guides often get extra money from happy customers, but they rarely ⁷*work / have / get* a bonus.

Doctor:

Pluses: Experienced doctors are generally well ⁸*paid / salary / wages*. They earn a high ⁹*pay rise / wages / salary* and can take between twenty and thirty days ¹⁰*flexible hours / overtime / paid holiday* per year.

Minuses: Training is long and expensive. Junior doctors work extremely ¹¹*long / low / regular* hours (they often do twenty-four-hour ¹²*shifts / hours / overtime*).

Office manager:

Pluses: Office managers ¹³*earn / do / work* an average salary and work regular ¹⁴*flexible / office / overtime* hours. Like other employees, office managers may get a small ¹⁵*pay / wage / salary* rise each year.

Minuses: Office managers rarely travel in their jobs.

TOP SOFT

Amber Jonstone
computer programmer

Topsoft (software development)
128 Regency Road,
London, SW1 EA8
(+44) 554 653 652
amberjst@topsoft.net

George Pendleton
architect

NEG Design (construction)
www.neggen.ch
(+41) 22 508 865 410

grpendleton@neg.com.ch

WORD STORE 6C
Confusing words – *job* and *work*

5 Complete the adverts with the words/phrases in the box. There are two extra words/phrases.

> a foreign company   advertising   apply for
> bonus   days off   finish   from home   have a job
> looking for   office   outside   ~~start~~   their hands

If you need extra cash before Christmas and you can ⁰*start* work very soon, then we need you. **We need people** who can do delicate work making simple jewellery with ¹_____ (you'll need short fingernails). **You can work** ²_____ – we will send everything you need to your home address. **This is an ideal job** for students or for people who already ³_____ but want to earn more money at weekends.
Call now to find out more: 609 343 210

Are you ⁴_____ a job that is creative AND physical?

Would you like to work ⁵_____ (in our clients' gardens)?

Do you want to ⁶_____ work early (e.g. before 2 p.m.)?

Why not become a professional gardener?
Visit our website for more details:
www.gardenpro.com

Euro-ad is looking for people to work in ⁷_____ (we design adverts for magazines and websites).

The jobs will be in our Berlin ⁸_____. If you would like to work for ⁹_____ in one of Europe's most exciting cities, send your CV to b.schmidt@euroad.com and ¹⁰_____ a job with us now.
(Interviews will be in March.)

6 Complete the sentences with the correct form of *job* or *work*.
1. My sister _____ for a big investment bank in Wall Street in New York.
2. After university I'm going to look for a _____ in hotel management.
3. Sandra is working in a café for the summer. She starts _____ at 6.00 a.m. but she finishes early, around 2.00 p.m.
4. Simon enjoys _____ with his hands. He wants to be a carpenter.
5. I didn't apply for that _____ in Paris. I didn't have the right experience for it.
6. Do you like _____ outside, Martin? You should get a job as a gardener.

REMEMBER THIS

Job (countable noun) means the regular paid work that you do to earn money.
Emma has a very well-paid job as a lawyer.

Work (uncountable noun) is often used to mean 'the place where you do your job'.
What time do you get to work? (e.g. to your office)

Work (uncountable noun) can also mean 'the activity of doing my job'.
I start work at 9.00 a.m. and finish at 5.00 p.m.

7 Read REMEMBER THIS and choose the correct options.
1. Sara applied for a *job / work* as a firefighter.
2. Mum will be late home from *job / work* tonight.
3. What time will you finish *job / work* tonight?
4. Jemma is looking for a summer *job / work*.
5. I enjoy *work / job* because I have lovely colleagues.
6. Mike left his computer at *job / work*.
7. My uncle lost his *job / work* when the factory closed.
8. What do you do all day at *job / work*?

SHOW WHAT YOU'VE LEARNT

8 Complete the words in the sentences. The first letter of each word is given.
1. Money is very important to me, so I want a job where I e_____ a h_____ s_____.
2. Jade wants to be her own boss. She wants to b_____ s_____-e_____.
3. Alfie enjoys working from nine to five and having evenings free. He likes w_____ r_____ o_____ h_____.
4. Piotr and Jacek are Polish but they work for Lufthansa. Most of the time, they like working for a f_____ c_____.
5. If you want more money, why don't you l_____ f_____ a j_____?
6. Erin loves the outdoors. She would hate to w_____ i_____ a_____ o_____.
7. Is Charlie a m_____? He's certainly handsome enough.
8. Mia w_____ a_____ the local hospital.
9. I w_____ f_____ m_____ f_____. There are advantages and disadvantages to having my dad as my boss.
10. Kathy's brother w_____ i_____ television. He's a cameraman.

/10

6.2 Grammar

Second Conditional

SHOW WHAT YOU KNOW

1 **Complete the First Conditional sentences with the correct form of the verbs in brackets.**

Zoe wants to go to the cinema with her friends, but:
0 if she _goes_ (go) to the cinema, she _'ll miss_ (miss) the last bus home.
1 if she _____ (not catch) the last bus, she _____ (have to) take a taxi.
2 it _____ (cost) a lot of money if she _____ (go) home by taxi.
3 she _____ (not have) any money for the weekend if she _____ (spend) it all tonight.
4 if she _____ (not have) any money at the weekend, what _____ (she/do)?

2 ★ **Read the article and choose the correct options.**

decisionsdecisions.com
helping teens with tricky choices

To go or not to go – that is the question!

We asked some teenagers:

What ¹would / did you miss about home if you ²went / 'd go to study in another country?

This is what they said:

Mark, 15:
My mum's cooking. I ³'d miss / missed her food if I ⁴'d live / lived anywhere except home. Can you put pierogi in the post?

Elle and Anna (twins), 17:
We ⁵'d never see / never saw our cats if we ⁶'d study / studied in another country. We really love them. If we ⁷'d get / got the chance to study in another country, we ⁸wouldn't / didn't leave without them.

Tom, 16:
If I ⁹'d do / did a course in another country, I ¹⁰wouldn't / didn't miss anything except my family. One day I want to live in the US or Canada for a few years.

Camilla, 17:
If I ¹¹went / 'd go to study in another country, I ¹²'d feel / felt lonely without my boyfriend. I can't imagine life on my own.

3 ★★ **Read the conversation and complete the Second Conditional sentences with the correct form of the verbs in brackets.**

A: I really like her, but I don't think I should tell her.
B: Wrong! You should definitely tell her.
A: Really? But, if I ⁰_told_ (tell) her, she ¹_____ (know).
B: Obviously! That's the idea.
A: But, if she ²_____ (know), I ³_____ (feel) totally embarrassed. I wouldn't even be able to look at her. Anyway, she probably doesn't even like me.
B: Look, Jason, I'll tell you a secret.
A: What?
B: Let's just say I had a very similar conversation with her yesterday. If I ⁴_____ (be) you, I ⁵_____ (tell) her.
A: What? Really?
B: She feels the same way about you! Will you please just go and find her NOW and ask her on a date?
A: Now? No way! What ⁶_____ (I/say) if I ⁷_____ (see) her now? I'm not ready.
B: Jason, you're nearly eighteen. It's time to be a man!

4 ★★★ **Rewrite the sentences. Use the Second Conditional.**

0 Ben doesn't have a job in the mountains this winter because he has exams soon.
Ben _would have a job in the mountains this winter if he didn't have exams soon_.
1 He doesn't have a job in the mountains, so he doesn't go snowboarding every week.
He _____.
2 He doesn't go snowboarding every week, so he's not good at it.
If _____.
3 He doesn't teach Charlotte to snowboard because he's not good at it.
He _____.
4 He doesn't teach Charlotte, so they don't spend time together.
If _____.
5 Ben's not very happy because he and Charlotte don't spend time together.
Ben _____.

SHOW WHAT YOU'VE LEARNT

5 **Complete the Second Conditional sentences with the correct form of the verbs in brackets.**

1 If Mandy _____ (be) a teacher, she'd get long holidays.
2 Adam _____ (not be) living with his parents if he had a job.
3 If Harry _____ (be) a mechanic, he'd fix the car.
4 If you worked for your father, _____ (you/argue) all the time?
5 We'd move out of our flat if the houses in our area _____ (not cost) so much money.
6 _____ (you/feel) depressed if our team lost the World Cup?

/6

6.3 Listening language practice

A great job • Words related to work

1 Read the conversation and text and choose the correct options. Then listen and check.

Extracts from Students' Book recording CD•3.5 MP3•92

1
A: I want to do your job.
B: Ah! Right. Well, why not? It's a great job. And we need more women in the ¹*profession / colleagues / qualification*. There aren't many female pilots. Did you know that only five percent of airline pilots are women?
A: That's terrible. Why is that?
B: I'm not sure. The ²*experience / overtime / training* is long and very expensive, but it's the same for men and women. Maybe women think it's a man's ³*work / job / employment*, so they don't apply for the training.

3
I'm the manager of a big supermarket and I really love my work. When I was at school, I really didn't know what I wanted to do. I wasn't very good at exams and studying has always been hard for me. So I didn't want to go to university and get a(n) ⁴*degree / experience / qualities*. I get on well with people and I worked on the checkout at a supermarket. It was great fun and I enjoyed meeting all the different people. I got ⁵*promotion / salary / profession* and they sent me on several courses. Now I'm the boss! To do this job, you need to be sensible and organised but most importantly, you need good social ⁶*qualifications / skills / experience*. I sit at a desk a lot, so I go jogging and swimming to keep fit too.

2 Complete the sentences with the words in the box. There are two extra words.

> colleagues   degree   experience   overtime
> profession   qualities   salary   ~~training~~

0 Dog *training* helps your pet behave better and can be fun for the dog and its owner.
1 The new education minister has over twenty years of _____ in politics.
2 Pat has one _____ in History and another in Literature.
3 What are the _____ of a good teacher? Knowledge, patience, tact, sense of humour …
4 How was your first day at work? What about the other people? Do you have any nice _____ ?
5 You need a high level of education and training to work in the legal or medical _____ .

REMEMBER THIS

When you learn new nouns, use a dictionary to check if they are countable or uncountable. Remember: some nouns can be both, depending on the context.

*You need lots of **experience** to become a professional footballer.* (uncountable – knowledge and skill learnt from time spent doing something)

*Working in the US was a great **experience**.* (countable – something memorable that happened to you)

3 Read REMEMBER THIS. Are the underlined nouns countable (C) or uncountable (U)?

0 training   *U*
1 advertising   ☐
2 profession   ☐
3 colleague   ☐
4 overtime   ☐

4 Read the sentences. Are the underlined nouns countable (C) or uncountable (U)?

0 We are looking for a hairdresser with at least five year's <u>experience</u>.   *U*
1 For most people, a gap year in Australia is an unforgettable <u>experience</u>.   ☐
2 What is more important for you when you buy food: <u>quality</u> or price?   ☐
3 In my opinion, the most important <u>quality</u> in a friend is honesty.   ☐
4 My girlfriend has long blonde <u>hair</u>.   ☐
5 Urgh! There's a <u>hair</u> in my soup.   ☐

WORD STORE 6D
Compound nouns – jobs

5 Complete the jobs. The first letter of each word is given.

Who can help you:

0 learn to drive?   d*riving* instructor
1 find what you are looking for in a shop?   shop a_____
2 get home on public transport?   b_____ driver
3 book a holiday?   t_____ agent
4 with paperwork and photocopying?   o_____ assistant
5 learn a winter sport?   s_____ instructor
6 get home late at night?   t_____ driver
7 buy a house or flat?   e_____ agent

6.4 Reading

Summer jobs • Collocations related to work • Phrasal verbs

Glossary

temporary (adj) = used to describe something you do for a short time only
proud (of) (adj) = feeling pleased about something you have done
rescue (v) = save someone or something from danger

first aid (n) = simple medical treatment given straight after an accident
shallow (adj) = you can stand with your head above the water in the shallow end of a swimming pool; you can't do this in the deep end

Summer jobs for active teenagers

Every year when school finishes for the summer, thousands of teenagers earn extra money by doing temporary summer jobs. We spoke to three young people who have had active, outdoor jobs and asked them about their experiences. This is what they told us:

Aaron, 16, Australia
Summer job: lifeguard, Sydney

I enjoyed my summer as a lifeguard. The beach was a great place to work and the views of the ocean were beautiful, but there wasn't much time to relax. It's a serious job and someone has to watch the swimmers all the time. It's hard for one person to concentrate for so long. That's why we always work with a partner. Each lifeguard watches for an hour, then has a break. I'm proud to say that my partner and I rescued seven people this summer.

As well as being very strong swimmers, lifeguards should be at least sixteen years old and have qualifications in first aid and water-rescue techniques. I did a training programme and learnt these skills before I started work. I'd recommend this job to anyone who lives near the coast. The pay is average and it can be stressful, but it feels great to rescue someone, and the 'office' is the best in the world!

Kuba, 19, Poland
Summer job: windsurfing instructor, Mazury

I started windsurfing when I was twelve, so I'm quite good. Last summer I trained as an instructor and this year I got a job at the lake near our village. There are lots of tourists in the summer and most of them are beginners. They generally spend more time in the water than on the board! A few silly people went out too far into the deep water, but we rescued them with the boat. Most sensible people stay where the water is shallow, so they don't have a problem. Plus, it's much easier to windsurf on a lake than on the sea because lakes don't usually have big waves.

It's not a very well-paid job, but I think it's cool if you can do something you love – and of course, it's a great way to meet girls.

Yasmin, 18, UK
Summer Job: activity leader, Devon

This summer I worked at a children's summer camp as an activity leader. It was exhausting but fun. We organised sports, games and activities for the kids, many of them in the huge camp swimming pool. We also took the older children swimming in the river. It was too dangerous for the younger ones though. In the evenings we organised discos and quizzes. Most of the time the kids were great and I worked with some lovely people and made some really good friends.

It is quite well-paid and you are so busy that you don't have time to spend any money. I lived for free in the camp accommodation. It wasn't very nice but at least we didn't have to pay. All our meals were free too, so I saved a lot of money over the summer.

1 **Read the article and choose the correct answer, A, B or C.**
   1 Lifeguards work in pairs because
      A there need to be two strong swimmers to help people.
      B the job is very stressful for one person.
      C they can take turns to watch the people.
   2 Beginners at windsurfing have problems if
      A they keep falling off the board.
      B they windsurf in the wrong places.
      C there are waves on the lake.
   3 Yasmin made a lot of money in her job because
      A she didn't have to pay rent.
      B she did some cooking too.
      C the salary was excellent.

2 **Read the article again. Are the statements (T) or false (F)?**
   1 Aaron found his summer job relaxing.
   2 Kuba worked close to his home.
   3 Yasmin liked the accommodation at the summer camp.
   4 All of the teenagers needed some sort of special training for their jobs.
   5 The three teenagers weren't very well-paid.
   6 All three teenagers enjoyed their summer jobs.

3 **Complete the crossword with the underlined words in the article.**

Across
2 an area of sand or small stones at the edge of the sea or a lake
5 bigger than a lake, smaller than an ocean
7 a large area of water surrounded by land
8 e.g. the Nile, the Amazon

Down
1 e.g. the Pacific, the Atlantic
3 the area where the land meets the sea
4 H_2O
6 lines of water that move across the sea; surfers surf on these

REMEMBER BETTER
You can record some groups of words on lines to show their relationship in terms of of an increasing/decreasing quality or chronological order.

Put the words in the boxes in the correct place on the lines.

1 [an average salary   a very high salary
    low wages   very badly-paid   well-paid]

a little money .... a lot of money

2 [apply for a job   get an interview
    get a job   look for a job   start a job]

first .... last

3 [finish work   get to work   go to work
    have a break   leave work   start work]

first .... last

4 [download music   go online   log off
    log onto a website   switch off the computer
    switch on the computer]

first .... last

WORD STORE 6E
Phrasal verbs

4 **Complete the questions with the phrasal verbs in the box.**

[find out   give up   set up
  sum up   throw out   work out]

0 When will you _find out_ if you got the job?
1 Sarah would like to have her own bookshop. Is it difficult to _____ a business?
2 I'll drive. Can you look at the map and _____ the fastest way to get there?
3 Karen, you were at the students' meeting yesterday. Can you _____ what happened please?
4 Grandma has bought you some new socks. Will you finally _____ all those old ones with holes in them?
5 Snowboarding is difficult at first, but it gets easier. Keep trying; don't _____ .

6.5 Grammar

Modal verbs for obligation and permission

SHOW WHAT YOU KNOW

1 Complete the sentences with *must* or *mustn't*.

0 I <u>must</u> do more exercise. I want to be fit and healthy.
1 We are lucky to have enough food and a warm house. We _____ complain about unimportant things.
2 I feel exhausted all the time. I _____ try to get more sleep.
3 We _____ be late again. We don't want the others to think we are unreliable.
4 I _____ stop biting my nails. They look terrible.

2 Complete the sentences with the correct form of *have to* and the words in brackets.

0 The gallery is free if you have a student card, so <u>students don't have to pay</u> (students/pay).
1 _____ (Emma/miss) school today because she's going to the hospital.
2 It's unfair. _____ (Alec/clean) his own bedroom, so why should I?
3 I can't concentrate on my homework. _____ (you/sing) so loud?
4 _____ (Nina/go) to school on Monday because it's a national holiday.

3 ★ Complete the sentences with the modal verbs in capitals. You do not need one of the verbs in each group.

1 NEEDN'T / HAVE TO / CAN'T
   a You _____ walk – why not save your energy? I'll take you in the car.
   b You _____ walk – it's freezing cold and you don't have a coat.

2 HAS TO / DOESN'T HAVE TO / CAN
   a Beth _____ bring food to the party, but it's not really necessary.
   b Beth _____ bring food to the party – we've already got plenty.

3 HAVE TO / MUSTN'T / DON'T HAVE TO
   a The students _____ revise – the exams are in three weeks.
   b The students _____ revise – the exams finished last week.

4 HAS TO / CAN / MUSTN'T
   a Katy _____ wear formal clothes – the wedding invitation says 'formal dress'.
   b Katy _____ wear formal clothes, but not everyone is going to be smart.

4 ★★ Choose the correct options.

1 Sarah *must / has to* be there at four o'clock. The others will be waiting for her.
2 I *must / have to* stop staying up so late. I fell asleep at school yesterday!
3 The sign says you *can't / needn't* park here.
4 I *can't / mustn't* forget to speak to Dad tonight. I need to ask him for some money.
5 Police officers *must / have to* wear uniforms.
6 You *can't / don't have to* go on this roller coaster if you are less than 1.4 metres tall.

5 ★★★ It's Julia's first day of work experience. Complete her conversation with William with modal verbs. Sometimes more than one answer is possible.

W: So, Julia, welcome to the chocolate factory. I'm William. Nice to meet you.
J: Hi. Nice to meet you too.
W: OK. Let's have a look round, first of all. There are a few rules in the factory – you ⁰<u>need to/have to</u> wear these special plastic shoes at all times and I'm afraid you ¹_____ wear any jewellery. Oh, actually, if you are married, you ²_____ take off your wedding ring, but no other jewellery, please.
J: OK, that's fine. I'm not married, so no problem.
W: OK. Follow me then, please … This is where we make the chocolate. We tell our workers that it's OK to eat as much chocolate as they like and, of course, they ³_____ pay – it's free.
J: Really? ⁴_____ I try some?
W: Of course, but you ⁵_____ use your fingers. Here, put this glove on.
J: Thanks. Mmm, it's delicious. Oh dear, I ⁶_____ eat too much though!
W: Don't worry. We usually find that after a few days, people have had enough.
J: Hmm, I'm not sure about that.

SHOW WHAT YOU'VE LEARNT

6 Choose the correct answer, A, B or C.

1 You ____ be seventeen to drive a car in the UK.
   A have to   B don't have to   C can't
2 Architects ____ be good at drawing.
   A mustn't   B need to   C needn't
3 I ____ remember to say thanks to Jenny.
   A must   B have to   C mustn't
4 You ____ be female to be a nurse.
   A need to   B mustn't   C don't need to
5 Students ____ make a lot of noise in a library.
   A can   B can't   C needn't
6 Women ____ become police officers if they want to.
   A can   B must   C needn't

/6

6.6 Speaking language practice

Asking for and giving advice

1 Choose the correct options.

1 I *think* / *don't think* Julia should become a primary teacher. She has no patience and she doesn't like young kids.
2 *It's* / *It's not* a good idea to ask for a pay rise. You've only worked there for two months.
3 If I were you, I *'d* / *wouldn't* take the day off. You look and sound really sick.
4 My best advice would be *to* / *not to* worry about it. Everyone makes mistakes.
5 Carlos *should* / *shouldn't* apply for more than one job. What if he doesn't get the first one?

2 Complete the conversation with the phrases in the box. There are two extra phrases.

> Do you have any tips on how to   It's a good idea
> I'm not sure that's a good idea   You should
> ~~What do you think I should wear?~~   That's really helpful!

A: Tomorrow is my first day of work experience. ⁰*What do you think I should wear?*
B: ¹_____ definitely wear a suit. Iron a shirt and clean your shoes. ²_____ to look smart on your first day.
A: ³_____ , Samantha.
B: Why not?
A: I'm going to work on a farm.
B: Oh.

3 Put the words in the correct order to complete the conversations. There is one extra phrase for each conversation.

A really / thanks, / helpful / that's
should / think / I / you
do / think / should / do / what / you / I?
have / tips / on / do / how / a / you / any / to

A: ⁰*Do you have any tips on how to* become a model?
B: ¹_____ keep yourself fit and look after your skin.
A: ²_____ .

B helpful / really / that's / thanks,
that's / good / a / sure / I'm / not / idea
about / any / you / how / do / have / to / ideas
you / why / don't

A: ³_____ get a summer job during the school holidays?
B: ⁴_____ come and work on my cousin's farm?
A: ⁵_____ . I have lots of allergies.

C should / you / what / think / do / I / do?
great / that's / thanks! / advice
do / to / you / have / tips / any / how / on
were / I / you, / If / I / 'd

A: I can't believe I forgot his birthday.
⁶_____
B: ⁷_____ call him and say sorry then buy him a nice gift.
A: ⁸_____ . What should I buy?

4 Complete the phrases in the conversation. The first letter of each word is given.

A local vet has just finished talking to Olivia and Toby's class about her job.

Vet: So, does anyone have any questions?
Olivia: Yes, I do. Thanks for your talk. I'd really like to become a vet. What ⁰d̲o̲ you t̲h̲i̲n̲k̲ I s̲h̲o̲u̲l̲d̲ do?
Vet: Well, ¹m_____ best a_____ w_____ be to work really hard in your Science classes! You'll need very good grades to get a place at a university veterinary school. ²W_____ d_____ you have a look online at some of the university websites?
Olivia: ³T_____ , that's really h_____ .
Vet: Anyone else?
Toby: Hi. Yeah, I have a question. ⁴D_____ you h_____ a_____ i_____ about h_____ to get some work experience as a vet?
Vet: Most universities expect you to have some experience, so ⁵i_____ a g_____ i_____ to try and work in a veterinary clinic, or perhaps a zoo during your school holidays. ⁶I_____ I w_____ you , I_____ email all the local ones and ask if they can help you. But, ⁷I d_____ t_____ you s_____ expect them to pay you, unfortunately! There is a lot of competition.
Toby: OK, well, that's ⁸g_____ a_____ . Thanks.

75

6.7 Writing
A letter of application

1 **Put the words in the correct order to form useful phrases for a letter of application.**

1 reference / with / your / advertisement / in … / to
   With reference to your advertisement in …

2 position / the / writing / I / am / express / my / to / in / interest / of …
   _____

3 experience / my / includes …
   _____

4 enclose / CV / my / for / information / I / your
   _____

5 advertisement / very / found / because … / I / your / interesting
   _____

6 would / suitable / because … / I / be / a / candidate / the / job / for
   _____

7 am … / currently, / I
   _____

2 **Match the sentence halves.**

1 I am writing in response to your advertisement — [f]
2 I would like to apply for the position of
3 At the moment,
4 I am particularly interested in your company because
5 As you will see,
6 I would be a suitable candidate for the job because

a I am in my final year at senior school.
b I volunteered for a charity last summer.
c I am responsible and creative.
d part-time sales assistant.
e I would like to work for an international organisation.
f in the *Student Times*.

3 **Replace the underlined phrases a–e in the letter with similar phrases from Exercise 1.**

Dear Sir or Madam,

ᵃ 1 I am writing in response to your advertisement in *Work and Travel Magazine*. ᵇ ___ I would like to apply for the position of Children's Activity Organiser at The Grand Hotel this summer. ᶜ ___ At the moment, I am preparing for my final exams and I will be available to start work from 5 July.

ᵈ ___ I am particularly interested in your company because I plan to do Hotel Management at university. I enclose my CV for your information. ᵉ ___ As you will see, I spent last summer working as a summer camp supervisor at a local middle school.

ᶠ ___ I would be a good candidate for the job because I get on well with children and am a responsible, creative and organised person.

I have provided my contact details on my CV and can be available for interview at any time.

I look forward to hearing from you.

Yours faithfully,

Mia Read

SHOW WHAT YOU'VE LEARNT

4 **You have seen the advertisement below on an international students' website. Write a letter applying for the job. Say where you saw the advert, give your reasons for applying and mention any relevant work experience.**

> **BIG MIKE'S BURGERS**
> REQUIRE **SUMMER STAFF**
> ✔ Are you a teenager looking for valuable work experience in the summer holidays?
> ✔ Can you cook, clean and take orders?
> We are looking for punctual, easy-going and trustworthy young people to join our team for the summer. Experience in customer service and kitchen work is an advantage.
> Contact Mike Pickles: bigmikepickles@bmb.net

Write your letter in about 100 words.

SHOW THAT YOU'VE CHECKED

In my letter of application:

- the beginning matches the end (*Dear Mr Smith* → *Yours sincerely; Dear Sir or Madam* → *Yours faithfully*). ☐
- I have said where I saw the job advert and why I am writing. ☐
- I have said what I am doing now and given reasons why I am interested in the job. ☐
- I have mentioned my CV and any relevant work experience. ☐
- I have given reasons why I am suitable for the job and said when I will be available for interview. ☐
- I have not used contractions (e.g. *I'm, aren't, that's*), emoticons (☺) or abbreviations (e.g. *info, CU, gr8*). ☐
- I have checked my spelling and punctuation. ☐
- I have written about 100 words. ☐

6.8 Use of English

Four-option multiple choice

1 Read the text below and choose the correct word (A, B, C or D) for each space.

Enjoy your work!

There are lots of surveys about jobs and why we choose them. Is it because they are ⁰___ ? Is it because we ¹___ work long hours? Or maybe it's because the job is interesting and we enjoy it. ²___ you ask most people today, they'll mention salary and enjoyment. After all, we need to ³___ an enormous number of hours at work, so it's better if we enjoy it!

Employers today have realised that relaxed employees work better than those who get stressed ⁴___ . Many of them are trying to ⁵___ the atmosphere in the workplace. In some ⁶___ there are games for the staff, like table tennis! If they start to feel stressed, the workers ⁷___ leave their desks and go and play a quick game! Other workplaces have regular fun activities during lunch breaks, such as quizzes or dance lessons.

It makes sense, really. If you can have a good ⁸___ at work, it's better for you and the company. It stops employees ⁹___ time off and also encourages them to work ¹⁰___ a team. A bonus for everyone!

0	A average salary	(B well-paid)	C self-employed	D part-time
1	A mustn't	B can't	C don't have to	D shouldn't
2	A Like	B When	C Often	D If
3	A give	B spend	C make	D put
4	A out	B off	C in	D over
5	A progress	B improve	C solve	D develop
6	A floors	B shifts	C offices	D work
7	A need	B allowed	C choose	D can
8	A time	B feeling	C experience	D enjoyment
9	A doing	B making	C taking	D asking
10	A like	B as	C for	D at

TIPS:

Question 2: Which word do First Conditional sentences usually start with?
Question 5: You need the verb which means 'make something better'.
Question 7: Which option, followed by an infinitive without *to*, can you use to show that someone has permission to do something?

Sentence transformations

2 Here are some sentences about a student who wants to work in the holidays. For each question, complete the second sentence so that it means the same as the first. Use no more than three words.

0 I must work this summer to earn some money.
  I must find a *job* this summer to earn some money.
1 I haven't got any experience, so I won't get high wages.
  If I _____ experience, I would get high wages.
2 I'm looking for work where it isn't necessary for me to get up early.
  I'm looking for work where I _____ to get up early.
3 It doesn't bother me if I need to do overtime.
  I don't _____ overtime.
4 I might reply to this advert for a job as a waiter.
  I might apply _____ job as a waiter.
5 My brother's worked in a restaurant for two years.
  My brother started working in a restaurant _____ .

TIPS:

Question 1: This is a Second Conditional sentence, so you need to change the tense.
Question 3: Be careful: the phrase you need to use is followed by an *-ing* form.
Question 4: What preposition usually follows *apply*?

6.9 Self-assessment

1 For each learning objective, tick the box that best matches your ability.

☺☺ = I understand and can help a friend. ☹ = I understand some, but have some questions.
☺ = I understand and can do it by myself. ☹☹ = I do not understand.

			☺☺	☺	☹	☹☹	Need help?
6.1	Vocabulary	I can talk about jobs and work.					Students' Book pages 72–73 Word Store page 13 Workbook pages 68–69
6.2	Grammar	I can talk about imaginary situations.					Students' Book page 74 Workbook page 70
6.3	Listening	I can identify specific detail in short conversations and monologues.					Students' Book page 75 Workbook page 71
6.4	Reading	I can understand the main points in short emails, notices and adverts.					Students' Book pages 76–77 Workbook pages 72–73
6.5	Grammar	I can express obligation and permission.					Students' Book page 78 Workbook page 74
6.6	Speaking	I can ask for and give advice about jobs and solving problems.					Students' Book page 79 Workbook page 75
6.7	Writing	I can apply for a summer job.					Students' Book pages 80–81 Workbook page 76

2 What can you remember from this unit?

New words I learned (the words you most want to remember from this unit)	Expressions and phrases I liked (any expressions or phrases you think sound nice, useful or funny)	English I heard or read outside class (e.g. from websites, books, adverts, films, music)

6.10 Self-check

1 Match the sentence halves.

1. I work for — f
2. Most office assistants earn
3. Nurses aren't usually
4. Ethan would like a job where he can
5. I'm contacting you to
6. I love my job because I get

a self-employed.
b work from home.
c apply for a job.
d an average salary.
e ten weeks' paid holiday.
f a construction company.

/5

2 Choose the correct options.

0. Lena has always wanted to work for a(n) *outside* / *(foreign)* / *overtime* company.
1. Carly's mum works *regular* / *shifts* / *overtime* office hours, so she always gets home at 5.30 p.m.
2. Dad didn't get a *wages* / *bonus* / *paid* this year, so we aren't going on holiday.
3. Molly works *in* / *for* / *at* Volkswagen.
4. You are so beautiful. Have you thought about working as a *mechanic* / *teacher* / *model*?
5. Susie had to give *up* / *out* / *in* skiing after she broke her leg.

/5

3 Find and correct the mistakes in the sentences.

0. I work ~~at~~ my father.   *for*
1. Leon has a summer work at the beach café.   _____
2. Alex works shift at the local chocolate factory.   _____
3. Professional sportspeople are generally well pay.   _____
4. Leah's brother is at IT.   _____
5. Natasha is the best secrety in the office.   _____

/5

4 Put the words in the correct order to complete the sentences. Add commas where necessary.

0. go surfing / I'd / lived / I / in Australia
   If *I lived in Australia, I'd go surfing* every weekend.
1. went / exhausted all the time / wouldn't / if / feel / she
   Rosie _____ to bed earlier.
2. invited / come / you / would / I / you
   If _____ to the party?
3. would / Laura and Kath / miss / worked from home / they
   If _____
   _____ their colleagues in the office.
4. wouldn't / if / were / I / go out with him again
   I _____ you.
5. give / if / you / won / some money / me / you
   Would _____ the lottery?

/5

5 Choose the correct options.

0. You *(don't need to)* / *mustn't* / *need to* be attractive to be a actor.
1. Soldiers *need to* / *mustn't* / *needn't* be fit and healthy.
2. Hotel guests *must* / *can* / *needn't* use the swimming pool for free.
3. Young children *needn't* / *can't* / *can* watch horror movies at the cinema.
4. I *have to* / *mustn't* / *must* remember to send Grandma a birthday card.
5. Students in our school *needn't* / *mustn't* / *need to* have uniforms on in the classroom, but they usually wear dark clothes.

/5

6 Choose the correct answer, A, B or C, to complete both sentences in each pair.

0. Visiting the Grand Canyon was a(n) _____ I'll never forget.
   I have _____ in customer service and kitchen work.
   A place   B *(experience)*   C holiday

1. Did you find ___ when Fiona starts her new job?
   Mum, did you throw ___ my favourite old T-shirt?
   A up   B in   C out

2. William's father is a(n) ___ agent.
   Roxy and Dave have just bought a house on a large housing ___ .
   A travel   B estate   C secret

3. What time does John start ___ ?
   I want to be an electrician because I want to ___ with my hands.
   A work   B job   C earn

4. Carl works ___ a very busy fast food restaurant. He hates it.
   My uncle works ___ marketing. He loves it.
   A in   B at   C for

5. We are trying to set ___ a Spanish club for the language students at our school.
   To sum ___ , I think all students should wear school uniforms.
   A about   B off   C up

/5

Total /30

7 SHOPPING

7.1 Vocabulary

Shops and services • Partitives • Shopping

SHOW WHAT YOU KNOW

1. Complete the names of the shops in the sentences. The first letter of each word is given.

   0. You can buy dolls and games in a **t**oy shop.
   1. You can buy bread and cakes at a **b**_____'s.
   2. You can buy jeans and jackets in a **c**_____ shop.
   3. You can buy magazines and newspapers at a **n**_____'s.
   4. You can buy used clothes and old books in a **ch**_____ shop.

2. Look at Amy's shopping list. Which shops does she need to go to? The first letter of each word is given.

   Shopping list
   - cat food — ⁰ **p**et shop
   - sausages — ¹ **b**_____'s
   - bananas — ² **g**_____'s
   - new boots ☺ — ³ **s**_____ shop
   - earrings for Mum — ⁴ **j**_____'s

WORD STORE 7A
Shops and services

3. Match the phrases in the box with the different areas in a supermarket 1–5. There are two extra phrases.

   > Electrical goods   Entertainment   Seafood
   > ~~Fruit and Vegetables~~   Health and beauty   Post office
   > Home and garden   Sports and leisurewear

   0. Fruit and vegetables
      bananas a_____
   1. b_____
      c_____
   2. d_____
      e_____
   3. f_____
      g_____
   4. h_____
      i_____
   5. j_____
      k_____

4. Write the words in box in the correct area of the supermarket a–k.

   > ~~bananas~~   carpets   strawberries   light bulbs
   > parcels   plants   swimwear   stamps   hairbrush
   > toiletries   trainers   vacuum cleaners

5. Complete the words in the adverts. The first letter of each word is given.

   Fantasyland
   ⁰ **T**heme **P**ark
   Try our amazing new roller coaster **The Monster!** All-day-all-rides ticket only £20 per person

   Las Vegas True Love Wedding ¹Ch_____
   For those who just can't wait to get married. Ceremonies every fifteen minutes. *Elvis, Harry Potter* and *Star Wars* themes available.

   The Pacific
   ² **A**_____
   Come and shake hands (eight of them!) with our newest arrival — Ollie, the giant octopus. Also, don't miss 'Meet the Sharks'.

   Natalie's Natural Nails
   Are you a nervous nail-biter who needs nice new natural nails? Pedicures (feet) and ³**m**_____ (hands). At Natalie's Natural Nails we know nails.

WORD STORE 7B
Partitives

6. Complete the phrases.

   0. a *pair* of skis
   1. a _____ of perfume
   2. a _____ of jam
   3. a _____ of flowers
   4. a _____ of biscuits
   5. a _____ of cola

WORD STORE 7C
Useful phrases – shopping

7 Read the conversations and choose the correct options.

Conversation 1
A: That's £29.99, please.
B: Erm … excuse me. This is a gift for my sister. Can I bring it back if she doesn't like it?
A: Certainly. Please keep your ¹*refund / bargain / receipt* and show it to the assistant if you bring the jumper back. You can exchange it for something else or get ²*a refund / a sale / an offer* if you prefer to get your money back.

Conversation 2
A: How about going shopping this afternoon, Mia? Do you need anything?
B: Well, I want a new watch. There's a beautiful one in the jeweller's in town but it's too expensive. I can't ³*keep / afford / pick* it.
A: Maybe we can just walk round and have a look for something cheaper. We can go ⁴*a refund / on special offer / window shopping*. It doesn't cost anything to look!

Conversation 3
A: Dad, we need a new vacuum cleaner, remember? The old one broke.
B: That's right, we do. Shall we go to the electrical goods store? I saw a sign saying they are having ⁵*a sale / a bargain / a refund* at the moment. Perhaps they have vacuum cleaners on special ⁶*bargain / offer / receipt*.
A: Did you say 'we'? I can't go. I'm meeting my … I mean, I've got too much homework.
B: Oh, right. That's a shame. I thought we could also go clothes shopping and pick up ⁷*an offer / a sale / a bargain* for you in the sales, but if you're too busy …
A: Oh. Well, maybe I can do my homework tomorrow.

WORD STORE 7D
Words for free – places in a town

8 Complete the words in the text message. Some letters are given.

> Meet u @ 14.00 @ the station ⁰c*ar* p*ar*k (I'll leave the car there). Remember u r seeing the ¹d_____t @ 13.30 – brush your teeth b4 u leave! I'm going to the ²d_____r about my headaches – finished by 2.00 p.m. Meet me outside the ³t_____e – we can pick up the tickets for the play on Sat night. Then coffee? The ⁴m_____m has a nice café + exhibition about ancient Egypt – a bit of culture?! We'll stop @ the ⁵s_____t on the way home 4 shopping. CU l8r. Mum.

REMEMBER THIS

Shop is both a noun and a verb.

We say **shop** (v) + **for** + the things you want to buy.
He usually shops for food on Saturdays.

We say **shop** (v) + **at/in** + the type or name of the shop.
I shop at/in Tesco.
We shop at/in the market.

9 Read REMEMBER THIS and choose the correct options.
1 Lucy often shops *at / for / in* clothes *at / for* Zara.
2 I never shop *in / for* big supermarkets.
3 I shop *in / for / at* fish and meat *in / for* the local market.
4 Alan shops *at / for* the twenty-four-hour petrol station. He doesn't have a healthy diet.
5 We shop *at / for / in* food online. It saves so much time.

SHOW WHAT YOU'VE LEARNT

10 Choose the correct options.
1 I need some new *swimwear / trainers / toiletries*. The old ones have got holes and I get wet and dirty feet when I go running.
2 Ann's little brother cried at the *shoe shop / post office / theme park* because he wasn't tall enough to go on the rides.
3 Who will water the *plants / carpets / pets* while we are away on holiday? We don't want them to die.
4 We need some more fruit. How about a nice *pair / can / bunch* of grapes?
5 Please save the empty *bottles / jars / packets* for Grandma. She's going to make jam again this year.
6 If you can't *afford / have / offer* it, you'll have to get a cheaper one.
7 Paula never *goes / picks / keeps* her receipts. What will she do if she wants to take something back to the shop?
8 I'm not happy with these shoes. I don't want a new pair, I want to get a *refund / bargain / sale*, please.
9 The sign says there are no spaces in the *theme park / museum / car park*. We'll have to leave the car somewhere else.
10 Most people shop at the *post office / supermarket / jeweller's* now, so a lot of the little shops in our area have closed.

/10

7.2 Grammar

The Passive

SHOW WHAT YOU KNOW

1 **Complete the sentences with the correct form of *be*.**

   0 My Dad *isn't* keen on shopping, but my Mum loves it.
   1 We haven't _____ to the new pet shop yet.
   2 Joel went to the newsagent's at 7 a.m. but it _____ open.
   3 Trainers _____ so expensive these days. Some of them cost over £100.
   4 My sister and I used to love playing 'shop' when we _____ little.

2 ★ **Read the fact file and choose the correct options.**

We love turkey!

Turkey facts! Did you know?

1 Archaeologists *have found / have been found* evidence of turkeys that lived 10 million years ago.
2 The first turkeys *brought / were brought* to England in 1526.
3 Turkey *has been eaten / has eaten* by ordinary UK families since the 1950s (before that it was too expensive!).
4 Around 10 million turkeys *sell / are sold* in the UK every Christmas.
5 About twenty percent of people in the UK *don't cook / aren't cooked* turkey for Christmas dinner. However, over eighty percent do.
6 Neil Armstrong and Buzz Aldrin *ate / were eaten* cold roast turkey when they landed on the moon.

3 ★★ **Rewrite the sentences in the Passive.**

   0 What language do people speak in the Netherlands?
   What language *is spoken in the Netherlands*?
   1 Special software protects the computer from viruses.
   _____ by special software.
   2 Who wrote *The Hobbit*?
   Who _____ by?
   3 A few people have seen the Loch Ness Monster since that moment.
   The Loch Ness Monster _____ .
   4 A famous chef has just opened a new restaurant in the city.
   _____ in the city by a famous chef.
   5 We don't sell used books here.
   Used books _____ .
   6 Did the sports teacher ask other students to play in the team?
   _____ by the sports teacher?

4 ★★★ **Complete the fact file with the correct passive form of the verbs in brackets. One sentence does not need the passive form.**

This month's fact file is all about Scotforth Senior School Student Snack Shop (or 6S, as we call it!).

- 6S ⁰*was opened* (open) by students three years ago.
- 6S ¹_____ (not start) to make money.
- Every year, the profits from 6S ²_____ (give) to a different charity.
- 6S ³_____ (make) over £2,000 for charity since it began.
- Unsold food from 6S ⁴_____ (not throw away); it's given to the local homeless shelter.
- Next year's charity ⁵_____ (not choose) yet, so please put ideas in the 6S suggestion box.

We hope that 6S will continue to be '6Sful' next year! ☺

5 ★★★ **Complete the text with the correct active or passive form of the verbs in brackets.**

Today in the UK and the US over fifty percent of shopping ⁰*is paid* (pay) for with plastic cards. The idea started in the US in the 1920s. The first cards ¹_____ (make) of paper and could only be used in a few specific shops and hotels. Then, in the 1950s, an American businessman called Frank McNamara had dinner at a restaurant one day, but ²_____ (not have) enough cash to pay for his meal. This ³_____ (give) him the idea for the Diner's Club Card and the first popular credit card ⁴_____ (invent). Since the 1950s plastic ⁵_____ (use) to make all credit cards. Today there are over 1.5 billion credit cards in the US. If they were all put one on top of the other, they would be over seventy miles high, which is taller than twelve Mount Everests!

SHOW WHAT YOU'VE LEARNT

6 **Choose the correct answer, A, B or C.**

   1 Smoking ___ in public places in the UK since 2007.
   A isn't permitted   B hasn't permitted
   C hasn't been permitted
   2 On busy days, over 100,000 people ___ Harrods of London.
   A visited   B visit   C is visited
   3 In 2003 a lottery win of $28.5 million ___ by anyone. The money went to the State of California.
   A wasn't collected   B isn't collected
   C hasn't been collected
   4 Last year, millions of unsold sandwiches from shops and cafés ___ to homeless people across the UK.
   A are given   B were given   C have been given
   5 The Walton family ___ Walmart, the world's largest group of shops, since it started in 1962.
   A is owned   B was owned   C has owned
   6 ___ in bookshops?
   A Are e-books sold   B Do e-books sell
   C Have e-books sold

/6

7.3 Listening language practice

Synonyms • Collocations

1 Put the words in the correct order to complete the interview. Then listen and check.

Extract from Student's Book recording CD•3.19 MP3•106

A: Hello and welcome to *Ask the Expert*. The topic of today's programme is buying presents and our expert is psychologist Amy Black. Thanks for joining us this afternoon Amy.

B: You're welcome. I'm pleased to be here.

A: Amy, can you tell us ⁰ what sort of person is good at choosing presents . (presents /at /good /person / sort of / what / is / choosing)

B: Well, it's true that ¹ _____
_____
(buying / really / presents / some / are / people / good at) and some people are really bad, but I don't think it's a question of personality. I think anybody can buy a good present but they have to do some research. […] ² _____
_____
(presents / are / the best / after /a lot of / chosen / thinking).

A: Do you think women are better than men at buying presents?

B: Well, I suppose women like shopping more than men and this means they don't mind spending hours in shopping centres or online. But as I said, ³ _____
_____
(buy / present / can / a good / anybody).

A: OK, let's read our first question. This was sent by Isabelle, seventeen years old, from Bristol. She says, 'My mum is going to be forty and ⁴ _____
_____
(want / special / get / I / to / her / something) to cheer her up.' What do you think, Amy?

B: Well, Isabelle, it's great that you want to get your mum something special. If you want to cheer her up, ⁵ _____
_____
(idea / good / toiletries / a / are / always). But be careful: your mum doesn't want to feel old. So don't buy face cream for the older woman. […]

2 Replace the underlined words in the sentences with the underlined words in the interview in Exercise 1.

0 Can we go home now, please? We've been in the shopping centre for ages/hours.
1 *Shopping Live* on the shopping channel is not a real TV show/_____ . It's more like one long advert.
2 The subject/_____ of the first chapter of the book is the oldest toy shop in the UK.
3 I don't really want to go shopping, but I guess/_____ we have to buy Lola a birthday present.
4 Which is nicer: modern furniture or antique furniture? Well, that's a matter/_____ of taste.
5 We're happy/_____ to say that we've already done all the Christmas shopping and it's only November.

REMEMBER THIS

buy/get/give **somebody** a present
My parents **bought/got/gave me** a present when I passed my exams.

get a present (**from somebody**) = receive a present
I **got a present** (from my parents) after I passed my exams.

3 Read REMEMBER THIS. Complete the second sentence so that it has a similar meaning to the first, using the word in capitals. Change the form if necessary.

0 My sister gave me a pair of socks for my birthday. **GET**
   I *got a pair of socks from my sister* for my birthday.
1 I got a puppy from my parents for Christmas. **BUY**
   My parents _____ for Christmas.
2 Matt gave Ann a necklace for her graduation. **FROM**
   For her graduation, Ann _____ Matt.
3 Vincent got a smartphone from Claire for his eighteenth birthday. **GIVE**
   Claire _____ for his eighteenth birthday.

WORD STORE 7E
Collocations

4 Complete the sentences with the words in the box. There are two extra words.

> a complaint   a living   a refund   the environment
> poverty   ~~some research~~   the shopping   the receipt

0 Excuse me. We're doing *some research* into shopping habits. Could I ask you a few questions?
1 You are a musician? What a wonderful way to make _____ .
2 I'm sorry, madam, if you didn't keep _____ , we can't give you a refund.
3 Will you come with me to do _____ ? It's easier to carry everything with two people.
4 We ask our customers to pay for plastic bags because we want to help protect _____ .
5 Please donate your change to help reduce _____ in third world countries.

7.4 Reading

Shopping • Antonyms • Word families

Glossary

queue (v) = stand in a line of people waiting to do something, e.g. pay in a shop
close down (phr v) = if a business closes down, it stops operating permanently
chain (of shops) (n) = a number of shops (also hotels, cinemas, restaurants, etc.) owned by the same company or person
store (n) = a large shop that sells many different things

1 Read texts 1–4 and match them with photos A–D.

A ☐ B ☐ C ☐ D ☐

2 Read the texts again and choose the correct answer, A, B or C.

Text 1
The author of the text
A advises readers to go shopping on Boxing Day.
B offers no advice on shopping on Boxing Day.
C advises readers to avoid shopping on Boxing Day.

Text 2
The owner of Safari
A is worried about her business.
B wants to close down her business.
C has moved her business recently.

Text 3
The boys 'looked at each other nervously' because
A there was no one else around.
B they saw the security guards.
C they were planning to break the rules.

Text 4
The advert says that secret shoppers
A work in one store.
B work in stores all over the country.
C work in the company's London office.

3 Read the texts again. Are the statements true (T) or false (F)?

1 Boxing Day is celebrated all over the world. ☐
2 Shops are open all night on Boxing Day. ☐
3 Safari hasn't closed down. ☐
4 Safari is located in a shopping centre. ☐
5 The shopping centre was closed when the boys met. ☐
6 There was no one else inside the shopping centre that morning. ☐
7 To do their job, secret shoppers need to travel. ☐
8 The advert asks you to send a CV to apply for the job. ☐

4 Match the underlined words in the texts with their opposites.

0 large ≠ small
1 finish ≠ _____
2 dangerous ≠ _____
3 save ≠ _____
4 interesting ≠ _____

Globalholidays.com   Home | Search | Contact

1

you searched for 'Boxing Day'

In Britain, Canada, New Zealand and parts of Australia, 26 December is **Boxing Day**. Originally, this was the day when rich people gave their servants small Christmas gifts, but these days **Boxing Day** is all about shopping. There are big sales with reductions on everything, and customers spend huge amounts of money. Shops and shopping centres open very early (some of them as early as 5 a.m.) and shoppers often start queuing for bargains in the middle of the night, hours before the sales actually begin.

Saveourcitycentre.net   discussion forum

2

Share your opinion and help save our city centre.

Safari _23 says: For the last ten years, I have owned a clothes shop called Safari on the main street of our town. About six months ago, a big shopping centre opened just outside the town and since then business has been bad. Every month fewer customers come into the shop and it is getting harder to make a living. I used to love my job, but standing there all day with hardly any customers is really boring. The little café opposite had to close down last month. I know that other small businesses on the street are having big problems too. Some of them have actually moved to the shopping centre recently. I am not sure what the solution is, but I feel sad and angry, and I'm afraid that I will have to close down my shop too.

84

3

The shopping centre opened at half past nine. They met by the entrance at twenty-five past. There was no one else around. They waited next to the sign that showed the centre rules: no smoking, no dogs, no radios, no skateboards. They looked at each other nervously. At half past, the cleaner unlocked the doors. They were still the only people waiting. It looked <u>safe</u>. It was time. Through the doors, boards ready and then suddenly, full speed! They flew through the shopping centre, the wheels of their skateboards speeding silently on the perfectly flat floor. The feeling was amazing, just as they imagined. And then they saw the security guard.

4

We are looking for

secret shoppers

to work for our large chain
of clothing shops.

Our secret shoppers travel around the UK, visit different stores and pretend to be real customers. On a typical visit, they go into one of our stores and ask questions about our clothes and shoes. Their main job is to check that our in-store sales assistants are friendly and know our products. Secret shoppers have to listen carefully, remember all the details and then send a report to our London office to describe their visit. If you are offered a job as a secret shopper, you will have to keep your job and identity secret.

For an application form, email
targetstores.gm@css.net.
Interviews start in October.

REMEMBER BETTER

Some words have more than one antonym. Use diagrams like the one below to help you remember them.

Complete the word webs with the words in the box. There are two extra words.

[<s>big</s>   clear   earn   end
  exciting   watch   unsafe]

0 small ········· large
           ····· <u>big</u>

1 start ········· finish
           ····· _____

2 safe ········· dangerous
           ····· _____

3 spend ········· save
           ····· _____

4 boring ········· interesting
           ····· _____

WORD STORE 7E
Word families

5 Choose the correct options.

1 Our latest example of *creative / creativity* at Pizza World is the Super Six, a six-cheese mega-pizza.

2 To be *honest / honesty*, I'd rather stay at home this afternoon. Why don't we do the shopping online instead?

3 You have already eaten three pieces of cake. Do you realise that *greed / greedy* is not an attractive quality?

4 Lena's mum bought her a new iPad for her birthday. I'm so *jealous / jealousy*.

5 I have no idea what Kevin is getting me for my birthday. It's a complete *mystery / mysterious*.

6 Complete the sentences with the correct form of the words in brackets.

0 I don't go shopping with Leo. He gets very <u>angry</u> (anger) if he has to wait in a queue.

1 The new wedding dresses by Chanel are extremely _____ (elegance) and extremely expensive.

2 Customer _____ (loyal) is very important for us. We want our customers to keep coming back.

3 We are _____ (passion) about customer service. We want our customers to love us.

4 I just saw a man put a jumper in his bag without paying. Call _____ (secure)!

7.5 Grammar

Quantifiers

SHOW WHAT YOU KNOW

1 Read the sentences. Are the underlined nouns countable (C) or uncountable (U)?

0 The teacher gave us <u>homework</u> to do over the holidays. It's so unfair. — **U**
1 It will take <u>time</u> to find the right pair of shoes for the wedding.
2 Our city has a major problem with traffic and the air <u>pollution</u> it causes.
3 Helen caught a very serious <u>disease</u> on holiday. Luckily, she's much better now.
4 Ian goes to the most expensive <u>school</u> in the city. His grades are not good though.
5 I love Thai <u>food</u> because it's hot, tasty and usually very healthy.
6 We don't get on with the <u>people</u> who live next door. They aren't very friendly.

2 ★ Read the conversation and choose the correct options.

A: Excuse me, may I ask you a few quick questions about your experience in the shopping centre today?
B: Er … will it take long?
A: No, not at all. Just ¹*a few / a little* minutes.
B: OK then.
A: Thank you. ²*How much / How many* shops did you visit?
B: Oh, I'm not sure exactly. Certainly ³*too much / too many*. My feet hurt!
A: Oh dear! Poor you. I'll write 'more than ten' on the form then. ⁴*How much / How many* time did you spend in the food zone today?
B: Oh, ⁵*very few / very little*. I stopped for a cup of coffee, but only for ten minutes.
A: OK, thanks. Just one more question, if you don't mind. ⁶*How much / How many* money did you spend today?
B: Only ⁷*a few / a little*. Most of the time I was window shopping.

3 ★★ Make the sentences negative using *not much* or *not many*.

0 Frieda has a lot of friends.
Frieda <u>doesn't have many</u> friends.
1 Peter goes to a lot of parties.
Peter _____ parties.
2 Chloe buys a lot of clothes.
Chloe _____ clothes.
3 Nick and Nancy watch a lot of sport.
Nick and Nancy _____ sport.
4 Jenny drinks a lot of juice.
Jenny _____ juice.
5 Edward and Eve write a lot of emails.
Edward and Eve _____ emails.
6 Francis eats a lot of fruit.
Francis _____ fruit.

4 ★★ Add *a* before *little* and *few* where necessary.

0 There is *a* little milk left, so you don't have to have black coffee.
1 I have ___ little interest in shopping. I prefer playing football, to be honest.
2 Leah wasn't going to celebrate her birthday, but then ___ few friends organised a party for her.
3 There are ___ few shops in the village, so most people travel to the city to do their shopping.
4 With ___ little luck, we'll find a bargain in the sales.

5 ★★★ Choose the correct answer, A, B or C.

1 I don't have ___ time. Can we be very quick in the shop?
  A much   B some   C a little
2 Adam doesn't have ___ male friends that like shopping.
  A some   B many   C much
3 On Fridays Lauren always buys ___ chocolate on the way home from school.
  A much   B any   C some
4 There are ___ snowboards to choose from. I don't know which one to buy.
  A too much   B too many   C not much
5 ___ people do their shopping online these days.
  A Lots of   B A little   C Any
6 Excuse me, do you have ___ blue T-shirts?
  A a little   B much   C any
7 Jo has ___ birthday money left, but she hasn't decided what to spend it on yet.
  A little   B a little   C a few
8 ___ of my friends actually buy CDs now. I think Lewis is the only one.
  A Few   B Little   C A few

SHOW WHAT YOU'VE LEARNT

6 Complete the sentences with *much* or *many*.

1 We don't have _____ customers in the shop on Sundays.
2 How _____ time do we have before the shopping centre closes?
3 There are too _____ cars in the city centre on weekdays.
4 Do you have _____ work in the hotel in the winter months?
5 Not _____ people do their shopping in the local shops these days.
6 We didn't buy _____ things in the winter sales.

/6

7.6 Speaking language practice

Shopping and making complaints

1 Put the words in the correct order to form questions. Then match them with answers a–e.

1. on / to / it / would / try / you / like?
   <u>Would you like to try it on?</u> — e
2. help / can / you / I?
   _____
3. would / how / pay / to / you / like?
   _____
4. size / are / what / you?
   _____
5. it / fit, / doesn't / I / refund / a / can / get / if?
   _____

a. By credit card, please.
b. I'm just looking, thanks.
c. I'm a medium.
d. No, I'm sorry, you can't because it's in the sale.
e. Yes, please. Where are the changing rooms?

2 Read the conversation in a shop and complete the phrases. The first letter of each word is given.

A: ⁰<u>Excuse</u> me, I'm l<u>ooking</u> f<u>or</u> a pair of dark blue jeans.
B: Sure, we have several different brands. What ¹s_____ are you?
A: I don't really know. I think I'm a ¹s_____ 32.
B: OK, I'll give you a few different ones to try. ²The c_____ r_____ are over there.

Five minutes later:

B: Do you like any of those?
A: I like these but they're a bit too big. Do you have them ³i_____ a s_____ 30, please?
B: Yes, we do. Just a moment. OK, here they are.
A: Thanks.
B: Are they better?
A: Yeah, I think ⁴I'll t_____ them. You know what? I'd really like to ask my girlfriend what she thinks. If I buy them and she doesn't like them, ⁵can I get a r_____ ?
B: Yes, for twenty-eight days you can. Make sure you keep your ⁶r_____ .
A: Great. How much are they?
B: They're £99.99. ⁷H_____ would you like to p_____ ?
A: What? 100 pounds for a pair of jeans? Er … look, I'm sorry, I have to go now. Maybe I'll … er … come back for them later, OK? I … er … I'm very late … yes … bye!

3 Choose the correct options.

1. What's wrong *to / for / with* it?
2. Do you *have / get / keep* your receipt?
3. We can exchange it *to / for / with* a new one.
4. I bought this last week but it *doesn't / isn't / hasn't* work.
5. I think it's *fault / faulting / faulty*.
6. *I'd / I'm / I* like a refund, please.

4 Complete the conversation in a pet shop with the sentences in Exercise 3.

A: Good morning, sir. Can I help you?
B: Yes, I hope so. ⁰<u>I bought this last week but it doesn't work.</u>
A: It doesn't work? But sir, it's a cat.
¹_____
B: Well, I've had it for a week and it hasn't caught one mouse. Not one. It just sleeps in front of the fire all day.
²_____
A: Faulty? But sir, it's a perfectly normal, healthy animal.
B: Well, I'm not satisfied with it.
³_____
A: A refund? For a cat? Er … well, we don't normally … Listen, I have an idea. Some new cats were delivered this morning.
⁴_____
B: I don't want a new one, I want my money back!
A: Well, I … er … well, I suppose …
⁵_____
B: Yes, I do. Here you are. Thank you. Now, tell me, do you sell guns?
A: Guns?!
B: For the mice.

87

7.7 Writing

A polite written complaint

1 Match the information to make customer problems.

1 I bought a watch from your website on 15 June.	a I paid for them on the same day, but when I tried to print them	i I am still waiting for them to be delivered.
2 I ordered a pair of skis from your company five days ago.	b When I checked my phone bill for this month	ii the system said 'You have not paid yet'.
3 On 24 November, I booked tickets for the *Monster Truck Show* on your website.	c You promised to send them to me the next day, but	iii I noticed a payment of three euros for this 'free' app.
4 Last month I downloaded your 'free' app *Friendtracker*.	d It arrived two days later, but	iv when I opened it, it was the wrong colour.

2 Complete the email with the words in the box. There are two extra words.

> bought   complain   disappointed   faithfully
> grateful   refund   sincerely   ~~Sir or Madam~~   wrong

Dear ⁰ *Sir or Madam*

I am writing to ¹_____ about the service provided by your restaurant.

I recently organised my seventeenth birthday party at JW's All-American Diner. I booked a table for 8.00, but when we arrived, the waitress said there was no reservation. We waited half an hour for a table. When we finally sat down, we were told that the chef was sick that day and we would have to wait at least an hour for our meal. The food arrived after seventy-five minutes and four out of ten orders were ²_____ . My vegetarian friend was given a steak!

I am very ³_____ with your service and feel sorry that I chose your restaurant for my birthday party. I would be ⁴_____ if you could send me a ⁵_____ for the cost of the meal or invite my friends and me for a free meal in one of your other restaurants.

Yours ⁶_____ ,
Kay Jones

---

3 Imagine you have received poor service or had a problem with a product you have bought. Tick the fair requests.

0 I would like a full refund of the money I paid. ✓
1 I would like an apology. ☐
2 I would like to eat for free at your restaurant forever. ☐
3 I would like you to close your business. ☐
4 I would like you to send me a new one that works. ☐
5 I would like you to send me the colour I ordered. ☐
6 I would like the waitress to lose her job. ☐
7 I would like to take you and your company to court. ☐

SHOW WHAT YOU'VE LEARNT

4 Read the information on the customer feedback form from a gym and fitness centre and write an email of complaint.

Sunshine Gym & Fitness

Feedback and suggestions
We are always keen to hear from our customers.
Tell us about your experience at Sunshine Gym & Fitness.

> I want to complain about your service. On 18 November, I paid 200 euros to join your gym for a year, but I am not happy. Half of the machines in the gym are broken or dangerous, the changing rooms are always smelly and dirty and the staff are rude. When I complained about the broken running machine last week, the man at the desk told me I should run home instead! I'm not going to come to your gym anymore and I want all my money back.

Write your email in about 100 words.

SHOW THAT YOU'VE CHECKED

In my email of complaint:

- the beginning matches the end (*Dear Mr Smith* → *Yours sincerely*; *Dear Sir or Madam* → *Yours faithfully*). ☐
- I have given my reason for writing. ☐
- I have explained the problem giving details (what? where? when?). ☐
- I have told the recipient what I expect them to do (and asked for something fair). ☐
- I have used polite language. ☐
- I have not used contractions (e.g. *I'm, aren't, that's*), emoticons (☺) or abbreviations (e.g. *info, cu, gr8*). ☐
- I have checked my spelling and punctuation. ☐
- I have written about 100 words. ☐

7.8 Word practice

Shopping

1 Choose the correct answer, A, B or C.

1 My little brother loves sharks. I'm taking him to visit the ___ this weekend.
   A post office   B zoo   C aquarium
2 You'll find a lot of bargains when you buy clothes in a ___ shop and your money will help someone.
   A designer   B charity   C clothes
3 We're going to the beach later, so don't wear your trainers; wear your ___ .
   A boots   B gloves   C sandals
4 Let's get this big packet of biscuits. It's more ___ than two small ones.
   A reduced   B expensive   C economical
5 I'm disappointed with this shirt I got. It wasn't cheap but the ___ is very poor.
   A value   B quality   C account
6 This magazine is awful. There's too much ___ and no information!
   A branding   B packaging   C advertising
7 I haven't got any money this week, so I'm just going to ___ at the weekend.
   A go window shopping   B reduce poverty
   C make a living
8 The colour of my husband's suit ___ everyone's attention at our wedding. It was green!
   A paid   B attracted   C picked up
9 Can I have two ___ of beans, please?
   A boxes   B bunches   C tins
10 This is the last packet of ___ we've got. We need to buy more.
   A water   B perfume   C tea
11 This online shopping site doesn't seem very ___ . I don't want to put my credit card details on it.
   A competitive   B secure   C passionate
12 Mr Mann is very ___ . He never talks about his past.
   A honest   B jealous   C mysterious
13 You need to stop shouting and control your ___ .
   A anger   B wealth   C creativity
14 It's OK to leave your passports at the hotel. You can trust them ___ all your documents.
   A with   B for   C on
15 We should focus ___ one idea at a time or we'll never decide!
   A at   B to   C on

2 Read the descriptions and write the words for shops and services.

1 You can buy toiletries and perfume in this part of a supermarket.
2 In Home and Garden you can buy these for your garden.
3 They sell light bulbs and vacuum cleaners in this department.
4 In Sports and Leisurewear you can buy this for swimming.
5 You can buy food for your dog in this shop.
6 You can buy second-hand clothes and books in this shop.
7 You can see fish, sharks and dolphins here.
8 You can go on a roller coaster or a ghost train here.

3 Find six partitives in the word square. Then use them to complete the phrases.

Q	W	R	J	T	Y	U	I
O	P	A	A	S	D	B	F
P	A	I	R	C	X	O	V
G	H	J	K	L	Z	T	B
U	P	A	C	K	E	T	N
T	R	E	A	W	Q	L	M
K	B	U	N	C	H	E	C

1 a _____ of jam   4 a _____ of biscuits
2 a _____ of perfume   5 a _____ of grapes
3 a _____ of cola   6 a _____ of shoes

4 Match 1–6 with a–f to make phrases about shopping.

1 have   a afford it
2 go   b a refund
3 keep   c window shopping
4 pick up   d a sale
5 can't   e the receipt
6 get   f a bargain

5 Complete the first and second columns of the table.

Adjective	Noun	Example
angry	anger	Rude people make me angry. Red is the colour often linked to anger.
creative		
	elegance	
greedy		
	honesty	
jealous		
mysterious		
	passion	
	security	
wealthy		

6 Write a sentence for each of the words in Exercise 5 in the third column of the table, as in the two examples.

7.9 Self-assessment

1 For each learning objective, tick the box that best matches your ability.

☺☺ = I understand and can help a friend.
☺ = I understand and can do it by myself.
☹ = I understand some, but have some questions.
☹☹ = I do not understand.

			☺☺	☺	☹	☹☹	Need help?
7.1	Vocabulary	I can talk about shops and shopping.					Students' Book pages 84–85 Word Store page 15 Workbook pages 80–81
7.2	Grammar	I can use the Passive to talk about trade and processes.					Students' Book page 86 Workbook page 82
7.3	Listening	I can identify details in an interview.					Students' Book page 87 Workbook page 83
7.4	Reading	I can find specific detail in an article.					Students' Book pages 88–89 Workbook pages 84–85
7.5	Grammar	I can understand countable and uncountable nouns and use appropriate quantifiers.					Students' Book page 90 Workbook page 86
7.6	Speaking	I can buy things in a shop and make complaints.					Students' Book page 91 Workbook page 87
7.7	Writing	I can make a polite written complaint.					Students' Book pages 92–93 Workbook page 88

2 What can you remember from this unit?

New words I learned (the words you most want to remember from this unit)	Expressions and phrases I liked (any expressions or phrases you think sound nice, useful or funny)	English I heard or read outside class (e.g. from websites, books, adverts, films, music)

7.10 Self-check

1 Complete the words in the conversations. The first letter of each word is given.

Conversation 1

A: Dad, Dad, Dad! Can we go the new ⁰t*heme* p*ark* on Saturday?

B: Hmm, I don't really like roller coasters. How about going to see a film at the ¹c_____ ?

Conversation 2

A: My nails are horrible. I'm going for a ²m_____ this afternoon.

B: Are you sure you can ³a_____ it? Do you have enough money left?

Conversation 3

A: I'm going to the Alps in February and I'd like a new ⁴p_____ of skis.

B: Certainly, sir. This pair is on special ⁵o_____ . They are half price at the moment.

/5

2 Choose the correct options.

0 On today's programme, a report on the *mystery* / (*mysterious*) disappearance of a teenage celebrity.

1 Please try to control your *anger* / *angry*. It doesn't help to scream and shout.

2 You looked so *elegance* / *elegant* in that dress. Did you take a photo?

3 Tim has got a really cool new pair of trainers. I'm *jealousy* / *jealous*.

4 We take *security* / *secure* very seriously at this bank.

5 At our company *creativity* / *creative* is more important than experience.

/5

3 Read the information and complete the names of the places. Some letters are given.

0 All shops and restaurants close at 9 p.m. s*hopping* ma*ll*

1 A diamond is forever. j_____'s

2 Please do not feed the fish. a_____m

3 Special offer: three packets for the price of two. s_____t

4 Guests of the bride, please sit on this side. w_____
_____l

5 You must be at least 1.3m tall to ride this roller coaster. t_____
_____k

/5

4 Complete the sentences with the correct passive form of the verbs in brackets.

0 Kyle *wasn't chosen* (not choose) for the football team.

1 Our new app, which _____ (design) by a teenager, came out two months ago.

2 _____ (you/give) a refund yesterday?

3 I'm sorry but the house _____ (sell) last week.

4 _____ (the parcel/deliver) yesterday morning?

5 The students _____ (not tell) about the new teacher yet.

/5

5 Find and correct the mistakes in the sentences.

0 There are too ~~much~~ things on the menu. I can't decide what to order. *many*

1 There is very few milk left. Can you drink black coffee? _____

2 How many snow is there in the mountains at the moment? _____

3 Very little people can afford to buy a private island. _____

4 Only few very good friends were invited to her party. _____

5 A lots of the students are sick this week. _____

/5

6 Choose the correct answer, A, B or C, to complete both sentences in each pair.

0 What time ___ you meet me tonight?
I'd like a(n) ___ of cola and a sandwich, please.
A do (B) can C are

1 Where can I find ___ bulbs, please?
You take the ___ bag and I'll carry the heavy one.
A light B garden C electrical

2 How ___ time do we have to get ready for the party?
You've put too ___ sugar in this coffee. It's really sweet.
A many B few C much

3 Two new shopping malls ___ built in this town last year.
When ___ flat screen TVs invented?
A was B were C are

4 Who is going to ___ the shopping this week?
We need to ___ some research to find out what our customers really want.
A do B make C keep

5 The classroom is dirty because the ___ is sick and couldn't come to work today.
We bought a new vacuum ___ because the old one broke.
A teacher B shampoo C cleaner

/5

Total /30

8 SOCIETY

8.1 Vocabulary

Politics • Crime • The justice system • Society

SHOW WHAT YOU KNOW

1 Complete the text with the words in the box. There are two extra words.

> city   elections   people   politics   population
> Prime   state   system   ~~United~~

FACTSFOCUS.COM — US politics

You searched for US politics.
Here are the best results:

There are fifty states in the ⁰*United* States of America. The total ¹_____ of the US is over 300 million. Washington D.C. is the capital ²_____. The political ³_____ is called a Federal Constitutional Republic. There isn't a ⁴_____ Minister in the US. The President is the head of the government and also the head of ⁵_____. The American people choose the president in presidential ⁶_____ every four years.

WORD STORE 8A
Crime and criminals

2 Read the news headlines and choose the correct options.

1 Police say last week's fire at the NuVu Cinema was **arson / arsonist**

2 'My life as a drug **dealer / dealing**' read our amazing interview with an ex-criminal

3 DVD **piracy / pirate** falls as more people download films legally online

4 Film star tells her terrible secret: 'I was a celebrity **shoplifter / shoplifting**.'

5 Police question students after **thieves / thefts** steal exam papers from city school

3 Look at the crime report and complete the sentences. The first letter of each word is given.

Last year's city crime figures:

5 people killed .... (up 20%)
68 houses robbed .... (down 17%)
43 people attacked and robbed .... (down 4%)
114 car thefts .... (up 12%)
122 buildings attacked (windows broken, graffiti, etc.) .... (up 1%)

Last year:
0 5 people were m*urdered*.
1 68 houses were b_____.
2 43 people were m_____.
3 114 cars were s_____.
4 122 buildings were v_____.

WORD STORE 8B
The justice system

4 Complete the court notes with the words in the box. There are two extra words.

> arrested   collected   ~~committed~~
> ended   guilty   innocent
> interviewed   sentenced   went

Case number 004256 — notes:

25/01 A crime (burglary) was ⁰*committed*.

26/01 A suspect was ¹_____.

26/01 The victim and suspect were ²_____.

27/01 Evidence was ³_____.

14/03 The case ⁴_____ to court.

14/03 The judge decided the man was ⁵_____.

16/03 The man was ⁶_____ to sixteen months in prison.

WORD STORE 8C
People involved in a crime case

5 Read the conversations and choose the correct options.

Conversation 1

A: Do you know any ¹*criminals / arsonists / judges*?
B: Yes, I do. My next door neighbour was arrested for drug dealing.
A: Really? What happened?
B: Very early one morning, five ²*muggers / burglars / police officers* came round and took her away. The case went to court and the ³*victim / suspect / judge* gave her five years in prison.

Conversation 2

A: Have you ever been a ⁴*suspect / victim / criminal* of crime?
B: Luckily not, but I have been a ⁵*murderer / pirate / witness*. I saw a man mug a woman and steal her handbag.
A: Wow! Did you tell the police?
B: Sure. I described the man and they arrested a ⁶*victim / suspect / judge*. I had to identify him in a photograph.

6 Complete the words in the email to the editor of *Channel 17 News*. Some letters are given.

Dear Editor,

I regularly watch *Channel 17 News*, but every time I switch on my television, I only hear stories about all the terrible ⁰c<u>riminal</u>s committing crimes around in the world.

This morning, for example (13 April), the first story was all about a man who put a bomb in a school because of his beliefs. There were interviews with the families of the ¹v____s – it was heartbreaking. Next was a story about how difficult it is for women to get in the top professions. For example, there are almost no women ²j____s in the British legal system today. The third story was about government ministers who accept money from big companies and ³p____ o____ who take money from ⁴s____s in criminal cases to ignore the ⁵e____ from important ⁶w____s.

Is there any good news in the world? Could you report some positive stories as well as negative?

Yours sincerely,

Simon Wallis

REMEMBER THIS
The structure **noun** + **crime** can be used to describe different types of crime.
car crime = stealing cars; **knife** crime = violent crimes where the weapon a criminal uses is a knife

7 Read REMEMBER THIS and match the types of crime with their definitions.

1 street crime — d
2 cyber crime —
3 war crime —
4 youth crime —

a crime committed using the Internet
b serious crime committed during military conflicts
c crime committed by children and teenagers
d crimes such as robbery committed in public places

SHOW WHAT YOU'VE LEARNT

8 Complete the sentences with the correct form of the words in brackets.

0 The same <u>robber</u> (robbery) stole money from five different post offices last month.
1 The attack on the World Trade Center in 2001 is perhaps the most famous example of _____ (terror).
2 Last night two _____ (thief) stole gold and diamonds from a local jeweller's.
3 In my opinion, if someone writes their name or paints a picture on a public building, they are a _____ (crime).
4 The police caught the _____ (burgle) who stole the jewellery from the museum last week.

9 Choose the correct answer, A, B or C, to complete both sentences in each pair.

1 The arsonist ___ fire to a school on Monday.
I'd like to ___ up my own business as a hairdresser.
A did   B set   C put

2 A detective interviews witnesses and ___ evidence.
My friend ___ stamps as a hobby.
A collects   B makes   C watches

3 The judge decided that both men were ___ and sentenced them to three years in prison.
I forgot to buy my dad a birthday present and now I feel really ___ .
A guilty   B innocent   C free

4 Three teenagers were arrested for dealing ___ in the nightclub.
The doctor gave my aunt some strong ___ to cure her illness.
A medicine   B items   C drugs

5 Lena's grandmother was ___ on the train.
Four men ___ a bank and then drove away in a blue van.
A stolen   B robbed   C mugged

6 A ___ was arrested today after a house was burgled on Vine Street.
The victim's husband is not a ___ in the murder case.
A man   B thief   C suspect

/10

8.2 Grammar

Past Perfect

SHOW WHAT YOU KNOW

1 Complete the sentences with the Past Simple form of the verbs in brackets.

1. When the alarm <u>went off</u> (go off), the security guard _____ (call) the police. Then he hid in the cupboard.
2. When the judge _____ (enter) the courtroom, the suspect _____ (not stand up). The judge was not pleased.
3. The police _____ (not arrest) the shoplifter when they _____ (arrive) at the supermarket. She was given a warning.
4. The vandals _____ (not run away) when I _____ (shout) at them. I ran away instead.
5. When the mugger _____ (attack) the woman, she _____ (hit) him in the face. Police said this was brave, but not a good idea.

2 ★ Complete the story with the Past Perfect form of the verbs in brackets.

Maggie lay in bed but couldn't fall asleep. She thought about everything that ⁰<u>had happened</u> (happen) that day. She thought about the robbery. It ¹_____ (be) perfect. No problems, no alarm, no police. She was also sure she ²_____ (not leave) any fingerprints. She ³_____ (get out) of the building before anyone realised what was happening. The diamonds were safe because she ⁴_____ (hide) them under the floorboards. Tomorrow was the delivery and then straight to the airport. ⁵_____ (she/really/do) it? She couldn't believe it.

3 ★★ Which action happened first? Write 1 or 2.

0. When the police arrived [1], the drug dealer threw away all the drugs [2].
1. When the police arrived [ ], the drug dealer had thrown away all the drugs [ ].
2. Because the owners came home [ ], the burglar jumped out of the window [ ].
3. When the owners came home [ ], the burglars had stolen their television [ ].
4. The murderer had already killed the victim [ ] when the witness saw him [ ].
5. The murderer killed the victim [ ] because she screamed [ ].
6. After the judge read the sentence [ ], the man began to cry [ ].
7. By the time the judge read the sentence [ ], the man had already begun to cry [ ].

4 ★★ Choose the correct options.

1. Did the judge give you a short prison sentence because you *didn't commit / hadn't committed* a crime before?
2. When he got home, the unsuccessful mugger realised he *had lost / lost* his own wallet.
3. The woman *hadn't shoplifted / didn't shoplift* before, so this time she wasn't given a prison sentence.
4. The bank had already been robbed by the time the unlucky bank robber *had arrived / arrived*.
5. Before he *had come / came* out of the changing room, the shoplifter had put the jumper on under his coat.
6. The suspect drove to the victim's house in a blue car. Where *did he steal / had he stolen* it from?
7. When police searched the house, they discovered the burglar *hid / had hidden* the jewellery in the freezer.
8. After the two women had robbed the post office, they *drove / had driven* away on a motorbike.

5 ★★★ Complete the story with the Past Simple or Past Perfect form of the verbs in brackets.

Liam sat on his bed and thought about the past. He ⁰<u>had been</u> (be) in prison for nearly three years. He was only half way through the six-year sentence the judge ¹_____ (give) him for dealing drugs. As usual, he ²_____ (feel) sad and lonely. White walls, one small window and nobody to talk to. He really ³_____ (miss) his parents and his brother. Before he was arrested, everyone ⁴_____ (try) to be his friend. Now he ⁵_____ (realise) that most of them ⁶_____ (just/want) to buy drugs from him. Of course, none of his old 'friends' ever came to visit him. He felt so depressed. Why ⁷_____ (he/start) dealing drugs in the first place?

SHOW WHAT YOU'VE LEARNT

6 Complete the sentences with the Past Simple or Past Perfect form of the verbs in brackets.

1. Julie _____ (not have) the car for long when the thieves _____ (steal) it.
2. _____ (Katie/finish) her homework last time you _____ (call) her?
3. I was half way to the party when I _____ (realise) I _____ (leave) your present at home.
4. By the time the bomb _____ (explode), the terrorists _____ (leave) the country.
5. The police _____ (not recognise) the suspect because he _____ (lose) a lot of weight.
6. When you _____ (go) upstairs at 9 o'clock, _____ (your little sister/go) to sleep?

/6

8.3 Listening language practice

Words and their definitions • Hobbies: noun + *spotting* • Antonyms

1 Read the interview with expert 'lie spotter' Martin Johnson and choose the correct answer, A, B or C, for questions 1–7. Then listen and check.

Extract from Students' Book recording CD•3.30 MP3•117

A: Can you tell us how you became involved in lie- ¹___?

B: Well, before I started working for the police, I'd studied Business and Psychology at university. On my course we studied ᵃbody language. I ²___ it fascinating, especially the way people behave when they're trying to hide something or tell a lie.

A: So, how exactly can you tell if someone is lying?

B: First, you need to watch the face. A fake smile is the first sign that something isn't right. It means somebody is trying to ᵇhide a real feeling. It's easy to do a fake smile – you just turn the sides of your mouth up. But a real smile changes a person's whole face – the eyes light up and the cheeks and eyebrows rise. And ³___ lines appear around the eyes.

A: I've heard that if someone is lying, they can't ⁴___ at you directly in your eyes. Is that true?

B: No, that's not true – in fact, if someone is lying, they often stare a little bit too ⁵___ in your eyes. […]

A: So the eyes can give you a lot of information.

B: Yes, indeed. The eyes can ⁶___ you a lot. But there are other signs that ᶜindicate a person is lying: crossed arms, for example, or a hand in front of the mouth. […] And then there are the things people say. […] They sometimes give too much information. A typical example is the suspect ⁷___ tells you that he had been at home all evening and then tells you ᵈin detail what he'd watched on television, who he had been with, exactly what time he'd gone to bed and so on. It's unnatural to give so much detail and I would be ᵉsuspicious. […]

1	A noticing	B spotting	C seeing
2	A remembered	B learned	C found
3	A much	B lots of	C a little
4	A see	B watch	C look
5	A few	B many	C much
6	A tell	B say	C speak
7	A who	B which	C what

2 Match the underlined words and phrases a–e in the interview with their definitions.

0 keep something secret or where others can't find it [b]
1 show or suggest that something is probably true ☐
2 you feel this way when you think that someone is guilty of doing something wrong or dishonest ☐
3 communication without words, through gestures, posture and face, especially eyes and smile ☐
4 with all the important information ☐

3 Complete the sentences with the underlined words and phrases in the interview. Change the form of the verbs if necessary.

0 James tried to *hide* his disappointment when he wasn't chosen to be the captain of the football team.
1 The witness told the police everything. She described the mugging _____ .
2 The teacher became _____ when William suddenly got top marks in every test.
3 Kelly didn't say anything, but her _____ showed that she was nervous.
4 Research _____ that most teenagers need more sleep than older adults.

4 Complete the sentences about hobbies with the words in the box. There are two extra words.

[bird   car   celebrity   cloud   dolphin   plane   ~~train~~   tree]

0 My uncle and his friends go *train*-spotting every Sunday. They sit by the railway station for hours.
1 Steve spends a lot of time at the airport because he loves _____-spotting.
2 If you want to do some _____-spotting, the expensive bars and restaurants in London are a very good place to start.
3 Chris is very keen on _____-spotting. He travelled all the way to Africa to see the pelicans and the flamingos that live there.
4 Until I started _____-spotting, I didn't realise that there are at least ten different types. I check the sky every time I go outside.
5 The _____-spotting boat leaves every morning at 10 a.m. Yesterday we saw them actually jumping up out of the water.

WORD STORE 8F
Antonyms

5 Complete the sentences with the words in the box. There are five extra words.

[~~boring~~   dishonest   fake   false   fascinating   genuine   honest   lie   true   truth]

0 Jack thinks Biology is *boring*. He skips the lessons regularly.
1 It's not a real Rolex watch. A _____ one costs thousands of pounds and I can't afford that.
2 _____ people don't tell lies, Emma. I hope you will never lie again.
3 How do I look, Mum? Please tell the _____ . If you don't like my dress, tell me.
4 I heard that Aaron asked you to go to the cinema with him. Wow! Is it _____ ?

8.4 Reading

Suffragettes • Synonyms • Word families

Glossary

opportunity (n) = a chance to do something
goal/aim (n) = something that you hope to do in the future
progress (n) = the process of getting closer to finishing something
honours degree (n) = a university degree that is above basic level
vital (adj) = extremely important

Newsinfocus.com

This week's iconic women: the Suffragettes

If you are a secondary school student, then quite soon you will have the opportunity to vote in your country's elections. If you are eighteen, you will have this right and of course, it will not matter if you are male or female. This might seem normal now, but one 100 years ago things were very different.

For example, in Britain, before 1918, it was against the law for women to vote in their country's elections. This meant that even intelligent, successful and well-educated women didn't have the chance to choose their political leaders. In contrast, any man had the right to vote. In 1897, a group of women decided to try to change things and the National Union of Women's Suffrage began. Their leader was a woman called Millicent Fawcett and their goal was to change the law to give women the same right to vote as men.

Millicent Fawcett believed in non-violent protest, but other women felt that her progress was too slow. In 1903 a woman called Emmeline Pankhurst started a different group: the Women's Social and Political Union (WSPU). They had the same aims as Fawcett's group, but they used more extreme and violent methods to attract attention to women's suffrage. The word *suffrage* actually means 'right to vote' and the women who supported the fight for this right became known as 'Suffragettes'.

As part of their protests, some women in the WSPU committed serious crimes. They attacked politicians, set fire to post boxes and churches and vandalised buildings. Most of the women who committed crimes were sentenced to prison, but many of them continued to protest by breaking prison rules or refusing food.

One of the most famous suffragettes was a woman named Emily Davison. As a student, Davison had already done something very unusual for a woman at that time. She had graduated from Oxford University with a first class honours degree. She was a passionate suffragette who believed in 'actions, not words'. Unfortunately, she is perhaps most well-known because, at a famous horse race in 1913 (probably as part of a protest, but no one really knows), she stepped in front of the King's horse and was killed.

In 1914 World War I began and Emmeline Pankhurst and the WSPU decided it was more important to help the country during the war than to continue their fight. While the men went to fight, women did men's jobs and kept Britain running. In 1918, helped by the vital role that women played during the war, the Suffrage movement had its first success and women over the age of thirty got the right to vote. By 1928, women were finally given identical voting rights to men.

When you reach voting age, take a moment to remember the people who fought for this right in the past. Don't miss the opportunity you have to express your opinion.

1 Read the article quickly and decide why it was written.
1 to encourage young people to vote in elections
2 to tell the story of how women got the right to vote
3 to explain why women and men should have equal voting rights

2 Read the article again. Are the statements true (T) or false (F)?
1 Millicent Fawcett was the leader of the group known as the WSPU.
2 Millicent Fawcett and Emmeline Pankhurst wanted the same thing.
3 Emily Davison believed that what people do is more important than what they say.
4 Emily Davison was well-educated.
5 Emmeline Pankhurst fought in World War I.
6 In 1918 the voting rights of men and women became equal.

3 Read the article again and choose the correct answer, A, B, C or D.
1 In Britain, before 1918, the following group had the right to vote:
   A well-educated women only
   B all men
   C all women
   D well-educated men only
2 The WSPU believed that
   A non-violent protest was not fast enough.
   B non-violent protest was the best method.
   C violent protest was too extreme.
   D violent protest was too slow.
3 The article says that in prison, many of the suffragettes
   A vandalised the prison building.
   B stopped protesting.
   C stopped eating.
   D attacked other prisoners.
4 In 1918
   A suffragettes were given the right to vote.
   B all women were given the right to vote.
   C women who helped in the war were given the right to vote.
   D some women were given the right to vote.

4 Match the underlined words in the article with their definitions.
0 peaceful — non-violent
1 say what you think — _____
2 enthusiastic — _____
3 illegal — _____
4 clever — _____
5 exactly the same — _____
6 carry on — _____

REMEMBER BETTER
To help you revise vocabulary, make revision cards. On one side, write an English sentence with the word you want to remember. On the other side, write either the word in your language or an English synonym. The cards will be easier to use for revision than long lists of words.

Complete the sentences with words from the glossary or underlined words from the article.
0 The information from the witnesses was *vital*. It helped us to catch the suspect quickly.
1 Like people, dolphins are extremely _____ animals. They have good memories, can solve problems and can communicate with each other.
2 Ken is _____ about the environment. He goes to meetings and protests every weekend.
3 Since they employed more officers, the police have made _____ fighting street crime in the area.
4 Your school wants you to _____ on the plans for a new cafeteria. Complete the questionnaire and tell us your preferences.
5 Peter and Greg are _____ twins. They look exactly the same, except Peter is slightly taller.
6 The _____ to learn a new skill in prison helps prisoners to find jobs when they finish their sentences.
7 In the UK it is _____ for anyone under the age of seventeen to drive.
8 Paul studied very hard at university and received a(n) _____ in Engineering.
9 The police investigate violent crimes such as mugging, and _____ crimes such as computer piracy.
10 The main _____ of organisations such as Amnesty International is to protect human rights.
11 If you _____ eating fast food every day, you'll become overweight and unwell.

WORD STORE 8E
Word families

5 Choose the correct options.
1 My brother's football team lost 10–0 on Saturday. He said he had never felt such *humiliation* / *humiliate*.
2 At this company, we do not *discrimination* / *discriminate*. Old or young, male or female, everyone is welcome to apply for a job here.
3 The *segregation* / *segregate* of male and female prisoners is very important for everyone's safety.
4 The *assassination* / *assassinate* of the Prime Minister has shocked the nation. He was killed outside his home on Friday evening.
5 The teachers had to *separation* / *separate* the two boys after they started fighting during the basketball game.

8.5 Grammar

Reported Speech

SHOW WHAT YOU KNOW

1 **Complete the sentences with the correct form of the verbs in brackets.**
  0 The judge _thinks_ (think) graffiti is a serious crime.
  1 The witnesses _____ (speak) to the police yesterday.
  2 We _____ (interview) the victim's family now.
  3 The suspect _____ (carry) a gun when the police arrested him.
  4 I'm looking forward to visiting Alcatraz. I _____ (never/be) inside a prison before.
  5 The drug dealer _____ (already/sell) all his drugs by the time the police arrived at the nightclub.

2 ★ **Complete the sentences with said or told.**
  0 The Prime Minister _said_ that he wanted to end discrimination in schools.
  1 The witness _____ the policeman that the burglar had been dressed in black.
  2 The thief _____ us that he had stolen the bread because he had been hungry.
  3 The lawyer _____ we probably wouldn't win the court case.

3 ★ **Choose the correct options.**
  1 'I don't usually shoplift.'
    The suspect said she *doesn't / didn't* usually shoplift.
  2 'My wife isn't answering her phone!'
    Mr Rey said that his wife *wasn't / isn't* answering her phone.
  3 'The witnesses are late.'
    The judge said the witnesses *were / are* late.
  4 'Two men are robbing the bank!'
    The guard said that two men *are / were* robbing the bank.
  5 'I can see the thief.'
    The woman said she *can / could* see the thief.
  6 'The police aren't doing enough.'
    Mrs Jackson said the police *weren't / aren't* doing enough.

4 ★★ **Complete the reported statements.**
  1 **Beth:** 'I locked the doors.'
    Seth: 'The burglar got in through the window.'
    Beth said she _had locked_ the doors.
    Seth told Beth the burglar _____ through the window.
  2 **Dan:** 'I've spent time in prison.'
    Anne: 'Everyone makes mistakes.'
    Dan told Anne he _____ time in prison.
    Anne said everyone _____ mistakes.
  3 **Bill:** 'I haven't told you the truth.'
    Jill: 'Sometimes I lie to you too.'
    Bill said he _____ Jill the truth.
    Jill said that sometimes she _____ to Bill too.

5 ★★★ **Read the news report and complete speakers' actual words.**

In the case of the stolen exam papers, the teenage suspect said ⁰*he was not guilty* of the theft. He said ¹*he had left his parents' house at 8 a.m.* that day and that ²*he had gone straight to his favourite café*. He told the court ³*he hadn't been near the school that day*. His parents said ⁴*their son was a good boy* and ⁵*he had never broken the law in his life*. They also told the judge that ⁶*he was studying hard for his exams*. The case continues.

  0 'I'm not guilty.'
  1 'I _____ house at 8 a.m.'
  2 'I _____ favourite café.'
  3 'I _____ near the school that day.'
  4 '_____ a good boy.'
  5 'He _____ the law in his life.'
  6 'He _____ hard for his exams.'

SHOW WHAT YOU'VE LEARNT

6 **Complete the reported statements.**
  1 'The vandals are breaking my shop window!' said Carly.
    Carly phoned the police and told them that the vandals _____ shop window.
  2 'I didn't hear the victim's screams,' said the witness.
    The witness said he _____ the victim's screams.
  3 'I don't want to go to prison,' said the man.
    The man told the court he _____ to go to prison.
  4 'There has been sexism in our office,' said the women.
    The women told the journalist there _____ office.
  5 'My father was a burglar,' Phillip said to Ella.
    Phillip told Ella that _____ a burglar.
  6 'We are educating the girls.'
    The volunteer said _____ the girls.

/6

98

8.6 Speaking language practice

Expressing and justifying an opinion

1 Put the words in the correct order to form sentences.

0 thief / shows / the / poster / car / a
  The poster shows a car thief.

1 the / it / on / hand, / one / shocking ... / looks
  _____

2 ... but / it / other / doesn't / the / on / hand, / real / look
  _____

3 find / don't / convincing / it / I / very
  _____

4 memorable / it's / that / is / main / I / the / think / advantage
  _____

5 good / as / think / don't / I / it's / as / this / one
  _____

2 Complete the conversation with the words in the box. There are two extra words.

> advantage   effective   important   like
> main   mind   ~~one~~   other   prefer

A: There's a new advert on TV about the dangers of drinking and driving. Have you seen it?
B: No, I haven't. What's it like?
A: Well, it shows real crashes that drivers had when they were drunk. They were filmed by CCTV cameras and it says that in each crash the driver was killed.
B: It sounds horrible.
A: Well, on the ⁰*one* hand, it gets your attention, but on the ¹_____ hand, it's so awful that it's actually difficult to watch. Mum and I had to look away. To my ²_____ , if you can't actually watch the advert, then it's not very ³_____ .
B: Well, I'm not sure. I think it's ⁴_____ to show the truth. I don't ⁵_____ these fictional adverts because I don't think they are very convincing.
A: Perhaps you are right, but I still ⁶_____ not to watch real accidents. For me, it's too shocking.
B: I know what you mean, but if it stops people drinking and driving, maybe that's the most important thing.

3 Complete the words in the conversation. The first letter of each word is given.

A: Have you seen the new poster on the computer room wall at school?
B: The one about switching off the computers when you leave?
A: No, the one about downloading music illegally.
B: No, I haven't.
A: It ⁰s*hows* statistics about the number of computers that get viruses after downloading.
B: Really?
A: Yeah, I like it ¹b_____ the statistics are quite interesting. It's amazing how many viruses there are in the files that people share and copy. I don't want my computer to get one, so I ²f_____ it quite convincing.
B: I don't think it's as convincing ³a_____ a poster that says that it's not fair to musicians. I usually buy music and support my favourite bands.
A: You're right. Anyway, when people download music illegally, another ⁴d_____ is that the quality of the files is sometimes really bad and then the music doesn't sound as good.
B: Yep. I ⁵p_____ to pay and get the best quality.

4 Read the conversation in Exercise 3 again. Which poster is on the computer room wall at school?

8.7 Writing
A reader's comment

1 Complete the phrases with the words in the box. There are two extra words.

> agree   also   fact   hand   on   personally
> ~~reason~~   what   why

1 For this _reason_, I …   C
2 _____, I believe that …
3 That's _____ …
4 I _____ agree that …
5 _____ is more, I think that …
6 In _____, …
7 _____ the other hand, I …

2 Mark the phrases in Exercise 1 as G for *giving an opinion*, A for *adding further points*, O for *giving an opposite opinion* or C for *concluding*.

3 Put the groups of sentences in the correct order.

Topic 1

a I believe that smoking in all public places should be illegal.   _1_
b However, I think that it is OK for adults to smoke in their own homes.
c I also agree that all cigarette advertising should be banned.
d Therefore, I don't think that cigarettes should be illegal.

Topic 2

a In fact, I think it is just the same as stealing a CD from a shop.
b Personally, I believe that downloading music illegally is a crime.
c On the other hand, I think music is very expensive to buy.

4 Read the comment and replace the underlined phrases with phrases from Exercise 1. Sometimes more than one answer is possible.

> I enjoyed your article about the irresponsible people who throw their rubbish in the streets, parks and rivers of our city.
>
> _2_ ᵃ<u>I think</u> dropping rubbish in the wrong place is definitely a crime. ᵇ___ <u>I also think that</u> the police should do much more to catch the people who do it. ᶜ___ <u>Moreover, I think that</u> people who are caught, should have to clean up all the rubbish in a certain area as a punishment. ᵈ___ <u>However,</u> I agree it would be helpful if there were more rubbish bins in our streets and parks. ᵉ___ <u>Therefore,</u> I think the city should invest more money in keeping our city clean, as well as catching the selfish people who drop rubbish.

SHOW WHAT YOU'VE LEARNT

5 You have just read the article below on a news website. Write a reader's comment giving your opinion and saying what you agree and disagree with.

> **NEWSFOCUS.com**
>
> **Daily discussion**
>
> **Kids who skip school – who is to blame?**
>
> Yesterday the parents of a teenage girl who skipped school over fifty times in one school year were fined €2,000. The judge said that the parents were responsible for the behaviour of their daughter. So who is to blame? Is it really the parents, the kids or the school that should take responsibility?
>
> Personally, I believe that parents should control the behaviour of their teenage children. However, it is impossible for mums and dads to know what their children are doing all the time. Most teenagers want to be treated as adults, so they should behave like adults and go to lessons, even if they find them boring. What is more, the school is also responsible for its students during school hours.
>
> I think the judge was wrong to fine the parents.
>
> **Join the Daily discussion** and tell us what you think in our **Reader's comments** section below.

Write your comment in about 100 words.

SHOW THAT YOU'VE CHECKED

In my reader's comment:

- I have given my opinion about the article.
- I have said what I agree with and why.
- I have said what I disagree with and why.
- I have used linkers such as *however* and *on the other hand* to show contrast.
- I have used words and phrases such as *therefore* and *that's why* to give a conclusion.
- I have checked my spelling and punctuation.
- I have written about 100 words.

8.8 Use of English

Four-option multiple choice

1 Read the text below and choose the correct word (A, B, C or D) for each space.

Where are the police?

Many older people today say that crime is increasing because the police aren't dealing ^{0}___ it well. They think that too many policemen ^{1}___ been taken off the streets. In the past they ^{2}___ to see policemen walking through town centres. Today a ^{3}___ of them are working at desks in the police station or driving around in cars. People think that because of this, we aren't as safe as before.

In fact, this isn't really true. Crime has changed a lot over the years. Today ^{4}___ use the Internet to organise and to ^{5}___ crimes. The police need to find new methods to track them. Also, instead of having policemen in the town centres and public places, there are cameras to watch and record crimes.

However, not everybody likes cameras. Sixty-year-old Martin Jones was ^{6}___ driving too fast by a camera last week. He ^{7}___ our reporter that he hadn't been speeding and that the camera had ^{8}___ ! He also said that he thought the police should focus on real criminals who had ^{9}___ the law and not try to get money from ^{10}___ people. What's your opinion? Post a comment after this article.

0	A of	B on	(C with)	D by
1	A are	B have	C had	D were
2	A needed	B had	C used	D often
3	A some	B lot	C little	D many
4	A burglars	B suspects	C pirates	D criminals
5	A rob	B commit	C do	D collect
6	A found	B taken	C reported	D caught
7	A said	B asked	C told	D complained
8	A mistaken	B faked	C gone	D lied
9	A broken	B crashed	C arrested	D committed
10	A true	B innocent	C victim	D loyal

TIPS:

Question 1: Which word do you need to complete this passive form?
Question 2: Which word do we use to talk about past habits or states?
Question 3: Be careful: only one of the words can be used with *a* for countable nouns.

Sentence transformations

2 Here are some sentences about going to the sales. For each question, complete the second sentence so that it means the same as the first. Use no more than three words.

0 I don't usually go to town when there are sales because it's crowded.
I usually avoid *going* to town when there are sales because it's crowded.

1 Last week Lara said, 'I want to go to the sales.'
Last week Lara said _____ to go to the sales.

2 I thought I might find something cheap, so I agreed to go with her.
I hoped to pick _____ , so I agreed to go with her.

3 It was the first time I had ever seen so many people in one shop!
I _____ so many people in one shop before!

4 I was happy because they had reduced a really nice laptop.
I was happy because a really nice laptop _____ .

5 I couldn't see an assistant, so I couldn't ask about the price of a printer.
There _____ assistants, so I couldn't ask about the price of a printer.

TIPS:

Question 1: Remember to change the tense in the reported statement.
Question 2: You need three words to complete this expression meaning 'buy something for less than its usual price'.
Question 3: You need to replace *ever* with *never* here.

8.9 Self-assessment

1 For each learning objective, tick the box that best matches your ability.

☺☺ = I understand and can help a friend.   ☹ = I understand some, but have some questions.
☺ = I understand and can do it by myself.   ☹☹ = I do not understand.

			☺☺	☺	☹	☹☹	Need help?
8.1	Vocabulary	I can talk about crime and punishment.					Students' Book pages 96–97 Word Store page 17 Workbook pages 92–93
8.2	Grammar	I can use the Past Perfect to talk about past events.					Students' Book page 98 Workbook page 94
8.3	Listening	I can identify specific detail in an interview.					Students' Book page 99 Workbook page 95
8.4	Reading	I can find specific detail in an article.					Students' Book pages 100–101 Workbook pages 96–97
8.5	Grammar	I can report what other people have said.					Students' Book page 102 Workbook page 98
8.6	Speaking	I can choose from options and justify my choice.					Students' Book page 103 Workbook page 99
8.7	Writing	I can give and support my opinion in writing.					Students' Book pages 104–105 Workbook page 100

2 What can you remember from this unit?

New words I learned (the words you most want to remember from this unit)	Expressions and phrases I liked (any expressions or phrases you think sound nice, useful or funny)	English I heard or read outside class (e.g. from websites, books, adverts, films, music)

8.10 Self-check

1 Choose the odd one out in each group.

0	prime minster	(elections)	president	queen
1	separation	assassination	humiliate	segregation
2	mugger	arson	burglary	drug dealing
3	thief	robbery	vandal	murderer
4	suspect	victim	witness	crime
5	shoplift	steal	vandalise	burglar

/5

2 Change the underlined words to give the opposite meaning. The first letter of each word is given.

0 I thought the programme about piracy was boring. — fascinating
1 This is the only place in the market where you can buy fake watches. — g_____
2 The celebrity shoplifter's court case will begin tomorrow. — e_____
3 The answer to question number 5 is true. — f_____
4 The judge in the corruption case said the minister was guilty. — i_____
5 Did he tell the truth? I'm not sure I believe him. — a l_____

/5

3 Complete the words in the sentences. Some letters are given.

0 Police have arrested three suspects in the murder case but they don't have a lot of evidence yet.
1 Last night a man was m_____d outside his home. Police say the dead man was a drug dealer.
2 V_____s sprayed graffiti and broke windows at a shopping centre on Friday evening.
3 Police are currently interviewing two w_____s who saw the thief when he was leaving the jewellery store.
4 The arsonist had set f_____e to the car while the owners were away on holiday.
5 S_____g is a real problem. Our chain of stores loses thousands of euros every year.

/5

4 Complete the sentences with the Past Simple or Past Perfect form of the verbs in brackets.

0 Connor had forgotten (forget) to wash his hands before he sat down for dinner.
1 Eliza _____ (be) sad because her boyfriend hadn't remembered her birthday.
2 When Neil arrived at the restaurant, everyone _____ (already/order) their food.
3 By the time Jill _____ (get) home, it had started to snow.
4 Linda felt much better after she _____ (speak) to her best friend about the problem.
5 Luckily, I had just left Jeanette's house when I _____ (realise) I didn't have my keys.

/5

5 Complete the reported statements.

0 Ross said, 'I am a witness.'
Ross told me he was a witness.
1 Abi said, 'I'm waiting for the police to arrive.'
Abi told us _____ for the police to arrive.
2 Nick said, 'I didn't tell the truth.'
Nick said _____ the truth.
3 Catherine said, 'I've never been a victim of crime.'
Catherine told them _____ a victim of crime.
4 Amy said, 'I didn't steal anything.'
Amy said _____ anything.
5 Mia said, 'I'm reading a crime story.'
Mia told me _____ a crime story.

/5

6 Choose the correct answer, A, B or C, to complete both sentences in each pair.

0 We are going to ___ the new James Bond film tonight.
I don't need a ___ because I've got the time on my phone.
A see   B clock   (C watch)

1 Jenny told ___ she was going to be late.
Hey! Those belong to ___ . You can't just use my things.
A me   B I   C that

2 The judge said the suspect was ___ guilty and sent him home.
I didn't recognise the man because I had ___ seen him before.
A definitely   B not   C never

3 Two men were arrested yesterday for dealing ___ at a party.
Grandma takes several different ___ each day to keep her healthy.
A cases   B pirate software   C drugs

4 The mugger ___ a knife in his jacket.
The suspect said she ___ left the building half an hour before the fire started.
A has   B had   C have

5 Police found ___ in the back of the woman's car.
___ suggests that teenagers need much more sleep than adults.
A witnesses   B courts   C evidence

/5

Total /30

103

EXAM STRATEGIES

Focus gives practice of the exam tasks found in upper secondary school leaving exams, as well as international exams like PET, Cambridge English: First (FCE), Trinity and PTE (Pearson Test of English). It includes exercises which will help you prepare for all parts of a typical exam – Listening, Reading, Grammar/Use of English, Speaking and Writing. In addition, in this section you will find some useful tips to help you confidently approach different types of exam tasks.

Listening
General guidelines
Do
- Before listening to a recording, read the instructions and statements/questions in the task carefully. Try to think about what kind of information you're going to hear (e.g. how many speakers there could be and what words/expressions they might use).
- When listening for the first time, look at the statements/questions in the task again and note down your answers.
- Before listening to the recording the second time, read all the questions again, especially those you didn't answer the first time. Note down your new answers and check your answers from the first listening.

Don't
- Don't worry if you don't understand some words. You don't need to understand all of the recording to do the task.
- If you don't understand part of the text at first, don't give up listening! Remember: there will be another chance to listen and your understanding of other parts of the recording will help you the second time.
- Don't spend too much time on the questions which you don't know how to answer. You can come back to them later. Move on to the next question.
- Don't leave any questions unanswered. If you're not sure, have a guess!

Multiple choice tasks
- Remember that the questions in the task usually come in the same order as the information in the recording.
- If you have picture options, look at the pictures and questions very carefully to check that you understand what the pictures show. This will give you an idea of what sort of information to listen for.
- When listening to the recording for the first time, note down your own answers to the questions. Then compare them to the options in the task and choose the ones which are closest in meaning to yours.
- Be careful of the answers which sound or look very similar to the information in the recording. They are often wrong. Something related to each option will be in the recording but only one option will answer the question correctly.
- With text options for multiple choice questions, the wording of the correct answer will not be exactly the same as in the recording. The correct answer will be said in different words.
- If you're not sure which option to choose, use the method of elimination: start by crossing out the answers which are definitely wrong, then those which you think are probably wrong, until you are left with only one option.

- Sometimes when you're answering a question or questions about a conversation, you need to remember to listen for the right speaker. The other options may be mentioned, but not by the person you are asked about.

True/False tasks
- Remember that the questions are usually in the same order as the information in the recording.
- When deciding if a statement is true or false, make sure that you use the information in the recording, not your personal opinions or knowledge.
- Remember that statements in exam questions don't usually use the same words as in the recording. Words and expressions from the recording are often rephrased.

Note completion
- You may need to listen for information to complete some sentences. Usually, you will need a maximum of a couple of words. You will definitely hear the words in the recording that you need to write.
- If you need to write a common word, you will be expected to spell it correctly. Sometimes a name that you need will be spelled for you in the recording. Listen carefully for this.
- Read the notes you need to complete carefully before you hear the recording for the first time so that you have an idea of what the recording is about. Try to predict from the sentences what sort of words or information you need to listen for. You might be able to guess that you need to listen for a place, a name, a number etc.
- Be careful about distraction in the recording. For example, if you think you need to listen for a number, there could be another number mentioned before or after the key information, but it will not be correct.

Reading
General guidelines
Do
- Before you start reading the text, read the instructions for the task carefully. Each task will ask you to do different things.
- Use the clues in the text to help you understand the context. The title and any photos or other visuals will help you with the main topic and the first sentences of paragraphs often summarise their content.
- Read the text through completely before you try to answer the question(s). This gives you a good idea of the general meaning and helps you with longer texts, where you need to answer a question about a particular section.
- Underline parts of the text which contain language relevant to the questions (single words, phrases, sentences, paragraphs).

Don't
- Don't try to understand every word in a text. You don't need to know every single word to do the task. You can try to guess the meaning of unknown words using different techniques (e.g. using the context to guess the meaning, noticing similarities to words in your native language).
- Don't leave any questions unanswered. If you are not sure, guess!

EXAM STRATEGIES

- Don't spend too much time on any one particular task. Remember that time in the exam is limited and you should try to do all of the tasks.

Multiple choice tasks
- With longer texts, decide which sections of the text have the answers to the questions.
- Focus on the detail of a paragraph or sentence. An incorrect answer might only differ from the correct one in a detail such as the verb tense used.
- Remember that the words in the correct option will not be the same as those in the text. They will be rephrased.
- Don't be attracted by options that use similar wording. Only one option will be exactly what you need.
- Eliminate the answers which you feel sure are wrong, then make your final choice.

True/False tasks
- Remember that the questions are usually in the same order as the information in the text.
- When deciding if a statement is true or false, make sure that you base your choice on the information in the text, not your personal opinions or knowledge.
- Remember that statements in exam questions don't usually use the same words as in the text. Words and expressions from the text are often rephrased.

Matching tasks
- You will need to match descriptions of people with different texts. Start by reading the descriptions and underline important information. Then do the same with the texts.
- Don't decide too quickly if you see one word that seems to match. Read the texts carefully to check if it's really correct.
- Remember that important information will be rephrased.

Grammar/Use of English
General guidelines
Do
- Before you start reading the text, read the instructions for the task carefully. The task will affect the way you read the text.
- When a text has a title, read it carefully as this can help you predict the main idea of the text.
- Where there are gaps in the text, read it through completely without worrying about the gaps to get the general idea of the text.
- There will be an example answer for each task. Make sure you look at it carefully as it will help you understand what you need to do.

Don't
- Don't try to understand every word in a text. You don't need to know every single word to do the task. You can try to guess the meaning of unknown words using different techniques (e.g. guessing on the basis of the context or the grammatical form, noticing similarities to words in your native language).
- Don't leave any questions unanswered. If you are not sure, guess!
- Don't spend too much time on any one particular task. Remember that time in the exam is limited and you should try to do all of the tasks.

Multiple choice cloze
- Read the text first to have an idea what each of its parts is about. Try to understand as much as you can while ignoring the gaps.
- Different types of words are tested in this exam task. For example, you may need to complete a phrasal verb, choose a correct linker or choose between words with similar meanings.
- Read the gap-fill options carefully before deciding which one to choose.
- When deciding which options to use to complete the gaps, look at the words before and after the gaps. They will give you clues about which option is correct (e.g. look for linkers, pronouns, adjectives and adverbs).
- Remember that the word you choose must fit grammatically into the sentence and must also have the correct meaning.
- When you've finished, always reread the text to see that it follows logically.

Open cloze
- Read the text first to have an idea what each of its parts is about. Try to understand as much as you can while ignoring the gaps.
- Different types of words are tested in this exam task. For example, you may need to complete a phrasal verb or find a correct linker, article, auxiliary verb, etc.
- When deciding which word to use to complete the gaps, look at the words before and after the gaps. They will give you clues about what sort of word you are looking for.
- Remember that the word you choose must fit grammatically into the sentence and must also have the correct meaning.
- When you've finished, always reread the text to see that it follows logically.

Word formation
- Read the text first to have an idea what each of its parts is about. Try to understand as much as you can while ignoring the gaps.
- You need to think carefully about how to change the word so that it fits grammatically into the sentence – is it an adjective, an adverb, etc.? You should also consider the meaning – for example, do you need a negative or positive meaning?
- Remember that as well as adding prefixes and suffixes to a word, you may also need to make other changes.
- When you've finished, always reread the text to see that it follows logically.

Key word transformations
- Make sure you read the first sentences carefully and understand the meaning. The second sentence must be as close to that meaning as possible.
- Read the parts of the second sentence which you have to complete carefully too, as parts of it will affect how you complete it. Look for any tense changes or whether you need a singular or plural verb, a negative or a question form, etc
- Remember that there is a word limit. Always check your number of words as if you have too many, it may mean that you've gone wrong somewhere. A contraction (e.g. *don't*) counts as two words, not one.

EXAM STRATEGIES

Writing
General guidelines
At this level exam tasks include writing a card, a note, a story or an email. You may have part of an email to reply to or some points to include in a card or notes. If you're writing a card or a note, the word limit will be quite short: 35–45 words. For the longer piece, it will be about 100 words.

When doing the writing tasks, you need to be careful that you write in the correct style. To help you do this we have provided a reference section in this Workbook (FUNCTION PHRASE BANK, pages 107–108).

Do
- Think carefully about what kind of writing task it is.
- Read carefully all the information that needs to be included in your writing.
- Write a plan noting down the information you want to include in each paragraph. Check that you have included all the information asked for in the question. Remember to use linkers so that your writing is easy to follow.
- Check the style of your writing and make sure it's right for the task (e.g. have you used formal or informal language?).
- Check that you have an introduction, a main body and a conclusion in your writing, that you have divided a longer piece of work into paragraphs and that you have written the right number of words.
- Finally, check your grammar and spelling.

Don't
- Don't write too much or too little.
- Try not to repeat the same information.
- Try not to use the same words and phrases more than once, use a variety of vocabulary and a range of grammatical structures.

Speaking
General guidelines
The FUNCTION PHRASE BANK (pages 109–110), the VOCABULARY BANK (pages 111–120) and the related PRACTICE EXERCISES (pages 121–127) will help you prepare for speaking tasks.

Do
- Listen carefully to the examiner's questions.
- If you are not sure whether you have understood what the examiner has said, ask them to repeat the question.
- If you need more time to decide what to say, ask the examiner to repeat the question and then repeat or paraphrase it, and use 'filler' phrases giving you time to think (e.g. *Let me think ..., It's difficult to say ...*
- If you cannot remember a word, don't panic! Try to use different words to say the same thing.).
- Make sure you remember that your partner needs to speak as much as you do! Try not to speak too much and prevent your partner from speaking. Also speak enough so that the examiner can assess your level.
- Remember that the examiner has a time limit for each part of the test. If he/she stops you while you're speaking, it's because you have spoken for longer than necessary.
- Try to keep speaking rather than finish your one-minute talk or discussion early. It is better to be interrupted because you're talking too much than to say too little.
- When you are asked to discuss something with your partner, make sure you interact by asking for his/her opinion. Don't take it in turns to give your ideas. It should be a real conversation.

Don't
- Try not to repeat the same phrases over and over. Show that you know a range of vocabulary and that you can use different grammatical structures. Don't ask the examiner to explain something. He/She can only repeat an instruction.
- Don't try to learn whole sentences or detailed answers to things you think you might be asked about. Speak and respond as naturally as possible.

FUNCTION PHRASE BANK, WRITING

Accepting suggestions

That sounds fantastic!
I'd love to go.
Well, it's worth a try.
I suppose it'll work.

Agreeing with opinions

I (completely) agree that/with …
I couldn't agree more that/with …
That's fine with me.
I think so too.

Apologising

Informal phrases

I'm really sorry (that) …
Sorry to bother you.
Sorry I haven't written for so long./Sorry for not writing for so long.
I'm writing to tell you how sorry I am to/about …
It will never happen again.

Formal phrases

I apologise for …
Please accept my apology for …

Closing formulas: emails and letters

Informal phrases

Best wishes,
Bye for now,
See you!
Love,
Take care,
All the best,

Formal phrases

Yours sincerely,
Regards,

Contacting people

Ways to contact people

If you have any information, please contact/call/leave a message for Alison on (0961224466).
If you are interested in …, call (John/Ms White)
To join us, call …
Call me on … for more details.

Maintaining contact

Drop me a line sometime.
I hope to hear from you soon.
Give me a call later.
Let me know if you can make it or not.
I was glad to hear about …

Describing lost property

I lost (my bag/passport/coat/dog).

Describing features

It is/was …
Size: huge/tiny/35 cm x 25 cm/big.
Shape: round/rectangular/square/narrow.
Colour: white/red and brown/light/dark green.
Material: made of leather/plastic/linen.
Age: new/young/old/six years old/modern/ancient.
It has/had (two handles/a leather strap/a blue cover/two pockets/short sleeves/a black tail).

Reasons for search

I keep (all my files there).
It was something I borrowed/got as a birthday present.
It is of great value./It's a really precious thing.
I can't live without it.
It means a lot to me.

Disagreeing

I disagree that/with …/I don't agree that/with …
I am totally against …
I see what you mean, but …
I see your point, but …
I'm afraid I can't agree with …
I'm not convinced about …
I don't think it's the best solution.

Encouraging participation

Come on, don't be afraid/it's not difficult/it's easy!
Why don't you come …?
Come and tell us what you think.
Come and have fun!
Don't miss it!

Ending an email/a letter

Informal phrases

It was good to hear from you.
Email me soon.
I'd better get going./I must be going now./Got to go now.
Looking forward to your news/to hearing from you again.
Say hello to …
Give my love/my regards to …
Have a nice (trip).
See you (soon/in the summer).
Write soon.
Keep in touch!

Formal phrases

I look forward to hearing from you/your reply.
I hope to hear from you soon.

Expressing opinions

I believe/think/feel (that) …
I really believe (that) …
In my opinion/view, …/To my mind, …
The way I see it, …
It seems/appears to me (that) …
My opinion is that …
As far as I am concerned, …

107

FUNCTION PHRASE BANK, WRITING

Expressing preferences

I really enjoy/like/love … because …
I prefer … to …
I'd like/I hope to …
I find … boring/dull.
I don't like/I can't stand/I really hate …
It's not really my thing.

Giving advice

You should/ought to …
You'd better …
If I were you, I would …
It might be a good idea (for you) to …
Why don't you …?
Have you thought of/about …?

Inviting

I'd like to invite you to …
I'd like you to come …
Would you like to come to …?
I'm having (a party).
I hope you can make it.
Would you like to come? If you want, you can bring a friend.
You are welcome to …
Join us today!
Come and meet me …
Why don't you come …?

Making requests and enquiries

Informal phrases

Can you …, please?/Could you …?
Do you think you could …?
Let me know if you can …
Could you tell me …?

Formal phrases

Would it be possible for you to …?
I'd be grateful if you could …
I wonder if I could ask you to/for …
I'm writing to ask for your help/advice …
I'm writing to enquire about …

Making suggestions

I think I/you/we should (go to) …
Perhaps I/you/we could (go to) …
What do you think about (going to) …?
What/How about (going to) …?
How do you feel about (going to) …?
Would you like me to …?
Why don't we (go) to …?
Let's (go to) …
Shall we (go to) …?
Do you fancy (going to) …?

Opening formulas: emails and letters

Informal phrases

Dear Margaret,
Hi Anne,

Neutral phrase

Dear Mr and Mrs Edwards,
Dear Ms Brennon,

Refusing suggestions

It doesn't sound very good.
I don't think I fancy it.
I'm sorry, but I can't join you.
I'm not really into …
I've got some doubts about it.
I don't see how it could work.
Actually, I would prefer not to.

Starting an email/a letter

Informal phrases

It was good to hear from you.
I hope you're doing well/you're fine/you're OK.
How are things with you?
I'm writing to tell you …
Thanks for your letter.
I wanted to/must tell you about …
Just a quick email to tell you …

Neutral phrases

I am writing to thank you for …

Telling a story

It all happened some time ago.
It was three years ago.
While I (was playing), …
First, …
Then …
Finally, …
Suddenly, …
Unfortunately, …
Fortunately, …

Thanking people

Informal phrases

I'm writing to thank you for …
Thank you so much.
It was so/really/very kind of you to …

Neutral phrases

I really appreciate your help.
Thank you for sending it back to me.
I am really grateful for your help.
It's very kind of you.

FUNCTION PHRASE BANK, SPEAKING

Unit 1

Saying you are similar

A: I love travelling and meeting new people.
B: Me too.

A: I don't really like rock or heavy metal.
B: Me neither.

Showing interest

A: I've got loads of friends and they want to meet you.
B: Really? That's cool!

A: I've just got one sister. She's a model.
B: Is she?

A: She's training to be a pilot.
B: Wow, that's interesting!

Saying you are different

A: I'm not very keen on tea.
B: Really? I love it.

A: I don't like travelling.
B: Don't you? Oh, I do.

A: I play the violin.
B: Do you? Right …

Unit 2

Telling a story

Using the right tenses

The sun was shining and I was enjoying myself.
The weather changed. I couldn't see the path.

Using linkers

To start with,/At first, …
Suddenly,/All of a sudden,/Luckily,/Fortunately, …
Unfortunately, …
In the end,/Eventually,/Finally, …

Saying how you felt

I was excited/frightened/relieved/surprised/shocked/worried.

Making a 'final comment'

It was the best/worst day of my life!
I'll never forget the look on his face!
I'll never do it again.

Listening to a story

Neutral response

Really?/Oh dear!/Oh no!

Strong response

That sounds amazing/funny/frightening!
What a great story/a nightmare!

Responding with questions

What happened?
What did you do?

Unit 3

Beginning a description

In this photo, I can see/there is/there are …
This photo shows …

Saying where (place)

There are …, so I think they're (in a bookshop/art gallery/ at a concert).

Saying where (in the photo)

in the background/in the middle/in the foreground
on the left/on the right
in front of/behind/next to

Speculating

He/She looks (shy/bored/tired)
She's probably …
Perhaps/Maybe/I imagine/I'm sure …

Giving your opinion

I think/I don't think …
Personally,/In my opinion, …

Unit 4

Making suggestions

Do you fancy (going to) …?
Let's (go to) …
What/How about (going to) …?
We could (go to) …
(I think) we should (go to) …
What about (going to) …?
Why don't we (go to) …?

Agreeing with suggestions

(That's a) good/great idea!
(That) sounds good/great!
Why not!

Disagreeing with suggestions

(I'm sorry,) I'm not keen on …
I don't really like …
I'd rather (go to) …
I'm not sure about that.
Let's (go to) … instead.

109

FUNCTION PHRASE BANK, SPEAKING

Unit 5

Giving an opinion

I think …
I don't think …
Personally, I think/In my opinion, …
I really believe …
If you ask me, …

Agreeing

I couldn't agree more.
That's a good point.

Disagreeing politely

I see what you mean, but …
That's true, but …
I'm not so sure.

Disagreeing

I totally disagree!
Oh come on! That's nonsense.

Unit 6

Asking for advice

What do you think I should do?
Do you have any tips/ideas on how to …?

Giving advice

You should …
I think you should …
I don't think you should …
Why don't you …?
My best advice would be to …
It's a good idea to …
If I were you, I'd …

Accepting advice

Thanks, that's really helpful.
That's great advice. Thanks!

Rejecting advice

I'm not sure that's a good idea.

Unit 7

Shopping for clothes

Shop assistant

Can I help you?
Would you like to try it on?
The changing rooms are over there.
How would you like to pay?
Make sure you keep your receipt.

Customer

Excuse me, I'm looking for (a top).
I'm a size 10.
Do you have this in a size 12, please?
I'll take it.
Cash, please./By credit card.
If it doesn't fit, can we get a refund?

Complaining

Shop assistant

What's wrong with it?
Do you have your receipt?
We can exchange it for a new one.

Customer

I bought this dress last week but the zip doesn't work.
I think it's faulty./It shrank./There's a hole in it.
The colour ran.
I'd like a refund, please.

Unit 8

Describing a picture

The picture shows …
On the one hand, … but on the other hand, …

Justifying your choice and rejecting other options

I prefer …
I don't like … because …
I don't find it very (convincing/interesting/shocking).

Giving your opinion

To my mind, …
I think it's important to …
I think the main advantage/disadvantage is that …
I don't think … is/are as (good/useful/effective) as …

VOCABULARY BANK

Translate the words and phrases.

People

Age
adult _____
elderly _____
old _____
teenage _____
teenager _____
young _____
youth _____

Personality
able to _____
adorable _____
arrogant _____
bad-tempered _____
boring _____
brave _____
bravery _____
caring _____
cheerful _____
clever _____
confident _____
cooperative _____
cowardly _____
crazy _____
creative _____
dishonest _____
disloyal _____
dull _____
elegance _____
elegant _____
experienced _____
fair _____
fit _____
friendly _____
funny _____
generosity _____
generous _____
good at _____
greed _____
greedy _____
grumpy _____
hard-working _____
helpful _____
honest _____
honesty _____
independent _____
inexperienced _____
insensitive _____
interesting _____
irresponsible _____
kind _____
laziness _____
lazy _____
liar _____
loyal _____
loyalty _____
mean _____
miserable _____
modest _____
modesty _____
mysterious _____
outgoing _____
passion _____
passionate _____
pessimistic _____
popular _____
positive _____
quiet _____
reliable _____
responsibility _____
responsible _____
selfish _____
sensible _____
sensitive to _____
serious _____
shy _____
sociable _____
stupid _____
successful _____
sure of yourself _____
talented _____
team-player _____
uncommunicative _____
uncooperative _____
unfair _____
unfit _____
unhelpful _____
unkind _____
unpopular _____
unsuccessful _____

Feelings and emotions
anger _____
angry _____
bad mood _____
bored _____
breathe a sigh of relief _____
crazy about _____
disappointed with _____
excited _____
excitement _____
exhausted _____
frightened _____
go crazy _____
inspired by _____
interested in _____
involved in _____
irritated _____
jealous _____
jealousy _____
keen on _____
laugh _____
negative about _____
nervous _____
obsessed with _____
proud _____
serious about _____
stressed about _____
tired _____

Body language
bite your nails _____
blink your eyes _____
cross your arms _____
fiddle with your hair _____
raise your eyebrows _____
stare at _____

Clothes and accessories
casual clothes _____
comfortable _____
designer clothes _____
dress smartly _____
fashionable _____
fit _____
formal clothes _____
friendship bracelet _____
hoodie _____
jacket _____

VOCABULARY BANK

jeans _____
jewellery _____
jumper _____
leisurewear _____
necklace _____
old-fashioned _____
purse _____
put on _____
skinny jeans _____
stylish _____
suit (n) _____
suit (v) _____
sweatpants _____
swimwear _____
T-shirt _____
take off _____
tie _____
uniform _____
wallet _____
wear _____
winter coat _____

Shoes
ballet flats _____
boots _____
flip-flops _____
high heels _____
sandals _____
slippers _____
trainers _____

Beauty
anti-aging _____
beauty products _____
face cream _____
get a tattoo _____
good-looking _____
have a haircut _____
have a shave _____
make-up _____
manicure _____
perfume _____
shampoo _____
toiletries _____
toothpaste _____

Home

Types of houses
apartment _____
bungalow _____
cottage _____
detached house _____
eco-house _____
flat _____
houseboat _____
semi-detached house _____
studio apartment _____
terraced house _____

Location
in a village _____
in the city centre _____
in the countryside _____
in the suburbs _____
near the sea _____
on a housing estate _____
on the edge of the city _____

Building materials
brick _____
concrete _____
mud _____
stone _____
wood _____

House and garden
back door _____
basement _____
bedroom _____
ceiling _____
floor _____
front door _____
kitchen _____
path _____
patio _____
pond _____
porch _____
roof _____
shed _____
sitting room/living room _____
skylight _____
stairs _____
stone wall _____
toilet _____
wall _____
windowsill _____

Furniture and equipment
armchair _____
beanbag _____
bed _____
bedside table _____
blinds _____
bookcase _____
bookshelf _____
carpet _____
central heating _____
cooker _____
couch _____
cupboard _____
curtain _____
cushion _____
desk _____
duvet _____
DVD player _____
electricity _____
floorboard _____
fridge/refrigerator _____
game console _____
interior décor _____
kitchen sink _____
light bulb _____
poster _____
rug _____
shelf _____
shower _____
single bed _____
solar panel _____
television/TV _____
uncluttered _____
vacuum cleaner _____
wardrobe _____
washing machine _____
wood-burner _____
worktop _____

Description
comfortable _____
cosy _____

VOCABULARY BANK

lots of natural light _____
modern _____
open-plan _____
peaceful _____
rural _____
spacious _____
traditional _____

Moving house
house-warming party _____
move (house) _____
neighbour _____
neighbourhood _____
share a room with sb _____

Housework
do the cooking _____
do the gardening _____
do the housework _____
do the ironing _____
do the shopping _____
do the washing _____
do the washing-up _____
make a mess _____
make dinner _____
make your bed _____
tidy (up) _____
tidy your room _____

School

Subjects and courses
Architecture _____
Art _____
Art History _____
Design and Technology _____
Engineering _____
English _____
Geography _____
Greek _____
Latin _____
Law _____
Maths _____
Medicine _____
Music _____
Physical Education (PE) _____
Reading _____

Science _____
Writing _____

Types of school
elementary school/primary school _____
nursery _____
secondary school _____
single-sex school _____
university _____

Places at school
canteen _____
classroom _____
gym _____
lab _____
playground _____
school gate _____

Education
ability _____
academic _____
apply for (a place) _____
attend a school _____
be a fast learner _____
classmate _____
compulsory _____
demanding _____
do a course _____
do a subject _____
do your homework _____
do/take an exam _____
drop a subject _____
educate _____
entrance exam _____
fail an exam _____
field trip _____
flexible timetable _____
focus on _____
gap year _____
get a place at university _____
get good marks _____
get into university _____
grade/mark _____
graduate (n) _____
graduate (v) _____
knowledge _____

learn by heart/memorise _____
leave school _____
literate _____
miss/skip lessons _____
pass an exam _____
pronunciation _____
revise _____
revision _____
rigid timetable _____
schedule _____
school uniform _____
schoolwork _____
study _____
swipe card _____
take a break _____
tuition fee _____
vocabulary _____

Work

Jobs
accountant _____
airline pilot _____
babysitter/childminder _____
banker _____
beautician _____
builder _____
bus driver _____
businessman _____
businessperson _____
camp supervisor _____
captain _____
carer _____
carpenter _____
computer programmer _____
cook _____
design consultant _____
doctor _____
driving instructor _____
electrician _____
engineer _____
estate agent _____
farmer _____
flight attendant _____
hairdresser _____
interpreter _____

VOCABULARY BANK

journalist _____
lifeguard _____
musician _____
nurse _____
office assistant _____
plumber _____
police officer _____
politician _____
receptionist _____
scientist _____
secondary school teacher _____
servant _____
shop assistant _____
skiing instructor _____
specialist _____
surgeon _____
taxi driver _____
tourist guide _____
travel agent _____

Looking for a job
apply for a job _____
candidate _____
communication skills/people skills _____
contact details _____
CV _____
driving licence _____
enclose _____
experience _____
get a good job _____
interview _____
job advert/advertisement _____
look for a job _____
self-confidence _____
university degree _____
work experience _____

Employment
banking _____
be badly-paid _____
be on your feet all day _____
be self-employed _____
be well-paid _____
be/work in (IT) _____
boss _____
building site _____

career _____
chairperson _____
chill out _____
colleague _____
conference call _____
director _____
do physical work _____
do/work flexible hours _____
do/work long hours _____
do/work overtime _____
do/work regular office hours _____
employee _____
employer _____
finish work _____
get a bonus _____
get/earn a high/an average salary _____
get/earn low wages _____
get/have a pay rise _____
get/have/take a day off _____
get/have/take five weeks' paid holiday _____
have a job _____
holiday job _____
income _____
make a living _____
male-dominated job _____
manager _____
manual job _____
marketing _____
office _____
oil industry _____
on duty _____
part-time job _____
personal skills _____
position _____
profession _____
promotion _____
retail _____
retire _____
staff _____
start work _____
take time off _____
training _____
work for (a construction company) _____

work for/at (Citibank) _____
work from home _____
work full-time _____
work in (a hospital/advertising) _____
work in/as part of a team _____
work outside _____
work with your hands _____

Family and social life

Family members
aunt _____
cousin _____
father-in-law _____
granddaughter _____
grandma/grandmother _____
grandpa/granddad _____
grandparents _____
grandson _____
husband _____
mother-in-law _____
nephew _____
niece _____
uncle _____
wife _____

Relationships
adapt to _____
admire _____
argue/fight _____
avoid sth _____
be friendly with _____
behave badly _____
care about _____
friendship _____
generation _____
get married _____
get on with _____
have sth in common _____
impress _____
inspire _____
keep a promise _____
make a good impression _____
marry _____

VOCABULARY BANK

meet up with _____
refuse to do sth _____

Free time
chat online _____
follow your interests _____
have a good time _____
have a party _____
invitation _____
invite _____
play computer games _____
_____
relax _____
socialise _____
spend time _____
text (v) _____

Food

Food and drink
apple _____
banana _____
beans _____
biscuit _____
bread _____
cake _____
calorie _____
carbohydrates _____
cheese _____
chicken _____
chips _____
chocolate _____
coffee _____
cola _____
crisps _____
cucumber _____
egg _____
fennel _____
fish _____
fruit _____
grapes _____
hamburger _____
ice cream _____
instant coffee _____
jam _____
lettuce _____
mayonnaise _____
meat _____

milk _____
mineral water _____
nut _____
onion _____
orange _____
pasta _____
pizza _____
protein _____
rice _____
roll _____
salad _____
salt _____
sandwich _____
seafood _____
soft drink _____
stew _____
strawberry _____
sushi _____
tea _____
tomato _____
vegetable _____
yoghurt _____

Eating out
café _____
canteen _____
dinner _____
fast food _____
local speciality _____
lunch _____
restaurant _____
tearoom _____

Shopping and services

Types of shops
baker's _____
bookstore/bookshop _____
butcher's _____
charity shop _____
clothes shop _____
department store _____
designer shop _____
electrical goods _____
jeweller's _____
newsagent's _____
pet shop _____

shoe shop _____
shopping centre/mall _____
_____
store _____
supermarket _____
toy shop _____

Shopping
advertising _____
attract attention _____
branding _____
buy on impulse _____
changing room _____
competitive _____
consumer _____
convincing _____
delivery _____
do some research _____
do the shopping _____
economical _____
effective _____
fit _____
go shopping _____
go window shopping _____
_____
goods _____
have a sale _____
logo _____
on (special) offer _____
out of stock _____
package _____
packaging _____
pay attention to _____
pick up a bargain _____
product _____
quality _____
reduced _____
sell out _____
sell-by date _____
service _____
shop online _____
size _____
subscription _____
suit _____
trust sb with sth _____
try on _____
value _____

115

VOCABULARY BANK

Complaints
broken _____
close your account _____
complain _____
complaint _____
damaged _____
exchange sth for sth _____
get a refund _____
keep the receipt _____
make a complaint _____
repair _____
replacement _____
return _____
send back _____
shrink _____
some parts are missing _____
_____

Money
bank account _____
cash _____
cheque _____
credit card _____
I can't afford it _____
invest _____
life savings _____
spend money on _____

Quantity phrases
a bottle of perfume _____
a bottle of shampoo/mineral water _____
a bunch of flowers _____
a bunch of grapes/bananas _____
a can of beans/cola/tomatoes _____
_____
a jar of jam/instant coffee/mayonnaise _____
a packet of biscuits/tea/crisps _____
_____
a pair of jeans/skis/scissors _____
_____

Travelling and tourism

Places in town
aquarium _____
bridge _____
café _____
canal _____
castle _____
church _____
cinema _____
harbour _____
library _____
monument _____
museum _____
palace _____
post office _____
public transport system _____
_____
restaurant _____
ruins _____
slums _____
square _____
statue _____
temple _____
theme park _____
waterfront _____
wedding chapel _____

Description
awesome _____
breathtaking _____
busy _____
crowded _____
fascinating _____
impressive _____
narrow _____
shallow _____
spectacular _____

Transport
air travel _____
bike/bicycle _____
car _____
caravan _____
carriage _____
ferry _____
flight _____
fly _____
gondola _____
GPS _____
helicopter _____
high-speed train _____
motorbike _____
on foot _____
petrol _____
ride _____
sail _____
speedboat _____

On holiday
a must _____
accommodation _____
adventure _____
attract tourists _____
attraction _____
camping _____
campsite _____
collect firewood _____
couch surfing _____
entertainment _____
forest walk _____
go backpacking _____
go climbing _____
go on holiday _____
historic site _____
host _____
local speciality _____
make a fire _____
nightlife _____
overseas _____
path _____
put up a tent _____
rock climbing _____
sailing _____
sights _____
sightseeing _____
souvenir _____
suitcase _____
suntan _____
tourist destination _____
tourist guide _____
travel agent _____
travel guide _____
view _____

VOCABULARY BANK

Culture

Art

- abstract
- art gallery
- artist
- black and white
- brush
- colour
- creation
- exhibition
- landscape
- museum
- (oil) painting
- paint
- painter
- photo/photograph
- photographer
- photography
- portrait
- sculptor
- sculpture
- street art
- studio

Film, theatre, books

- act
- acting
- animation
- author
- award-winning
- based on
- best-seller
- book/film review
- camera
- central character
- chapter
- costume
- dialogue
- direct
- filming
- give a good performance as …
- hold your attention
- lead actor
- literary critic
- movie
- novelist
- perform
- performance
- play the role of …
- playwright
- plot
- poem
- poet
- scene
- screenplay/script
- scriptwriter
- setting
- soundtrack
- special effects
- stage
- storyline
- suspense
- take place in
- tension
- violence
- writer
- X-rated

Types of books and films

- action film
- adventure film
- autobiography
- biography
- cartoon
- classic
- cookbook
- crime story/film
- documentary
- encyclopedia
- fairy tale
- fantasy novel/film
- ghost story
- historical drama
- horror
- musical
- novel
- play
- poetry
- romantic comedy
- romantic fiction
- science fiction novel/film
- short story
- silent film
- thriller
- travel guide
- war film
- western

Music

- album
- band
- band member
- the charts
- classical music
- composer
- concert
- drummer
- folk
- gig
- guitar
- headphones
- heavy metal
- hip-hop
- hit
- house
- instrument
- jazz
- live
- music award
- music festival
- opera
- piano
- play the guitar
- pop
- punk
- R & B
- record company
- reggae
- rock
- singer
- song
- songwriter
- symphony
- track
- verse
- vocal range

117

VOCABULARY BANK

TV and media
celebrity _____
comedian _____
episode _____
journalist _____
newspaper article _____
reality show _____
report _____
reporter _____
sitcom _____
TV presenter _____

Description
amazing _____
amusing _____
boring _____
brilliant _____
emotional _____
enjoyable _____
entertaining _____
excellent _____
factual _____
funny _____
great _____
inspiring _____
moving _____
perfect _____
predictable _____
relaxing _____
true-life _____
unoriginal _____
unrealistic _____
wonderful _____

Sport

Types of sport
bungee jumping _____
football _____
golf _____
horse-riding _____
kite-surfing _____
scuba diving _____
skiing _____
snowboarding _____
sumo _____
swimming _____
tennis _____
triathlon _____
volleyball _____
yoga _____

Doing sports
go for a run _____
keep fit _____
lose _____
push-ups _____
referee _____
ring _____
skier _____
sports centre _____
stretch _____
sumo wrestler _____
team _____
team mate _____
train _____
training session _____
triathlete _____

Health

Illness
deaf _____
disease _____
drug addict _____
get ill _____
leukemia _____
sick _____
unhealthy _____

Treatment
antibiotics _____
blood _____
dentist _____
doctor _____
first aid _____
get better _____
healthy _____
hospital _____
medicine _____
nurse (n) _____
nurse (v) _____
operation _____
surgeon _____
therapist _____

Science and technology

Computers and phones
attach a photo _____
battery _____
broadband _____
chat _____
click on (an icon) _____
crash _____
desktop computer _____
digital _____
download music _____
dropdown menu _____
e-book _____
e-ink _____
electronic _____
email _____
emoticon _____
FAQ (Frequently Asked Questions) _____
follow sb on Twitter _____
go dead _____
go online _____
hang up _____
icon _____
Internet server _____
keyboard _____
laptop _____
log on _____
mobile phone _____
mouse _____
music download _____
open a document _____
password _____
screen _____
scroll up/down _____
search engine _____
social networking site _____
switch on _____
tablet _____
text message _____
tweet _____
update your profile _____

VOCABULARY BANK

username _____
visit a website _____

Science

analyse _____
analysis _____
ancestor _____
archaeologist _____
archaeology _____
carry out _____
chemicals _____
chemist _____
chemistry _____
collect evidence _____
come up with _____
data _____
discover _____
discovery _____
do experiments _____
do research _____
ecologist _____
ecology _____
engineer _____
environment _____
evolution _____
evolve _____
exploration _____
explore _____
figure out _____
find a cure _____
find a solution _____
fix a problem _____
geologist _____
geology _____
imagination _____
imagine _____
interactive _____
invention _____
jet engine _____
make a discovery _____
(marine) biologist _____
(marine) biology _____
mathematician _____
mathematics/maths _____
nature _____
nuclear power _____
observation _____

observe _____
oxygen _____
physicist _____
physics _____
preservation _____
radar _____
researcher _____
robot _____
science _____
scientist _____
solution _____
solve _____
technology _____
vision _____

Space exploration

astronaut _____
astronomy _____
atmosphere _____
black hole _____
capsule _____
commander _____
communications satellite _____
_____
explosion _____
fuel tank _____
gravity _____
launch _____
mission control _____
moon _____
on board _____
orbit _____
parachute _____
planet _____
space _____
spacecraft _____
splash down _____

The natural world

Landscape

altitude _____
beach _____
canyon _____
cloud _____
coast _____
field _____
foggy _____

forest _____
hill _____
island _____
limestone _____
mountain _____
natural wonder _____
ocean _____
rainforest _____
reef _____
river _____
rock _____
sea _____
soil _____
spring _____
summit _____
valley _____

Animals and plants

camel _____
chicken _____
farm animals _____
flower _____
marine life _____
pig _____
seaweed _____
shell _____
tree _____

Environmental protection

climate change _____
compost _____
contaminate _____
ecologist _____
ecology _____
global warming _____
pollution _____
preserve _____
protect the environment _____
_____
recycling _____
throw out _____
waste _____

State and society

Society and politics

background _____
black community _____
Board of Education _____

VOCABULARY BANK

capital city _____
citizen _____
community _____
constitutional monarchy _____
_____
declare _____
democracy _____
developing country _____
_____
discriminate _____
discrimination _____
empire _____
equal _____
fight for _____
foreign _____
freedom _____
general elections _____
head of government _____
_____
head of state _____
human race _____
human rights _____
humiliate _____
humiliation _____
identity _____
make/give a speech _____
_____
market _____
national anthem _____
native _____
Nobel Peace Prize _____
_____
peace _____
political system _____
politician _____
population _____
president _____
Prime Minister _____
racial discrimination _____
racial segregation _____
reduce poverty _____
run a campaign _____
secure _____
security _____
segregate _____
segregation _____
separate _____

separation _____
slave _____
slave trade _____
slavery _____
statistics _____
survey _____
tax _____
the Supreme Court _____
trade _____
trading centre _____
unemployment _____
vote _____
wealth _____
wealthy _____

Charity
charity _____
collection _____
donate _____
donation _____
fundraising _____
homeless _____
soup kitchen _____
voluntary work _____
volunteer _____

Crime
appear in court _____
arrest _____
arson _____
arsonist _____
assassinate _____
assassination _____
break into _____
break the law _____
bully _____
burglar _____
burglary _____
burgle _____
car crime _____
case _____
catch _____
collect evidence _____
commit a crime _____
community service _____
crime scene _____
criminal _____

damage public property _____
_____
deal drugs _____
drug dealer _____
drug dealing _____
gang _____
graffiti _____
guilty _____
hacking _____
illegal _____
innocent _____
interview a criminal _____
_____
judge _____
justice _____
mug _____
mugger _____
mugging _____
murder _____
murder rates _____
murderer _____
mystery _____
online piracy _____
pirate _____
police officer _____
prison _____
punish _____
report a crime _____
rob _____
robber _____
robbery _____
search _____
sentence _____
set fire to _____
shoplift _____
shoplifter _____
shoplifting _____
steal _____
suspect _____
theft _____
thief _____
vandal _____
vandalise _____
vandalism _____
victim _____
witness _____

VOCABULARY BANK – PRACTICE EXERCISES

People

1 Read the horoscopes and match the descriptions with the adjectives in the box.

> boring brave caring cheerful confident
> crazy ~~creative~~ generous grumpy hard-working
> helpful independent irresponsible lazy loyal
> modest outgoing passionate quiet reliable
> selfish shy unhealthy unfit

Aries: You are good at writing and drawing. ⁰_creative_
But you never feel like working. ¹_____
Taurus: You will leave a young child alone near a swimming pool. ²_____
But when the child falls into the water, you will rescue him. ³_____
Gemini: You are always smiling and happy. ⁴_____
You don't need help from other people. ⁵_____
Cancer: You never cheat a friend or betray them. ⁶_____ But you easily get irritated. ⁷_____
Leo: You like excitement and adventures and don't think about the consequences. ⁸_____ You never exercise. ⁹_____
Virgo: You take hot soup to your grandmother when it's cold. ¹⁰_____
You never lose your self-belief. ¹¹_____
Libra: You always help your friends. ¹²_____
You don't say much. ¹³_____
Scorpio: You don't take a break until the job is finished. ¹⁴_____
You always have strong feelings. ¹⁵_____
Sagittarius: You always buy great birthday presents. ¹⁶_____ You like meeting new people. ¹⁷_____
Capricorn: You don't like exercise but you love your food. ¹⁸_____
People can trust you. ¹⁹_____
Aquarius: You think about yourself but not about how other people feel. ²⁰_____
You also talk about the same things over and over again. ²¹_____
Pisces: You feel uncomfortable meeting new people. ²²_____
You don't like to talk about your abilities. ²³_____

2 Complete the sentences with *about*, *with*, *by* or *in*.

0 I always get stressed _about_ meeting new people.
1 My sister is very interested _____ science.
2 I was inspired to write a poem about a sunny day _____ the river.
3 Jo's boyfriend is obsessed _____ planes.
4 At this age all children are negative _____ school.

Home

1 Match the types of houses with their definitions.

1 semi-detached house — **h**
2 cottage
3 detached house
4 bungalow
5 houseboat
6 studio apartment
7 terraced house
8 apartment

a a house in a line of houses joined together
b a house with only one floor
c (US) a set of rooms for living in
d a small house in the country
e a house which is not joined to another house
f a small apartment with one main room
g a house on water
h a house joined to another house on one side

2 Choose the correct answer, A, B or C.

0 The place in the house which is below the ground floor is called a
  A shed. (B basement.) C toilet.
1 A porch is a place under a small roof
  A under the stairs. B on the top floor of a building.
  C outside the front or back door.
2 The room in a house where you relax and watch TV is called a
  A living room. B shed. C porch.
3 A skylight is a kind of
  A door. B window. C floor.
4 You use a vacuum cleaner to clean the
  A windows. B carpet. C dishes.
5 You prepare meals on a
  A bean bag. B couch. C worktop.
6 A wardrobe is a large
  A storage area. B room. C armchair.
7 You cover yourself in bed with a
  A cushion. B duvet. C poster.
8 To keep warm in winter, you turn on the
  A game console. B light bulb.
  C central heating.
9 You hang curtains in front of a
  A window. B front door. C fridge.
10 A small carpet is called a
  A floorboard. B blind. C rug.
11 You wash the dishes in the kitchen
  A sink. B cupboard.
  C washing machine.
12 The ceiling is the part of a room
  A under your feet. B above your head.
  C where you hang pictures.
13 You usually put a solar panel on the
  A ceiling. B roof. C floor.
14 A piece of furniture with open shelves is called a
  A cooker. B cupboard. C bookcase.

121

VOCABULARY BANK – PRACTICE EXERCISES

School

1 Match 1–10 with a–j to make phrases.

1	attend	c	a	homework
2	take		b	good grades
3	study		c	school
4	drop		d	from university
5	graduate		e	lessons
6	get		f	a break
7	learn		g	an exam
8	skip		h	at university
9	pass		i	by heart
10	do		j	a subject

2 Tick (✓) the true sentences and cross (✗) the false sentences. Then correct the false sentences.

0 A *gap year* is a break between primary school and secondary school. ✗
   A gap year is a break between secondary school and college or university.

1 A *timetable* is a list of the times when classes in school take place.

2 *Learning by heart* means 'memorising'.

3 An *entrance exam* is an exam you have to take at the end of your education.

4 A *tuition fee* is the money you pay for college or private school.

5 A *swipe card* is a special plastic card that you use to get into a building or open a door.

6 A *uniform* is what you wear on the beach or at a swimming pool.

7 *Vocabulary* is all the verbs in a language.

8 *Pronunciation* is the way you say a word.

3 Complete the sentences with the words in the box. There are two extra words.

> classmate   gym   knowledge   literate
> nursery   revise   ~~Science~~   single-sex

0 What did you do in your *Science* class today?
1 _____ schools are only for girls or only for boys.
2 We normally have PE outside or at the _____ .
3 A _____ person can read and write.
4 A _____ is a place where parents leave their small children when they go to work.
5 When you have your final exams, you will need to _____ a lot for them.

Work

1 Read the descriptions and write the people's jobs. The first letter of each word is given.

0 'Some people think it's an unimportant job, but in my case it's just the opposite – it seems I'm responsible for everything – phone calls, emails, my boss's coffee and even ordering pens and pencils.'
   of f i c e **a**s s i s t a n t

1 'I've always been good at numbers, but it is not what people think; it's not that you only have to count in this job. Calculators and computers count, but we use intelligence to make good business decisions.'
   a_ _ _ _ _ _ _ _ _

2 'I make people happy in my job. My clients are usually women. I make their skin look younger and healthier. I also paint their nails and put their make-up on before a special occasion.' **b**_ _ _ _ _ _ _ _

3 'I'm self-employed, but I can't work from home. In my job I visit people's flats and houses, but I never enter the living room. I'm always invited straight to the bathroom or kitchen, where I fix problems with water and pipes.' **p**_ _ _ _ _ _

4 'People call me or visit my office when they want to buy, sell or rent a flat, a house or a piece of land. I help them find the best offer and negotiate the price. I don't have many clients in a month, but when I sell or buy a house for someone, I earn a lot.'
   e_ _ _ _ _ _ _ **a**_ _ _ _ _

5 'My job is very stressful. I often go to conferences and have to speak in front of a lot of people. I change a person's words from one language into another when they speak. I never do it in writing because I think it's boring this way.' **i**_ _ _ _ _ _ _ _ _ _

6 'I can work for a newspaper, a magazine, television or radio. I like my job because every day is different. I usually go to places where something interesting is happening and then write a news report. This means I have to travel a lot to collect information and then I work from home when I write.' **j**_ _ _ _ _ _ _ _ _

7 'Summer is a busy time for me. I work ten hours a day, seven days a week when it's warm and sunny. I spend the whole day at the beach and can sunbathe, which is great! But I can't fall asleep because I'm responsible for the lives of all the people swimming and playing in the water.' **l**_ _ _ _ _ _ _ _

2 Match the verbs with the words/phrases in the box. Some verbs go with more than one word/phrase.

> a living   a pay rise   an average salary
> ~~badly paid~~   a bonus   from home   full-time
> low wages   on duty   outside   overtime
> physical work   shifts   self-employed

1 be   *badly-paid,* _____   4 get   _____
2 do   _____   5 make   _____
3 earn   _____   6 work   _____

122

VOCABULARY BANK – PRACTICE EXERCISES

Family and social life

1 Complete the letter with one word in each gap.

> Dear Amanda,
>
> I've got a problem and I don't know what to do. I can't adapt ⁰to my new school. All my classmates are friendly ¹_____ new students and I know they all meet ²_____ after school, but I don't get ³_____ with anyone! I've tried talking to a few boys, but we have nothing ⁴_____ common. They listen ⁵_____ hip-hop all the time and play basketball three times a week. I love classical music and going ⁶_____ the cinema. The teacher doesn't seem to care ⁷_____ newcomers like me. What can I do? Please help!
>
> Patrick

2 Choose the correct answer, A, B or C.

0 When you *admire* someone, you
  A like them because they have done something good.
  B dislike them because they have done something bad.
  C don't respect them.
1 When you *text* somebody, you
  A read what they have written.
  B send them a short message on your mobile.
  C send them a letter.
2 When you *socialise*, you
  A argue with people.
  B avoid other people.
  C spend time with other people.
3 When you *chat* with somebody, you
  A talk to them about unimportant things in a friendly way.
  B talk to them about business in an official way.
  C talk to them to make a good impression on them.
4 When you *refuse* to do something, you
  A say you won't do something.
  B say you can do something.
  C say you will do something.

3 Complete the sentences with family words.

0 My mother's sister is my *aunt*.
1 My uncle's son is my _____.
2 My brother's son is my _____.
3 My husband's father is my _____.
4 My son's son is my _____.
5 My sister's daughter is my _____.
6 My wife's mother is my _____.

4 Match 1–6 with a–f to make phrases.

1 get   f   a computer games
2 behave   □   b a party
3 have   □   c badly
4 keep   □   d time
5 spend   □   e a promise
6 play   □   f married

Food

1 Choose the correct answer, A, B or C.

0 Which of these is an example of seafood?
  A fish   **B** beans   **C** butter
1 Which of these is not a dish to be eaten?
  A stew   **B** mud   **C** sushi
2 Where do schoolchildren typically eat lunch?
  A in a restaurant   **B** in a canteen   **C** in a café
3 Which of these is not fruit?
  A grape   **B** lettuce   **C** strawberry
4 Which of these is not made from milk?
  A ice cream **B** mayonnaise **C** cheese
5 Which of these do most people never have for breakfast?
  A yoghurt **B** eggs   **C** pasta
6 Which of these are not vegetables?
  A nuts   **B** beans   **C** onions
7 Which of these is not a drink?
  A cola   **B** milk   **C** café
8 Which of these do you never put in a salad?
  A jam   **B** cucumber **C** salt
9 Which of these is not a type of meat?
  A beef   **B** chicken   **C** a roll
10 Which of these are not sweet?
  A crisps   **B** cakes   **C** biscuits

2 Match 1–6 with a–f to make compound nouns. Then use the nouns to complete the sentences.

1 mineral   f   a drink
2 instant   □   b cream
3 ice   □   c coffee
4 soft   □   d speciality
5 local   □   e food
6 fast   □   f water

0 Don't drink cola – *mineral water* is much healthier.
1 Hamburgers and chips are the most popular types of _____ .
2 You must try the Piora cheese here; it's a(n) _____.
3 _____ is prepared by adding hot water.
4 A(n) _____ does not contain alcohol.
5 I love vanilla _____ .

123

VOCABULARY BANK – PRACTICE EXERCISES

Shopping and services

1 Match 1–6 with a–f to make a shopping list.

1	a pair of	f	a	tomatoes
2	a can of		b	biscuits
3	a bunch of		c	milk
4	a jar of		d	bananas
5	a packet of		e	face cream
6	a bottle of		f	boots

2 Where can you buy the things in Exercise 1?

1. shoe shop: _____
2. greengrocer's: _____
3. baker's: _____
4. supermarket: _____ , _____ , _____

3 Complete the text with one word in each gap.

> Yesterday my mum gave me a shopping list and sent me to the nearest department ⁰*store*. She asked me to buy a birthday present for my brother and food for the birthday party. I didn't want to go because I always buy ¹_____ impulse and spend too much ²_____ unnecessary things. I prefer sitting at my computer and shopping ³_____. When I was passing a clothes shop, I saw a dress ⁴_____ special offer, so I decided to try it ⁵_____. Unfortunately, it didn't ⁶_____ me and the dress in my size was ⁷_____ of stock. On my way to the toy shop, I passed a jeweller's. I saw a bracelet which attracted my ⁸_____. The price was reduced – I had never picked ⁹_____ such a bargain! I didn't have my ¹⁰_____ card with me, so I paid in ¹¹_____ with my mum's money. When I left the shop, I realised it was almost closing time. I quickly bought some food from the shopping list and a toy car for my brother. When my mum saw what I'd bought, she was mad – the toy was broken and the food was past its sell-by ¹²_____. I couldn't return the food or exchange the toy ¹³_____ something else because I hadn't kept the ¹⁴_____. She will never trust me ¹⁵_____ her shopping again!

4 Choose the correct answer, A or B.

0. When you *complain*,
   A you are happy about something.
   B you are unhappy about something.
1. When you get a *refund*,
   A the shop gives you the money back.
   B the shop offers you something at a reduced price.
2. When parts of something are *missing*,
   A there are too many of them.
   B there aren't enough of them.
3. When someone is *convincing*,
   A you believe they are right.
   B you don't believe they are right.

Travelling and tourism

1 Choose the correct answer, A, B or C.

0. An area of calm water next to the land where ships can stay is called a
   A church.   B castle.   **C harbour.**
1. The part of a town next to the sea or river is called a
   A chapel.   B waterfront.   C bridge.
2. An official home of a king or queen is called a
   A temple.   B palace.   C monument.
3. A large open area in the city centre is called a
   A square.   B slum.   C statue.
4. A place where you borrow books is called a
   A theme park.   B post office.   C library.
5. A place where you go on holiday is called a
   A local speciality.
   B tourist destination.   C tourist attraction.
6. A way that people made by walking from one place to another is called a
   A site.   B path.   C walk.
7. A mobile home you can pull behind your car when you go on holiday is called a
   A caravan.   B gondola.   C carriage.

2 Match 1–8 with a–h to make compound nouns. Then use the nouns to complete the sentences.

1	air	h	a	climbing
2	tour		b	site
3	rock		c	surfing
4	couch		d	guide
5	speed		e	walk
6	historic		f	transport
7	forest		g	boat
8	public		h	travel

0. *Air travel* is the only way of getting from Europe to New Zealand if you get seasick on ships.
1. I've logged onto a(n) _____ site as a host and next week a girl from Japan is coming to visit me.
2. Let's all go on a(n) _____ at the weekend and pick some mushrooms.
3. _____ can be a very dangerous sport.
4. In the future I'd like to become a(n) _____ and show people around my home town.
5. The royal castle in Warsaw is a well-known _____.
6. My father rented a(n) _____ and gave us a ride to the other end of the lake.
7. The underground is the fastest form of _____.

3 Choose the odd one out in each group.

0. carriage   ferry   (path)   car
1. backpacking   sailing   sightseeing   wedding
2. camera   view   campsite   sight
3. tent   flight   caravan   campsite
4. ruins   souvenir   castle   museum
5. accommodation   harbour   waterfront   bridge
6. aquarium   canal   ferry   suitcase

124

VOCABULARY BANK – PRACTICE EXERCISES

Culture

1 Write the words in the box in the correct group. Some words can go in more than one group.

> acting   animation   artist   author   ~~biography~~
> cartoon   celebrity   chapter   comedian
> composer   cookbook   documentary   drummer
> episode   exhibition   fairy tale   gig   hit
> movie   novel   performance   play (noun)
> playwright   poet   poetry   R&B   reality show
> reggae   review   script   sculptor   short story
> singer   sitcom   songwriter   special effects
> street art   symphony   the charts   track

1 Things you can read: *biography* _____
_____
2 Things you can see/watch: _____
_____
3 Things you can listen to: _____
_____
4 People: _____
_____

2 Complete the film types. The first letter of each word is given.

0 a film about elves and dragons:
   a f*antasy* film
1 a film in which two countries fight against each other:
   a w_____ film
2 a film in which people live on Mars:
   a s_____ f_____ film
3 an old film in which you can't hear any words:
   a s_____ film
4 a film about funny people and humorous situations:
   a c_____
5 a film in which dangerous and exciting things happen:
   an a_____ film

3 Choose the correct adjective from the box to describe a book. There are two extra adjectives.

> amusing   boring   excellent   ~~factual~~
> inspiring   unoriginal   moving
> predictable   relaxing   unrealistic

0 It's based on what really happened. *factual*
1 It makes you fall asleep. _____
2 You know what will happen and what the characters will do. _____
3 It makes you feel strong emotions. _____
4 It's funny. _____
5 It motivates you to do something special. _____
6 It's not based on facts. _____
7 It makes you feel good when you're stressed. _____

Sport and health

1 Match 1–7 with a–g to make compound nouns. Then use four of the nouns to complete the sentences.

1 bungee	[g]	a centre
2 training	[ ]	b diving
3 sports	[ ]	c aid
4 first	[ ]	d wrestler
5 sumo	[ ]	e mates
6 team	[ ]	f session
7 scuba	[ ]	g jumping

0 The best place for *bungee jumping* is a high bridge.
1 During the match one of my _____ broke his leg.
2 When an accident happens, everyone should be able to give _____ .
3 If you want to be a _____ , you need to go on a special high-fat diet.

2 Choose the correct answer, A, B or C.

0 Who doesn't work with the sick?
   (A) skier   B nurse   C surgeon
1 Which is not a person?
   A referee   B triathlete   C push-up
2 Which is a disease?
   A leukemia   B ring   C deaf
3 What do we use as a type of medicine?
   A blood   B aid   C antibiotics
4 Which word doesn't mean the same as 'ill'?
   A healthy   B unhealthy   C sick

3 Read the descriptions and write the sports.

0 There are two teams, eleven players in each of them, and one ball. They play on a large green area called a pitch. *football*
1 You do exercises on a mat to control your mind and body and relax. _____
2 You do it in winter. You go down a hill on a special flat piece of wood or synthetic material. _____
3 It must be windy to do this sport. You hold some ropes in your hands. At the end of the ropes there is something flying in the air. You stand on a board and move across water. _____
4 It's played on a large green area which usually isn't flat. Players hit a small white ball into holes. _____
5 You must be very fit to do this because you have to run, swim and cycle long distances. _____

125

VOCABULARY BANK – PRACTICE EXERCISES

Science and technology • The natural world

1 Choose the correct options.

0 *Archaeology* / *Archaeologists* have just discovered some human bones in the ruins of the city.
1 *Biologist* / *Biology* is the study of life on earth.
2 Animals must *evolve* / *evolution* to survive climate change.
3 Authors use their *imagine* / *imagination* when they write.
4 The ship broke down and some dangerous *chemists* / *chemicals* got into the sea.
5 Scientists *discover* / *discovery* new drugs every day.
6 *Physics* / *Physicist* was my least favourite subject at school.
7 Before the scientists could decide how to cure the disease, they had to do a genetic *analyse* / *analysis* of the virus.

2 Complete the puzzle. What's the hidden word?

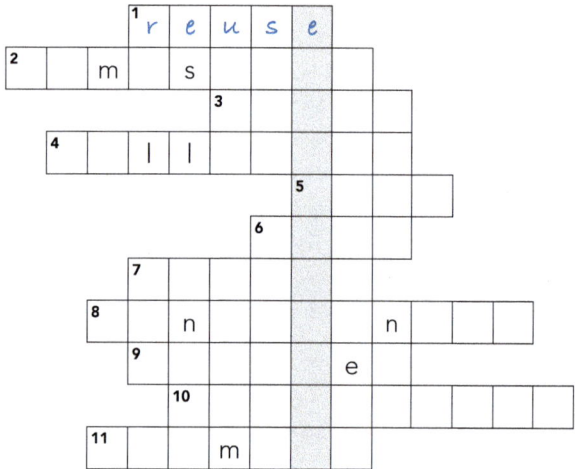

1 use something again
2 a type of rock that contains calcium
3 the Thames or the Mississippi
4 dangerous chemicals in the air or water
5 sharp rocks made of coral in tropical seas
6 where plants grow
7 connected with the sea
8 make a place or substance dirty
9 a plant that grows in the sea
10 a forest in a tropical area where it rains a lot
11 it is changing everywhere in the world because of global warming

Hidden word: _____

3 Match 1–6 with a–f to make collocations.

1 make — f
2 protect
3 fix
4 find
5 do
6 collect

a experiments
b a problem
c evidence
d the environment
e a solution
f a discovery

4 Choose the correct answer, A, B or C.

0 A system of sending information online at a very high speed is called
   A broadband.   B a blog.   C a desktop.
1 If your computer suddenly stops working, it means it has
   A splashed down.   B crashed.   C tweeted.
2 If a camera records information in the form of numbers, it means it's
   A technological.   B electronic.   C digital.
3 If a battery stops working because there is no power, it means it's
   A dead.   B switched off.   C scrolled down.
4 A secret group of letters or numbers is called
   A a document.   B e-ink.   C a password.
5 A special word that shows who you are and allows you to enter a computer system is called
   A a search engine.   B a username.   C an icon.
6 When you add new information to your profile, you
   A update it.   B follow it.   C download it.

5 Complete the definitions. The first letter of each word is given.

0 A **h**ill is a small mountain.
1 A **v**_____ is an area between two mountains.
2 A **s**_____ is the top of a mountain.
3 A **s**_____ is where a river begins.
4 An **i**_____ is a small piece of land in the sea.
5 A **c**_____ is where rain comes from.

6 Write the words in the box in the correct group. Write two words in each group.

> black hole   ~~camel~~   canyon   engineer   field
> fuel   geologist   keyboard   moon   scanner
> nuclear power   pig   server   website

1 Animals: *camel,* _____
2 Computer equipment: _____
3 Energy: _____
4 Internet: _____
5 Jobs: _____
6 Landscape: _____
7 Space: _____

VOCABULARY BANK – PRACTICE EXERCISES

State and society

1 Read a politician's speech and complete the words. Some letters are given.

'Dear ⁰c̲i̲t̲i̲z̲e̲n̲s, I feel that we need to change a lot in this country and the next general ¹e _ _ c _ _ _ _ _ _ is a chance to do so. We must have a new head of ²g _ _ _ _ _ n _ _ _ _ _ _. The Democratic Party has decided to run a ³c _ _ _ _ _ _ i _ _ _ against corruption. Too many people are hungry and have no jobs – we are going to fight against ⁴p _ _ _ _ r _ _ _ and ⁵u _ _ _ _ p _ _ _ _ _ _ _ _ _ _. We know that our ⁶c _ _ _ _ _ a _ city can become the main trading ⁷c _ _ _ _ r _ on the continent, with more work for everyone who needs it. We want the poor to become ⁸w _ _ _ l _ _ _ y. The ⁹t _ x _ _ we pay now are much too high. We want to eliminate organised ¹⁰c _ _ _ m _ _ and make everyone feel ¹¹s _ _ _ u _ _ _ in their homes. If you feel and think the same, ¹²v _ _ _ e for us!'

2 Match the nouns in the box with their definitions. There is one extra noun.

> assassination background charity community
> democracy discrimination donation freedom
> fundraising humiliation identity justice
> ~~market~~ monarchy peace population
> segregation slavery

0 an area where a country or company sells its products. _market_
1 a political system in which a king or queen decides about the most important things in the country _____
2 a situation in which everyone is treated fairly _____
3 a situation in which everyone has the right to do what they want _____
4 the number of people living in a country _____
5 an organisation which helps people in need _____
6 a situation in which people are treated differently – some better than others _____
7 someone's history – their family, education, work, etc. _____
8 a situation when you feel shame because someone has made you look stupid _____
9 a system in which some people belong to others and have to work for them for no money _____
10 a time without wars _____
11 who you are _____
12 a situation in which an important person e.g. a politician, is killed _____
13 a political system in which everyone has the right to vote to elect the government _____
14 collecting money to help people in need _____
15 a situation in which people have to live, work, study, etc. separately because of their race, sex or religion _____
16 the money you give to a person or organisation to help them _____

3 Match 1–6 with a–f to make collocations.

1 developing   [f]   a race
2 human   [ ]   b trade
3 political   [ ]   c kitchen
4 slave   [ ]   d work
5 soup   [ ]   e system
6 voluntary   [ ]   f country

4 Answer the questions.

What do you call a criminal who:
0 has killed someone? _murderer_
1 has set fire to a building? _____
2 has stolen something from a shop? _____
3 has stolen money from a bank? _____
4 sells drugs? _____
5 has broken into a house? _____
6 has attacked someone in the street to steal their mobile? _____
7 illegally downloads music from the Internet? _____
8 has damaged public property? _____

5 Match 1–5 with a–e to make collocations.

1 collect   [e]   a a crime
2 interview   [ ]   b in court
3 commit   [ ]   c the law
4 appear   [ ]   d a criminal
5 break   [ ]   e evidence

6 Choose the correct answer, A, B or C.

0 When you think that someone is a criminal but you don't have the evidence yet, you call them a
  (A) suspect.   B witness.   C volunteer.
1 Someone who has stolen something is called a
  A victim.   B judge.   C thief.
2 A problem which is analysed and solved in court is called a(n)
  A search.   B case.   C interview.
3 When you try to frighten someone weaker or smaller than you, you
  A bully them.   B rob them.   C vandalise them.
4 Everyone should be treated in the same way because everyone is
  A foreign.   B equal.   C secure.
5 The most important national song in a country is a(n)
  A anthem.   B sentence.   C prize.
6 The head of government in many countries is called the
  A Judge.   B President.   C Prime Minister.

127

SELF-CHECKS ANSWER KEY

Unit 1
Exercise 1
1 inexperienced 2 unpopular 3 lazy
4 uncooperative 5 dishonest
Exercise 2
1 about 2 at 3 for 4 about 5 in
Exercise 3
1 sensible 2 healthy 3 outgoing
4 caring 5 successful
Exercise 4
1 C 2 B 3 A 4 B 5 B
Exercise 5
1 to learn 2 playing 3 to carry
4 studying 5 walking/to walk
Exercise 6
1 C 2 B 3 A 4 C 5 A

Unit 2
Exercise 1
1 click 2 download 3 follows 4 raise
5 switch
Exercise 2
1 text message 2 username
3 search engine 4 keyboard
5 Broadband
Exercise 3
1 analyse 2 evolution 3 observes
4 solve 5 exploration
Exercise 4
1 was doing, called 2 were sleeping, rang
3 Did they find, closed 4 were dancing, stopped 5 Was Shelly waiting, crashed
Exercise 5
1 ~~used to go~~ went
2 ~~used~~ use
3 ~~used to play~~ played
4 ~~use to be milk~~ milk use to be
5 ~~used to were~~ used to be
Exercise 6
1 B 2 A 3 A 4 A 5 C

Unit 3
Exercise 1
1 classical 2 crime 3 adaptation
4 portraits 5 funny
Exercise 2
1 literary 2 tales 3 episode 4 scene
5 emotional
Exercise 3
1 playwright 2 autobiography 3 band
4 photographer 5 unrealistic
Exercise 4
1 I've just finished … 2 Eileen has already seen … 3 Has Rosa looked at a travel guide for Spain yet? 4 Mum's already paid … 5 We haven't met any of the other guests yet.
Exercise 5
1 too 2 fit 3 furthest 4 more 5 the
Exercise 6
1 A 2 C 3 B 4 C 5 C

Unit 4
Exercise 1
1 cooker 2 pond 3 washing-up
4 eco-house 5 bookcase
Exercise 2
1 harbour 2 decision 3 ironing
4 porch 5 suburbs
Exercise 3
1 cosy 2 bridge 3 countryside/country
4 mud 5 single
Exercise 4
1 The statue of the King has been in the square since 1754. 2 Their pond hasn't had fish in it for two years. 3 The cat has sat on the windowsill since this morning. 4 Nina has lived in a flat for ten years. 5 I haven't felt well since last weekend.
Exercise 5
1 A 2 B 3 C 4 A 5 A
Exercise 6
1 B 2 A 3 A 4 C 5 A

Unit 5
Exercise 1
1 rid 2 home 3 nervous 4 reply
5 station
Exercise 2
1 take off 2 get on with 3 won't fail
4 carry on 5 meets up with
Exercise 3
1 compulsory 2 decide 3 isolation
4 explain 5 tried
Exercise 4
1 'll rent 2 'll save 3 get
4 won't pass 5 fails
Exercise 5
1 which/that 2 where 3 that/who
4 that/which 5 that/who
Exercise 6
1 C 2 A 3 C 4 B 5 C

Unit 6
Exercise 1
1 d 2 a 3 b 4 c 5 e
Exercise 2
1 regular 2 bonus 3 for 4 model
5 up
Exercise 3
1 ~~work~~ job 2 ~~shift~~ shifts 3 ~~well pay~~ well-paid 4 ~~at~~ in 5 ~~secretry~~ secretary
Exercise 4
1 wouldn't feel exhausted all the time if she went 2 I invited you, would you come 3 Laura and Kath worked from home, they would miss 4 wouldn't go out with him again if I were 5 you give me some money if you won
Exercise 5
1 need to 2 can 3 can't 4 must
5 needn't
Exercise 6
1 C 2 B 3 A 4 A 5 C

Unit 7
Exercise 1
1 cinema 2 manicure 3 afford 4 pair
5 offer
Exercise 2
1 anger 2 elegant 3 jealous 4 security
5 creativity
Exercise 3
1 jeweller's 2 aquarium 3 supermarket
4 wedding chapel 5 theme park
Exercise 4
1 was designed 2 Were you given
3 was sold 4 Was the parcel delivered
5 haven't been told
Exercise 5
1 ~~few~~ little
2 ~~many~~ much
3 ~~little~~ few
4 ~~few~~ a few
5 ~~A lots of~~ Lots of/A lot of
Exercise 6
1 A 2 C 3 B 4 A 5 C

Unit 8
Exercise 1
1 humiliate 2 mugger 3 robbery
4 crime 5 burglar
Exercise 2
1 genuine 2 end 3 false 4 innocent
5 lie
Exercise 3
1 murdered 2 Vandals 3 witnesses
4 fire 5 Shoplifting
Exercise 4
1 was 2 had already ordered 3 got
4 had spoken 5 realised
Exercise 5
1 she was waiting 2 he hadn't told
3 she'd never been 4 she hadn't stolen
5 she was reading
Exercise 6
1 A 2 B 3 C 4 B 5 C